Local History and the Library

J. L. Hobbs's
Local History and the Library

Completely revised and partly rewritten by
George A. Carter, F.L.A.
Borough Librarian, Warrington.

 ANDRE DEUTSCH/A Grafton Book

942.009

First published January 1962 by
André Deutsch Limited
105 Great Russell Street London WC1

Second impression December 1962
Second revised edition 1973
Copyright © 1962, 1973 by John L. Hobbs
and George A. Carter

Printed in Great Britain by
Ebenezer Baylis and Son Ltd
The Trinity Press, Worcester, and London

ISBN 0 233 95615 8

Contents

List of Illustrations

Introduction to Second Revised Edition

I wish to acknowledge the help I have received during the revision of the present book. As was the case when the first edition was written by the late John L. Hobbs, a questionnaire was circulated to the librarians of many public library authorities. Two hundred and fifty-three completed returns were received. Gratitude must be expressed at the outset, therefore, to all those librarians who responded to this questionnaire so readily, and especially to those who supplied comments and information in far greater detail than I hoped to receive. It is now hoped that a major part of the information submitted has been incorporated in this revision of what many librarians have come to regard as a useful guide to local collection practice. For this new edition about half the book has been rewritten, the remainder extensively revised and a new index of the Special Collections mentioned in the text has been added.

A particular debt of gratitude is owing to all those who read the typescript and made valuable comments and suggestions in consequence. Mr E. T. Bryant, M.A., F.L.A., Borough Librarian of Widnes was especially helpful after reading the typescript in its entirety. The chapters dealing with manuscript records and archives were submitted to the Secretary of the Royal Commission on Historical Manuscripts, Mr Roger H. Ellis, M.A., F.S.A., F.R.Hist.S., and through him to the Assistant Secretary to the Commission, Mr H. M. G. Baillie, M.B.E., F.S.A. The suggestions made in consequence were of great value, as were those of Mr Brian C. Redwood, M.A., County Archivist of Cheshire County Council, who also read these chapters.

The first three chapters were read by Mr R. H. Bartle, B.Litt., M.A., F.L.A., Principal Lecturer at Manchester Polytechnic, Faculty of Commerce, and the chapter on 'Local History in County Libraries' was read by Miss O. S. Newman, F.L.A., County Librarian of Shropshire County Library and Mr S. G. Berriman, F.L.A., Director of Libraries and Museums, Cheshire County Council.

Helpful advice and comment has also been received from Mr T. S. Broadhurst, M.A., F.L.A., Deputy Librarian, the University of Liverpool; from Mr M. Cook, M.A., University Archivist, the University of Liverpool and from Mr K. Jermy, M.A., of the Warrington and District Archaeological and Historical Society.

It was necessary to visit and correspond with many colleagues and others on matters of detail and I have nothing but praise to offer for the forbearance and helpfulness displayed by all who were asked to help at various times and especially to: Mr Philip Hepworth, M.A., F.L.A., City Librarian, Norwich; Mr Paul Sykes, D.M.A., F.L.A., City Librarian, Nottingham; Mr R. G. Charlesworth, A.L.A., Deputy City Librarian, Plymouth; Mr M. F. Messenger, F.L.A., Borough Librarian and Curator, Shrewsbury; Mr M. W. Devereux, F.L.A., Borough Librarian, Swinton and Pendlebury, all of whom were hospitable when visited by the writer. Also a special word of thanks must be given to: Mr S. H. Barlow, F.L.A., Borough Librarian, Nuneaton; Mr J. Bebbington, F.L.A., City Librarian of Sheffield; Mr G. Bradley, F.L.A., Borough Librarian of Newcastle-under-Lyme; Dr G. Chandler, M.A., F.L.A., F.R.Hist.S., City Librarian, Liverpool; Mr D. I. Colley, M.A., F.L.A., City Librarian, Manchester; Mr G. B. Cotton, F.L.A., Lecturer, Manchester Polytechnic, Faculty of Commerce; Mr A. B. Craven, F.L.A., City Librarian, Leeds; Mr Donovan Dawes, F.R.Hist.S., A.L.A., Principal Keeper, Guildhall Library; Mr K. C. Harrison, M.B.E., F.L.A., City Librarian, Westminster; Mr J. Hoyle, F.L.A., Director, Libraries, Museums and Arts Department, Dudley; Miss D. H. McCulla, A.L.A., Head, Local Studies Library, Birmingham; Mr T. S. McNeil, F.L.A., Borough Librarian, Swindon; Mr C. E. Makepeace, Local History Librarian, Manchester; Miss Bettie Miller, Secretary, Standing Conference for Local History;

Mr J. A. Miller, F.L.A., Borough Librarian, Crosby; Mr C. S. Minto, F.L.A., City Librarian, Edinburgh; Mr Colin Muris, M.A., F.L.A., County Librarian, Bedfordshire County Library; Mr D. Phillips, M.A., Dip. Ed., A.L.A., Lecturer, the Polytechnic of North London; Mr W. J. Smith, Hon. Secretary, British Records Association; Mr Peter Walne, M.A., F.S.A., F.R.Hist.S., County Archivist, Hertfordshire County Council; and to Mr M. Yelland, B.A., A.L.A., Research Officer, the Library Association, all of whom replied readily and helpfully to my letters.

Permission to reproduce *M.H.L.G. Circular No. 44/62 – Local Government (Records) Act 1962* has been given by the Controller of Her Majesty's Stationery Office and the policy statement, 'The Place of Archives and Manuscripts in the Field of Librarianship', is reproduced with the consent of the Library Association, from the *Library Association Record*, January 1969. Photographs reproduced are published with the consent of the following authorities: City of Liverpool, City Libraries; City and County of Norwich, City Library as well as the Norfolk and Norwich Record Office in the Norwich Central Library; Borough of Nuneaton, Public Library; City of Plymouth, City Libraries; City of Sheffield, City Libraries; County Borough of Warrington, Municipal Library.

Finally, for services rendered beyond the normal call of duty, I wish to thank members of the staff of the Warrington Municipal Library who helped me considerably – Mr N. Viney, F.L.A., Deputy Librarian; Mr D. Rogers, A.L.A., Reference Librarian, and Mrs S. Pargeter, A.L.A., Local History Librarian, and especially Mr A. Hartley, A.L.A., Cataloguer, who compiled the index and assisted in compiling the bibliography.

To my wife, Joy, I owe most of all for persuading me to undertake this revision after I had been invited to do so, and for her unselfish help in many ways during the period in which the book was written, and not least for the no slight labour of typing the manuscript.

July 1972   GEORGE A. CARTER

Chapter 1

Local History: Its Value and Use

'In recent years there has been an enormous growth of serious interest in local history all over England – not least in extra-mural classes which are doing so much original work,' said Professor W. G. Hoskins in an inaugural lecture delivered in the University of Leicester on 3rd March 1966.[1] Further evidence of this growing interest is shown throughout the British Isles in villages, towns, cities, counties and London boroughs by the formation during the past ten years of many new societies for the study of local history.

Nearly half of the local authorities of the country report the formation of such societies in the years 1960–70 and give details showing that these new societies vary from those likely to be concerned with all aspects of local history such as the Camden History Society; the Fenland Historical Society; the Offa's Dyke Association; the High Wycombe History Society; the Warrington and District Archaeological and Historical Society; and the Durham County Local History Society to societies formed for the study of more specialised aspects of local affairs. These more specialised societies include the Hallamshire Buildings Society and the Bath Buildings Record, which exists to make accurate drawings, plans, photographic and research records of buildings and areas scheduled for demolition; the Watford Industrial History Society; and the Bolton Society for the Study of Local Industrial History which is helping with the cataloguing of a collection of engineering drawings acquired by Bolton Public Libraries.

1. W. G. Hoskins. *English Local History: the Past and the Future.* Leicester University Press, 1967. p. 9.

Dudley reports the formation of a Teachers Archive Study Group and Swindon a Swindon (Public Libraries) Railways Society all of which supports the comment of one librarian that 'Local studies are now a booming industry'.

Certainly the variety of these recently formed societies supports another statement made by Professor Hoskins in his inaugural lecture, namely that:

To the true local historian no human record, whatever its form – a hedge-bank, a wall, a street, a headstone, a farmhouse, an old man's gossip, wills and tax assessments and the thousands of other written things, a memorial tablet on a church wall – a multitude of evidence in every shape or form – no human record fails to tell him something about the past.[2]

At the same time the emergence of new local history societies in so many different localities also supports Professor V. H. Galbraith when he writes:

It has often been said that all history is local history, and Domesday Book reminds us that the history of England includes that of every single estate or manor in the country. Nevertheless local history as a separate study is implied in our whole, age-long administrative structure.[3]

'When the intellectual and cultural history of the present epoch comes to be written, a not insignificant place will have to be occupied in its perspectives by the remarkable development in this country of the studies we are accustomed to include under the heading of local history', wrote the reviewer of Professor Hoskins's book *Local History in England*[4] in the *Times Literary Supplement*. 'The pursuit of such studies', he added, 'in one form or another has of course attracted antiquaries, and some who deserve to be called historians, ever since the sixteenth century; . . . but it is only of recent years that the subject has become really popular – a matter of keen and widespread interest among education classes and Women's Institutes.'[5]

There has, then, been a considerable revival of interest in

2. Ibid. p. 20.
3. V. H. Galbraith. *An Introduction to the Study of History*. C. A. Watts, London, 1964. p. 34.
4. Longmans, London, 1959.
5. *T.L.S.* August 1959. p. 470.

local history during the post-war years, both as a subject of study and as a basis for research, and it is not unreasonable to equate this with the success of the movement for making local research materials more widely available through libraries and record offices. This revival has been greatly accelerated since the last war and from being a mere appendage to national study it has become a subject for study in its own right and recognised as such in our universities. The field is no longer monopolised by the university professor, a few professional writers and clerics, nor is the local historian today regarded with amused tolerance by the man in the street as a potterer and a dabbler. The tremendous growth and spread of education during the twentieth century is undoubtedly a contributory factor while Professor Hoskins suggests that another may be that 'as the modern world becomes bigger and more incomprehensible people are more inclined to study something of which they can grasp the scale and in which they can find a personal and individual meaning'. The enormous range of topics available to the student and would-be writer of local history is another of its fascinations.

The active interest in local history through universities, extra-mural courses, public lectures, archaeological excavations and other activities has been accompanied by a no less significant passive interest in this sphere on the part of the general public. The popularity of the many radio and television programmes on archaeology, geography, place-names and similar topics illustrates this, as does the increasing number of articles and correspondence on different aspects of local history that have been published in newspapers and magazines.

At the same time there has been a gradual, yet perceptible, increase in the seriousness of the approach to history, which has not been confined to one section of the population. The vast increase in the amount of research material made available in recent years has opened a wider field to the professional historian and teacher of history. They, in their turn, have conveyed this to the student and the amateur historian. In particular the influence of men like Stamp, Hoskins and Finberg has been to widen the scope of local studies and to improve the quality of published research. Again, specialist historians such as Chaloner of Manchester, Beresford of Leeds and Simmons of

Leicester have helped to increase public interest by studying
and publishing industrial, agricultural and transport history.
The effect has been to wean the amateur away from pre-
occupation with family, manorial, ecclesiastical and military
history into the more fascinating and rewarding byways of
economic and social development.

There is still a tendency for local historians, particularly those
working on their own, to place excessive emphasis upon the
manor and its history and pedigrees of landed families to the
neglect of the growth of the village itself as exemplified in its
surviving fields, houses and landmarks, and the manner in
which its development has been governed by local conditions of
soil, climate and water supply. It is this tendency that modern
local historians are seeking to counter by emphasising that the
really important things in history are those which had a direct
impact on the village or which affected and changed the lives of
ordinary people.

One result of this is that the librarian today faces problems in
local history work which are quite distinct from those which
faced his predecessor of a generation or two ago. The local
collection of the past, catering for a select band of clerics and
schoolmasters and based on the county antiquarian society,
consisted chiefly of the rag-bag publications of the antiquaries,
plus the county and family histories. The local librarian today
needs to be something of a palaeographer, map expert,
medievalist, archaeologist and economic historian, but above
all he must develop a keen interest in the current events of his
own locality and be equipped to ensure that a record of these
events is properly maintained as they occur.

In the past the approaches to local history were limited to
three. Firstly, there was the attempt to discuss the subject as a
reflection of national events, resulting in a catalogue of local
occurrences. Then there was the study of particular records,
such as churchwardens' accounts, resulting in a concentration
upon curiosa rather than essentials. There was also the determined and scientific collection of facts from many and varied
sources which resulted in the best of the eighteenth- and nineteenth-century local histories. Today local history attempts to
study the growth of the locality and the development of its
institutions logically and in all its manifold aspects by fieldwork,

co-operative study and the examination of original records, and much of our social and economic history is being rewritten as the study of local sources adds to our knowledge of these subjects.

Although it is no longer a mere handmaiden of national history, local history *can* explain and elucidate our national affairs at many points. The manor and the parish have been autonomous units of local government for centuries, and national movements cannot be properly understood without reference to their history and records. Indeed, as J. E. Neale points out, the medieval system of government *was* local government because 'the monarch had not the means to plan and maintain a centralised and uniform system of institutions. The localities had been left largely to themselves, to their old folk institutions and the feudal institutions grafted on to them.'[6]

The generalisations on which many of our national histories were founded are succumbing to the minute investigation of detail made possible by local studies, and the exceptions to these are seen to be many and various, far more than the older historians, their vision and outlook limited by reliance upon centralised records, realised. Local history can be of the greatest value to national history when it gathers together instances of events illustrating social trends or tendencies which are otherwise difficult to find. Each area can be shown to have contributed something to the commonweal which is the basis of our constitution. Indeed, the very causes of national events, when studied in detail, are often shown to lie in the personalities behind them, which again are determined by local conditions and affairs. Dr Finberg has shown how the Barons' Wars of Stephen's reign had their origin, or at least a contributory cause, in the struggle between Glastonbury Abbey and a local baron for the small manor of Uffculme, in Devon. This episode in its otherwise uneventful story 'throws a wholly new searchlight on the tempestuous reign of Stephen. . . . We are growing accustomed', says Dr Finberg, 'to the thought that places otherwise obscure may have had their moments of historical importance. Generations of scholars have explored the main sources of our history, but new information may still emerge

6. 'English Local Government' in *Essays in Elizabethan History*. Cape, London, 1958. p. 204.

from detailed local studies, and sometimes the data thus brought to light will modify our conceptions of well-known historical events.'[7]

The view which regards local history merely as the lantern slide which illuminates national affairs is, however, a shortsighted one. Local history today is approached, not as an aid to the study of national or international history, nor even as a microcosm of the national story, a corpus of evidence gathered together to illustrate general trends, but as a subject worthy of study in its own right. It can, indeed, claim to be the most advanced form of historical study. It antedates national history, for national states were comparatively latecomers on the stage of history, while local communities can be traced back to the earliest communal settlement, and its study can give a sense of 'belonging' and continuity which can serve as an antidote to the rootlessness of our twentieth-century society. This view propounded by Dr Finberg in 'The Local Historian and His Theme',[8] and put into practice in the Department of English Local History at Leicester University, asserts that local history is distinct from national history in both space and time and that the origins, development and success or decline of a local community constitutes a field of study quite apart from that of the national historian. 'Local communities had existed before the nation and had come into being since, and they had their place within the nation, as the nation had its place within the world. Local, national and international history might be pictured as concentric circles, and local history was not a less perfect circle for being enclosed and surrounded by others.'[9]

So far as the library is concerned, local history work today has a fourfold aspect, and it is necessary to consider its place in formal education, in adult education, in university and postgraduate research and, finally, the assistance which can be given to the amateur historian.

In schools and training colleges, where it offers an alternative

7. 'Uffculme' in *Devonshire Studies* by W. G. Hoskins and H. P. R. Finberg. Cape, London, 1952. pp. 59–77.

8. In *Local History: Objective and Pursuit* by H. P. R. Finberg and V. H. T. Skipp. David and Charles, Newton Abbot, 1967.

9. H. P. R. Finberg. 'The Meaning and Scope of Local History' in *Report of the 11th Annual Meeting of the Standing Conference for Local History, Held on Friday, 13th November, 1959*. National Council of Social Service, London, 1959. Duplicated.

to the dead generalisations of textbooks, local history is being given increasingly greater prominence, and there are few modern teachers who do not introduce it into the curriculum at some point. History, geography and various other studies are associated with the topographical, social and economic environment of the pupil in the realisation that the child's world lies within a short distance of his home. The past of his own village or town is more comprehensible than that of ancient civilisations or of national history, and the force of local example drives home the lessons of history in the dullest mind far better than the ablest textbook. The facts of national history, too, are related more intimately to the child's world, for there are few national movements which cannot be linked in some way to the immediate locality. Education is thus transferred from the classroom to the world of reality, and the teacher and librarian became guides and active participators rather than academic tutors. The development and value of local history in schools is discussed by Robert Douch in his book *Local History and the Teacher* (Routledge, London, 1967) and the author also considers the opportunities and the difficulties which the study and teaching of historical aspects of the local environment present.

The approach naturally differs, however, in industrial and rural areas, and also in the various types of school. The secondary modern school, where the curriculum is not so conditioned by the need to prepare for public examinations usually gives greater attention to this local approach to history than does the grammar school. But the pupil of the latter, hoping to advance to university or training college, also needs the practical experience of working on original sources which can only be gained locally. A Department of Education and Science pamphlet, entitled *Archives and Education* (Education Pamphlet no. 54, HMSO, London, 1968) indicates how such records can be used in schools to further educational projects, while Mr F. G. Emmison, formerly County Archivist of Essex, has written a practical guide to the use of local records, *Archives and Local History* (Methuen, London, 1966), for the amateur and academic with the increasing demands of students and teachers in mind. Many schools now organise lectures, excursions, field clubs, exhibitions and 'Local History' weeks, in all of which local studies play their part. School museums, too, are best organised on a local basis.

An outstanding feature of the past decade has been the advance in the development of a wide variety of photographic processes and machines for copying written and printed documents with speed and at relatively cheap rates so that most record offices and libraries now possess machines which enable them to reproduce and duplicate original material for study purposes. Wallets containing reproductions of original documents, together with explanatory notes are now made up by a number of librarians and archivists in a similar manner to the 'Jackdaw' wallets on historical events published by Jonathan Cape and some, like the Archive Teaching Units, prepared in the Department of Education, University of Newcastle-upon-Tyne, have been printed and published. These wallets are available for use in schools, and those librarians and archivists who have prepared such photographic aids to the study of documents in their care are clearly enthusiastic about this new ability to widen the availability of material that too often in the past could only be used under repository conditions. The general editor of the Newcastle Archive Teaching Units, J. C. Tyson, expresses the hope in the general preface that the units will offer schools 'the opportunity to work with selected documents which, though not the originals, are as close to the originals as technical skill can make them'.

Adult education has been long recognised as a legitimate function of the public library service, and it is in the sphere of local history that this reaches its zenith and makes its greatest impact on the community. The library service must accept, in partnership with the education service, the lead in stimulating and helping to mould the desire to know more about the immediate neighbourhood, in its past or present state, which is latent in any community, be it an historic town with a long tradition, a rural village or a satellite town of modern development. No longer is the librarian and archivist simply the passive provider of basic materials, but it is abundantly clear that in many towns and counties both librarians and archivists have actively encouraged local history studies through the formation of groups and societies to promote this purpose.

Although it is evident that many British universities are

actively concerned with local history studies, Professor W. G. Hoskins, the Hatton Professor of English History at Leicester University in his inaugural address delivered in 1966 said:

Though the study and the writing of local history in England is now some 400 years old, and has produced an immense literature, the University of Leicester is still the only university to recognize the subject as one worthy of serious academic pursuit. Founded now nearly twenty years ago as the Department of English Local History, it was from the first designed to take the whole of England within its purview. It is therefore not merely local history confined to Leicestershire or even to the Midlands. It is not a School of Regional Studies such as one or two other universities now tentatively possess. It takes all England, the most diverse and complex country in the world in relation to its area, within its province.[10]

The department publishes the *Journal of Transport History* and the University of Leicester's Prospectus 1971–72 states that: 'The Hatton Collection of books in the University Library covers all the counties of England and is one of the most extensive local history libraries in the country.' Following the lead given by Leicester, the University of Hull offers a Diploma in Local Historical Studies requiring the completion of a three-year tutorial course in local history organised by the Department of Adult Education and the submission of an essay of not less than seven thousand words. Regional studies are being developed by the University of Lancaster which has on its staff a Reader in the Regional History of North-West England. The University of Liverpool offers a B.Phil. for research in local history, and Birmingham, Exeter, Leeds, Newcastle and Nottingham are among other universities where local historical studies are encouraged.

The publications of many university presses also indicate the extent to which local and regional studies are pursued throughout the British Isles, and so great an interest has been engendered in these studies that in recent years there has been a spate of publishing concerned with the reprinting of rare and out-of-print items, as well as the emergence of a number of publishers who devote themselves almost exclusively to the production of new local studies. Important reprints have included the Victoria History of the Counties of Lancashire,

10. op. cit. p. 3.

Surrey and Warwick by Wm. Dawson & Sons Ltd.; the First
Edition of the One Inch Ordnance Survey, in the process of
being republished in collaboration with the Ordnance Survey
by David and Charles, who have done so much to advance
industrial archaeological studies through their publishing
activities; a series of Urban History Reprints under the
editorial direction of Dr G. H. Martin has commenced publication by S. R. Publishers Ltd. in association with the Standing
Conference of National and University Libraries; and a series
of books on English linguistics 1500–1800 selected by Dr R. C.
Alston of Leeds University and produced by the Scolar Press
Ltd. of Menston, Yorkshire. Dr Alston has also produced
between 1965–69 the first six volumes of a comprehensive
*Bibliography of the English Language from the Invention of Printing
to the Year 1800* (E. J. Arnold, Leeds, 1965–   ) and research
into dialect, linguistics and phonology conducted at Leeds
University has resulted in the publication of a *Survey of English
Dialects* (E. J. Arnold, Leeds, 1962–   ) by Professor Harold
Orton and Professor Eugen Dieth which is still in progress.
Also at Leeds Maurice Beresford has searched for and tracked
down deserted medieval villages and examined the causes of
medieval depopulation in many parts of the country, a study
which has led to the founding of the Society for Medieval
Archaeology, and under the auspices of the School of History
a new scholarly review, *Northern History*, concerned with the
history of the six northern counties of England commenced
publication in 1966. This review, *inter alia*, includes a record of
archive accessions to northern repositories and record offices.

Manchester University, which has the oldest chair of economic history in Great Britain, is a leading centre in research and
teaching on the subject. It was at Manchester that Professor
T. S. Ashton established himself as a leading economic historian
and produced so many economic history studies of immense
local value.

One of these studies, *An Eighteenth-century Industrialist, Peter
Stubs of Warrington* (Manchester University Press, 1939), which
was based on a collection of original business papers now housed
in the Manchester Central Library, has quite recently afforded
an interesting example of the inspiration communicated by
Professor Ashton to those with whom he was associated as a

teacher, and has provided at the same time an example of a growing tendency of the amateur as well as the student to pursue local studies in some depth. One of Professor Ashton's former students, Colonel E. Surrey Dane, who retired recently from the management of the firm of Peter Stubs Ltd. decided to spend the first few years of his retirement on pursuing further research on the Stubs papers and has now submitted the result of his research as a thesis for a doctorate on 'Peter Stubs and the Lancashire Hand Tool Industry to 1840'.

The English Place-Name Society in which Sir Frank Stenton of Reading University played a leading part, now with Professor K. Cameron as Honorary Director, is at University College, London; whilst the Museum of Rural Life at Reading University is a national centre for the collection of material relating to the countryside and combines the functions of a research institute and a reference centre. In the field of archives the Borthwick Institute of Historical Research of the University of York is a record office specialising in ecclesiastical archives which are valuable sources for the local historian.

It is nevertheless striking that of all the purely local studies published by British universities only those emanating from the Department of English Local History at Leicester deal with localities far removed from the seat of the university and have included Occasional Papers on localities as widely separated as Lancashire and Southampton.

The London University Institute of Historical Research, founded in 1921 by Professor A. F. Pollard, is a centre for advanced work in history, devoted exclusively to post-graduate work. The Institute admits teachers and research students from other universities, and other historians and archivists engaged in research. Amongst many other functions the Institute also administers the Victoria History of the Counties of England. Since 1930 it has been responsible for an annual list of theses both completed and in progress, which initially appeared as part of its *Bulletin* but since 1967 has been separately published as *Historical Research for University Degrees in the United Kingdom*. Much of the published work which emanates from professors and historians at the universities is based upon guided investigations and researches of undergraduates, and many would readily admit not only the enormous assistance afforded to their work by the collection of research materials in record offices and libraries, but also to the groundwork done upon these sources by students working under their tutelage. Detailed investigation of this nature is the foundation of modern historical study and it is not untrue to say that the local historian is today engaged in rewriting the history of England.

Only the library with a substantial amount of original research material can assist the professional historian to any great extent, and in the smaller local collection it is the student and the amateur worker who benefit most from the collections. We have intimated that, until recently, local history was regarded as the province of the amateur and, notwithstanding the advances on the academic side, this is still largely true today. Dr Jacob tells us that it 'has been founded upon private and often co-operative enterprise, supported by amateurs and written by amateurs', adding that 'the remarkable thing is that before those fuller developments in archival science and in the calendaring of documents . . . before there was any systematic investigation of family and local government records, local historians and local academies had achieved the results they had.'[11] An American writer expresses a similar view. 'It is not, after all, the highly trained historian who will write the local history of each community in this vast country. Not only is the field too great but usually the trained historian is primarily interested in larger areas of research, such as state, regional and national history.'[12] Professor Hoskins, too, states that 'the amateur has made a large contribution to English local history in the past, and there is still plenty of room for him (or her) in this vast and still largely unemployed field'.[13]

Concomitant with, or perhaps inspired by, the greater interest in this subject in academic circles has been a revival of interest in local history as a basis for study and practical work in the rural areas, where it has been fostered and encouraged by rural community councils, Women's Institutes, Young Far-

11. E. F. Jacob. 'Local History: the Present Position and Its Possibilities'. An Address to the inaugural meeting of the Standing Conference for Local History, December 1948.

12. Donald D. Parker. *Local History: How To Gather It, Write It, and Publish It*. Rev. ed. by Bertha E. Josephson. Social Science Research Council, New York, 1944. Introduction, p. xi.

13. W. G. Hoskins. *Local History in England*. p. 3.

mers' Clubs and parish councils. The recording of material by
such groups of people untrained in the historical sciences is
quite a modern phenomenon, these pursuits having hitherto
been the province of the vicar, the squire and a sprinkling of
antiquarians, and centred on the county archaeological society.
Now, with the necessary impetus and guidance supplied
by university extra-mural tutors of LEA and WEA organising-
tutors, the entire energies of a village may be, for a time,
devoted to a 'survey' of the village life and culture and the
results, though variable, are sometimes of considerable historical value. Even more important than the actual results,
which are often regarded as 'unscientific' by the professional
mind, are the intangible benefits conferred upon the community by the sense of a corporate endeavour and a unity of
purpose, while the process of research is, of itself, stimulating
and rewarding. Many local groups have decided to compile
and publish local histories, following successful adult courses,
while others have successfully sorted, examined and listed
borough and parochial records.

Intelligent study of the past promotes not only pride in
former achievements, but also in current progress. It contributes
to a fuller understanding of those principles, inherent in the
past, upon which our future progress ultimately depends, and is
essential if we are to appreciate our surroundings and to
improve them. It can also, as Dr Jacob has pointed out,
'deepen appreciation of art and architecture and help to promote an intelligent interest in design'.[14] It makes an important
contribution, too, to the social sciences and it is not without
significance that the National Council of Social Service has
played a leading role in fostering local history studies through
the formation of the Standing Conference for Local History and
its constituent county committees, and also that, in the United
States, the Social Science Research Council has performed a
similar task.

A sub-committee of the National Council of Social Service,
committed 'to assist the development of the study of local
history in rural areas, through Rural Community Councils and
other suitable bodies and to administer any fund that may be
made available for this purpose' came into being soon after the

14. op. cit.

formation in 1929 of the first county local history committee in Lindsey. This sub-committee obtained a grant from the Carnegie Trust which it used to promote local history studies until the outbreak of the Second World War. The sub-committee was revived and reformed in 1947 and developed within one year into the Standing Conference for Local History which meets annually in London and also holds a regional meeting each year in a different area of England or Wales.

The aims and objects of the Standing Conference are defined as follows:

(a) to encourage the study of local history, and the provision of necessary services for its furtherance,
(b) to bring together representatives of local and national authorities and organisations in membership of the Standing Conference, and where desirable to co-operate with other bodies to that end.

Membership consists of representatives of national authorities and organisations (including the Library Association), of universities, county committees and of individual members having special knowledge of local history. Local history societies or groups are allowed to join as non-voting associate members.

It was recognised that the co-ordination of viewpoint and of activities was equally as desirable at local as at the national level, and efforts were made to stimulate the formation of county committees. These now (1972) exist in forty-one counties in England and Wales, and each is entitled to elect two representatives annually to the Standing Conference. They are intended to plan the local activities in each county by bringing together the societies and organisations already working in this field, by encouraging research and the recording of facts and by placing the resultant records in some place accessible to students. The services of county and municipal librarians and of county archivists are therefore very valuable and have been made available to many of the committees. The library of the county town is, we suggest, an appropriate meeting place for the committee. A typical county committee would include representatives of the county archaeological or historical society, the naturalists' society or field club, local branches of the Historical Association, the Geographical Association, the Workers' Educational

Association, Women's Institutes, Townswomen's Guilds, Young Farmers' Clubs, the National Farmers' Union and the National Union of Teachers, and of local authorities, libraries and record offices, linked through the rural community council which often provides both headquarters and secretarial assistance.

Not the least important feature of the work of the Standing Conference has been its success in demonstrating the inter-action of the various forces which have forged the past of any community, and the interdependence of social, economic, industrial and historical factors. Annual sessions of the Conference have been devoted successfully to the consideration of different aspects of local history, such as town history, transport history, agrarian history, business history, etc. Although such was not its direct intention, another of the more encouraging results has been that it has brought together the professional and the amateur local historian. By providing a meeting ground where they may discuss and understand each other's viewpoint and problems, it has helped to resolve the mistrust and the conflict between them. The different levels of research are continually coming closer together as the universities and local education authorities reach out into the rural areas to encourage and stimulate local groups, and the local history committee provides the means of integration.

In urban areas similar co-ordination is often achieved through an Arts Federation, a local Arts Council or an Arts Centre. Examples of such bodies are to be found in Dudley, Norwich, Swindon, Weymouth and elsewhere. The Swindon Arts Centre which dates from 1946 (and which has proved so successful that a new and much larger Arts Centre, including a six-hundred-seat theatre, was opened in 1971) has the following functions:

(a) To provide a home for the various societies sponsored by the Arts and Recreation Committee which are given free accommodation.
(b) To be available for hire (very cheaply) to other societies in the town, working in related fields.
(c) To provide a venue for events directly sponsored by the borough council such as Wednesday chamber music concerts.

Societies in the first category include the Swindon Public Libraries historical, archaeological, and geological societies.

The part which the public library has played and is capable of contributing to the developing interest in local history will be considered in subsequent chapters, but it should be noted here that a majority of libraries are well aware of the fact that one of the best contributions they can make to the well-being of the community is to interest the ordinary man and woman in local history, and to provide the means by which he can develop and increase that interest. Evidence of this awareness is provided by the fact that about 24 per cent of the local authorities responding to a questionnaire, circulated in 1970 to more than three hundred authorities, reported that their local history libraries had been given separate housing in new buildings, or in alterations to old buildings, during the past ten years. It was also reported that of the many new local history societies formed in the same period, either the library authority or the library staff was actively involved with the society in a majority of cases and in many instances had played a major role in the inauguration of the society.

This does not mean, of course, that the value of local history libraries is fully appreciated, either by the library profession as a whole, or by all the local authoritier responsible for the provision of public library services. Even the Library Association in its last quinquennial review of librarianship *Five Years' Work in Librarianship 1961–1965* (Library Association, London, 1968) failed to find any space to review the work of local history libraries. It is true that a section devoted to work in archives was included but this was confined to archives and record offices, and whilst other specialised library services – reference, technical, commercial and work with children and young people – all found their place, the vast amount of serious work in local history (in many instances in departments no less specialised than the commercial or technical library) was not mentioned.

It is scarcely surprising, therefore, that in too many guides to research facilities, many excellent local history libraries are either overlooked or overshadowed by details concerning record offices and collections of archives, and yet it is in the sphere of local history that public libraries are in a position to contribute most to research and serious study. Apart from substantial research collections in at least twenty large cities and many of the recently formed London boroughs, there are by no means inconsiderable collections in many more towns and counties.

Not a few of these local history libraries have been painstakingly collected and organised by librarians possessing a vocation for their work, some of whom were derided by their colleagues for over-indulgence in antiquarian leanings.

Many of those who created the most useful local history libraries, however, were also often the most active members of the library profession in other spheres. William Elliott Doubleday, who died in 1959 in his ninety-fifth year, for example, was a staunch advocate of the worth of local collections. Intensely interested in the history of his native Nottingham he compiled, at intervals throughout his working life, a vast index-bibliography of the city on cards, which is a tool of immense value in the Nottingham City Library, to whom he presented it and where, with regular updating, it now contains about half a million cards. A noted librarian, he built up an excellent library service at Hampstead, wrote useful early manuals of library practice, was general editor of the pre-war Library Association manuals published by Allen and Unwin, and edited the *Library Association Record* for several years. He also lectured at University College, London, on librarianship and served on many committees, and as Chairman of the Library Association Council negotiated the Net Book Agreement, a landmark in British librarianship. Then there was George Roebuck at Walthamstow, a man of scholarly tastes, keenly interested in local affairs who, in an article written towards the close of his career, made a plea for the inclusion of local record work amongst the duties of a public librarian.[15] A man of culture and wide learning, he also built up an excellent all-round library service and found time to play a prominent part in the affairs of the professional body, taking the initiative in action for the abolition of the crippling 'penny rate' restriction in 1919, and leading the fight for its repeal. We think of others, too, W. H. K. Wright, Ernest Axon, James Duff Brown, W. Benson Thorne,

15. 'The Collection and Preservation of Local Records in the New Areas'. *Library Association Record*, vol. 38, November 1936. pp. 546–51. See also his obituary by W. Benson Thorne in *Library Association Record*, vol. 55, April 1953.

H. Tapley-Soper of Exeter, George Stephen of Norwich, John Warner of Newport, H. M. Cashmore of Birmingham, James Ormerod of Derby, Miss E. Gerard of Worthing, Charles Madeley of Warrington, the founder of the North West Branch of the Library Association, A. J. Hawkes of Wigan, the great Jast himself, a pioneer in local history, as in many other fields, who compiled a local history classification, Ernest Savage, whose Edinburgh Collection exhibited many novel features, and Berwick Sayers, who built on Jast's foundation at Croydon and published an excellent book on this subject.[16]

All of these, and many more,[17] though staunch advocates of library local collections, played a leading part in the life and work of the Library Association, and were foremost in inventing and adopting new techniques and ideas. Librarianship has in recent years become more of a career and less of a vocation, and has lost as well as gained something in the process.

Even today a live local history department is hardly ever an alternative to good library service in other directions. There are few, if any, bad libraries with good local collections and vice versa. The more modern the librarian in his outlook, the better his local collection tends to be. It would be invidious to give instances, but examples will readily occur to the discerning reader. Time is perhaps the greatest inhibiting factor to the full development of many local collections, and inadequacy of staff, both numerically and qualitatively, militates against this to a greater extent than shortage of money. A successful local history library and a lively interest in these activities by the library inevitably evokes a great emotional response from the local authority and from members of the public which, by increasing goodwill, benefits the whole library service.

But the real reason why the librarian should participate in this work of collecting local historical materials is simple. He really has no alternative: it is a duty – one thrust upon him by

16. W. C. Berwick Sayers. *Library Local Collections*. Allen and Unwin, London, 1939.

17. One should also remember the former Borough Librarian of Shrewsbury and the original author of this book, John Leslie Hobbs, whose early death was a tremendous loss to local studies and who was remembered by Philip Hepworth, the present City Librarian of Norwich, in the dedication of his book *How To Find Out in History* (Pergamon, Oxford, 1967) in these simple terms: 'John Leslie Hobbs 1916–1964 who spent his life furthering local history in libraries' [George A. Carter].

the logic of circumstance and by virtue of his position as custodian of the literature which is of potential interest to the community he serves and which gives him his livelihood. Local history material constitutes a vital part of this literature and the librarian who neglects it is not fulfilling his whole duty to his community.

There is, in the average community, no other body willing or able to assume these functions *in toto*, although there are organisations which can help or share in the work, such as the museum, record office and local historical society. In America, state and local historical societies are extremely active in this field, to the virtual exclusion of public libraries in many areas, but in the small town in this country there is no one and if the library disregards or neglects its duty vital historical data is in danger of being lost for ever. The supreme virtue possessed by the library in this connection is that of continuity. Societies rise and wane, they often tend to be dominated by individuals or sectional interests, and individuals and isolated groups need a focus for their activities. There are many variant approaches to local studies today which are often inter-active and interdependent and these need an umbrella organisation under which they may all flourish and through which they may cooperate. This the library, through its local history department, can provide. It is true that the librarian is not always free from private interests and partial affections and that fluctuations may occur occasionally through changes in personnel, but the local historian can always make his needs known to the library committee and the council. This will ensure that the librarian has full support for any claims made on their behalf, and that collections built up by earlier librarians are not neglected or former policies discontinued. The librarian, for his part, will seek to knit together the multifarious threads by co-operating with anyone sharing an interest in the subject and by co-ordinating local activities to the best of his ability.

The rest of this book will consider the development and administration of a local history collection, whether accompanied by archive material or not, and the part which the library can play in this spreading movement. By developing its services in this field the library will acquire a reputation as a research centre, and active participation in the affairs of such bodies as the Standing Conference for Local History, the British Records Association and the National Register of Archives will bring librarians into close touch with archivists, scholars, educationists, dons and historians, and with other organisations which can help in the work.

Chapter 2

The Local Collection Today

The response of the majority of municipal and county librarians to the challenge provided by the growth and development of local studies in recent years indicates a healthy awareness of current needs but leaves no room for complacency.

A questionnaire concerning local history collections was circulated in June 1970 to 309 library authorities and it was evident from the returns received that projects affecting the organisation or development of 64 per cent of these collections in libraries throughout the British Isles had taken place during the past decade. New buildings have included separate housing for local history collections and have often been accompanied by the provision of specialist staff. Other schemes have included the classification, cataloguing and indexing of collections hitherto neglected; the addition of new material, especially of photographs, illustrations and maps; and in a few cases the commencement of new local history libraries from virtually nothing.

Collections still vary enormously in range and size from the research collections of primary and documentary sources maintained by large city and some town libraries, to small assemblies of printed material occupying only a few shelves in the reference section of the smaller independent libraries. The largest municipal collections at Birmingham, Norwich, Nottingham, Cardiff, Westminster, Sheffield, Plymouth, Edinburgh, Glasgow, Belfast, Leeds, Bradford, Liverpool, Manchester, Derby, Leicester, Newcastle, Bristol, Oxford, Exeter and York are all well known and well used and vary in size from around

20,000 items to well over 100,000 items, excluding archives in each case. Sizeable collections are also maintained in many of the new London boroughs notably at Bromley, Camden, Croydon, Hackney and Waltham Forest; whilst, again excluding archives, collections of more than 20,000 items are maintained at Brighton, Burnley, Chester, Dudley, Grimsby, Harrogate, Huddersfield, Northampton, Warrington and Wigan.

The size of a collection is not always a fair indication of usefulness, however, as unless it is maintained in a 'live' state it can tend to 'fossilise'. The absence of any code of practice too has meant that each collection has grown up, sometimes haphazardly, sometimes along organised lines, often over a long period of time. Frequently moulded by local conditions, such as the interest, or lack of it, on the part of successive librarians and committees, the stimulus of local societies or the munificence of private collectors, no collection can be said to be 'typical'.

In order to meet the needs of those who now wish to pursue local history studies, however, the development and maintenance of adequate local history collections depend above all upon the efforts that can only be made by staff who are either exclusively devoted to the purpose, or by those whose interest leads them to devote a considerable part of their time and energy to the same objective. The lack of separate staff or the absence of interest is painfully apparent in the returns from libraries which have failed to show any considerable development during the past ten years. Localities and towns have changed considerably during this period and these alterations should be reflected in local history collections. Those which are well maintained show surprising uniformity in increases in the number of photographs which record changes in areas that are being demolished, developed or redeveloped. There has also been a large increase in the acquisition of micro-photographs of printed and manuscript material, in many cases indicating a determination to meet the needs of the increasing number of students pursuing local studies 'in depth', as well as many increases in map and archive collections sometimes owing to recent changes in the local government structure. Sheffield, for example, reports that the number of photographs and illustrations which totalled 2,300 in 1960 had increased to 25,000 a decade later; and a detailed account of a successful co-operative venture whereby a systematic photographic survey commenced in 1963 in Chester has been written by the City Reference Librarian.[1] The urgent need for a photographic record of areas scheduled for demolition was emphasised in the initial stages of the Chester project, but one authority (Walsall) states that: 'New buildings, estates etc. are photographed as soon as possible so that the image presented to future historians is not one of decay and ruin.' Leicester reports that the size of its entire local history collection has more than trebled in the past ten years; Northampton and Oxford, both with collections of more than 12,000 photographs and illustrations, report considerable growth in their photographic collections in recent years; Batley, although reporting that the 'Collection only started in 1968 and so still in infancy', is nevertheless able to record the acquisition of 1,400 printed books and pamphlets, 100 maps, 50 photographs and illustrations, 12 tape-recordings, 4 films and a file of newspapers and newspaper cuttings from 1968, together with an index to them. It would seem, however, that possibly the greatest achievement of the period must be that of the Borough Librarian of Crosby (Mr J. A. Miller) who writes: 'This is a department that has come into being in Crosby since 1960' and goes on to report that 'in 1961 there were less than 250 local books and pamphlets; very few maps; no transactions of historical societies; no microfilms; there were, however, some 1,000 photographs but no coloured slides'. He then records that the Crosby local history collection at June 1970 contained 3,500 printed books and pamphlets; 2,500 photographs and illustrations; 130 maps plus bound volumes of O.S. maps; 1,174 colour transparencies; 67 microfilms, mostly of local newspapers; 5 tape-recordings; 3 films; about 2,000 deeds and documents; 62 volumes of Local Boards of Health and U.D.C. minutes; about 150 typescripts of papers given to the Historical Society as well as photocopies of wills, court rolls and other documents. All this in addition to planning and opening a new central library in the same period.

A large majority of county libraries have now built up

1. Yvonne Fennell. 'Chester Photographic Survey'. *Library Association Record*, vol. 72, May 1970. pp. 197-9.

centralised collections of county literature for reference purposes and most of them also have collections of loanable
material. In some counties there are also smaller collections
situated in regional centres and at main branch libraries.
Examples of 10,000 items or more can be found in Buckinghamshire, Cornwall, Dorset, Dumfriesshire, East Sussex, Norfolk
and Westmorland, indicating that a considerable number of
county collections are of major importance. Their role and the
contribution they make to local studies will be considered in
Chapter 10.

Although a few small library authorities still report that the
local history collection is inadequately housed far from the
reach of users – 'in a basement store', 'in the office' or 'in the
Secretary's office' – at least one standard appears to have
emerged in recent years, in so far as separate housing for the
local history collection has been included almost invariably in
the new central libraries erected during the past decade, as
well as in the plans of those projected for the immediate future.
Many library extension schemes have also incorporated
separate accommodation for the local history collection. Fifty
municipal library authorities now report that their collections
have been rehoused since 1960 or are about to be located in
separate accommodation.

A comparison of the proportion of municipal libraries to have
provided a separate department for the local history collection
in recent years with the proportion to have provided specialist
staff in the same period (a ratio of approximately three to one)
leads to the conclusions that it is either much easier to persuade
a local authority to erect a new building than to convince an
establishment committee that additional staff are an equal
necessity; or, that there are still librarians who remain un-
convinced of the need for full-time local history librarians. In
far too many instances the staffing dilemma remains unresolved
and contains the following perplexity: that on the one hand, a
local history collection will not develop in the most balanced
and most useful manner unless properly directed by the interest
and enthusiasm of those who are employed to do this in a full-
time capacity; and on the other, that it is not until a balanced
and useful collection has been acquired that users will be
sufficiently numerous to justify the appointment of full-time

staff. The second horn of this dilemma unfortunately contains the circumstance most likely to be accepted in a majority of local authorities when the appointment of full-time staff is being considered, and by this time, of course, any full-time staff appointed would discover that so much of their time had to be devoted to the day-to-day user requirements and enquiries that the further development of the collection would be in danger of neglect.

The extent to which a wide and extensive range of useful material can be collected by a librarian with interest and enthusiasm has been demonstrated by the Librarian of Crosby, as it was in the previous decade by Mr G. B. Cotton, former Borough Librarian of Swinton and Pendlebury. In both cases the local history collections, so admirably developed from a negligible basis, have now been accorded separate housing with adequate seating for users in new central libraries. It is hoped that the efforts of such librarians, together with the evidence of the lively growth of local history studies provided in the first chapter of this book will provide a stimulus to all those local authorities where the local history collection is failing to meet current needs.

Those who use local history collections are mostly residents of the locality. With surprisingly few exceptions the librarians who have kept records of their users are able to affirm that from 85 per cent to 95 per cent of these users belong to the locality. These records have been kept in libraries serving populations varying in size from 20,000 to 160,000 people and include places as widely separated as Stalybridge and Falkirk, Dartford and Bolton, as well as Gravesend and Huddersfield. Generally, it is only in the much larger cities such as Nottingham, Newcastle, Leicester and Belfast, where the collections have been developed on more regional lines, that local use is reported to represent between 50 per cent and 75 per cent of the total, although there are a number of smaller towns and cities also possessing well developed and widely used regional collections.

This reaffirms the truth that there is a need for a local history collection in the smallest library, because the materials of the history of each locality will be sought for in the local library, if anywhere. This is the one field in which the smallest library cannot rely upon its large city neighbour, its county library or upon special libraries in the area, nor indeed the county branch upon its headquarters. No library should claim that it is providing a service on the basis of ill-assorted material acquired haphazardly over whatever length of time.

Indeed recent evidence on the areas covered by local history collections seems to point in a direction which is likely to prove inescapable in some libraries if present user trends continue. This is a tendency on the part of some authorities, which in the past have collected material for an area or region and, in one instance, a country, to concentrate instead on the immediate locality or a smaller region. The City Librarian of Belfast, for example, writes:

The main point of interest regarding this Library is that it began as an Irish collection and for many years an attempt was made to collect all material on the whole of Ireland; this wide coverage did not permit of an 'in depth' acquisition policy for material relevant to the immediate local area, and many items were missed. Consequent upon a recent Organisation and Methods Study of our service we are in the process of re-organising the collection as a true Local History Library which in our case means all material relating to Northern Ireland and in particular the City of Belfast.

Birkenhead reports 'less emphasis on Cheshire material and more on Wirral and Merseyside'; Gateshead that 'prior to 1961, this Library was the officially recognised repository for records relating to Northern Durham. Since the opening of Durham County Record Office, we have restricted ourselves to the area of the County Borough only'; Shrewsbury that 'we do work in fairly close co-operation with the County Record Office now and we have an agreement with them concerning the geographic areas which the respective organisations cover, without prejudice, of course, to existing holdings.' Concerning co-operation with Shrewsbury Borough Library the County Librarian of Shropshire says that 'Local enquiries which cannot be met from our resources are passed to the Borough Library. An agreement exists between the Borough and ourselves, that they are to be regarded as the centre for local studies in the geographical County, and in return general reference services will be the responsibility of the County Library. This agreement works well.'

Concern about the geographical areas covered by local history collections has been expressed by a number of librarians where the competition of Town, County and University for the same items is tending to increase the cost of collecting often, it is feared, somewhat needlessly. A deeper concern has also been expressed concerning the fate of the local history collection in the eventuality of the widespread reformation of local government boundaries. Certainly the fear that a well-developed and locally well-used collection might be moved to a more remote administrative centre does not seem to have been an inevitable result in those schemes of local government reorganisation that have already taken place, and the realisation of the need for well-developed collections in each locality seems generally to have been appreciated. Clearly it is extremely difficult to lay down any rules concerning the most appropriate geographical restrictions, since even many of the librarians who report that the use of their particular collection is 'mainly local', qualify this by explaining that 'mainly local' may mean anything from a five-mile to a twelve-mile radius of a particular centre. Thus a certain amount of overlapping is bound to occur in many areas and this would appear to demonstrate a need for reasonable discussion between those responsible for the administration of library services in the areas concerned.

One recent co-operative venture in connection with the acquisition of local material is worthy of imitation. This is a Northern Ireland scheme whereby a checklist of books and articles on Northern Ireland is issued by Belfast Public Libraries in co-operation with all other public and university libraries in the Province. The idea came from the Standing Committee of Deputy Librarians in Northern Ireland and aims to be both a 'current awareness' tool to draw the attention of librarians to recently published material and, eventually, after cumulation and subject-indexing, a current bibliography of Northern Ireland. It is produced at two-monthly intervals and is still (at the time of writing) in the third experimental year. The issue for March 1970 entitled *Northern Ireland Local History* contained 119 entries consisting of recently printed books, pamphlets, brochures and periodical articles. A review of periodical literature and occasional publications relating to Northern England, similar in scope but in somewhat greater detail than the

Northern Ireland list, appears in each issue of *Northern History*, which is published annually under the auspices of the School of History, the University of Leeds.

It is, however, in the pursuit of archival material and the acquisition of rare printed items that conflict is most likely to arise between those whose interests overlap. Here it can only be emphasised that the allocation of funds for the purchase of rare items can help to ensure that a greater number of rare items find their way into public rather than private hands in the first instance, and that once an item, or collection of items, has been acquired by a local history library it is then possible for another competing authority to obtain photographic copies of one kind or another. Only about thirty library authorities appear to have funds specifically allocated for the local history collection, however, and these vary from budgets at Norwich, Newcastle and Nottingham, which not only include provision for separate staff, but also include the annual expenditure of around £1,000 on the purchase of books and other material, to those libraries having small sums allocated specially for photographic and microfilm programmes. Several librarians stress that the money spent is governed by the material available, and that the small amounts spent betoken a scarcity of material rather than unwillingness to make expensive purchases. In the words of one, 'No specific sum is allocated for purchase of material, but we do not hesitate to buy from reference library funds any item which would be a useful addition and the amount spent could vary between wide extremes over the years.' There is little doubt, however, that where a specific sum is set aside there is no real difficulty in spending it on microfilm or photographic programmes in particular, as well as on the growing number of useful local reprints and on items gleaned from second-hand catalogues which regrettably indicate the increasing but inevitable rise in prices owing to growing competition for local history material.

Wider divergencies of policy appear to exist in the field of archival material than in any other aspect of the local history collection. Apart from the county authorities where the responsibility for archives, with one or two notable exceptions, is the province of the county record office, the policy pursued by other local authorities is fourfold. A few authorities have joint arrangements with a county record office, especially when this office is situated in the same town or building as an independent public library. Examples of joint arrangements with a record office are to be found at Norwich where the Colman and Rye MSS. have been separately administered since 1963 by the Norfolk and Norwich Record Office, which is situated in the new Norwich Central Library and where for the City side, the Libraries Committee is the controlling committee; at Lincoln, where the Lincolnshire County Archives Office is the recognised depository for archive materials and where close collaboration is maintained between this office and the city library; at Shrewsbury where an agreement has been reached concerning the geographic areas which the respective organisations cover without prejudice to existing holdings; at Newport, Monmouthshire, where there is a joint scheme with Monmouthshire County Archives; and at Carlisle where the Cumberland, Westmorland and Carlisle Record Office is situated. Somewhat similar schemes apply at Bury St Edmunds which has joint arrangements with West Suffolk; at Ipswich where the arrangement is with East Suffolk; and at Lichfield where the joint record office in the library is controlled by a committee consisting of representatives from Staffordshire County Council, Lichfield City Council and the Bishop of Lichfield, with the county archivist and city librarian as joint officials.

In some other cities and large towns, archive departments are administered as separate city record offices under the aegis of the town clerk or a records officer. Such separate record offices are to be found in Bristol, Canterbury, Coventry, Chester, Newcastle, Southampton and Winchester as well as in Edinburgh and Glasgow, whilst at Belfast the Public Record Office of Northern Ireland is the official repository. There are also a few authorities where archival functions are exercised by the museum rather than the library. This is so at Leicester, Hastings, Guildford, Maidstone and at the Manx Museum, Douglas, Isle of Man.

The most usual policy in municipalities, however, is for archival material to be administered as a part of the local history collection or as a separate record office within the central library, and archivists are employed in addition to professional librarians by those authorities possessing the largest collections such as are to be found in the cities of Birmingham, Liverpool, Manchester, Sheffield, Exeter, Westminster, Leeds, Gloucester, Plymouth, Nottingham, Cardiff and York, as well as in some large boroughs such as Halifax, Wigan, Bromley, Camden and Lambeth. A large collection of archival material requires the services of a professional archivist and it is of interest that as a result of the implementation of the Local Government (Records) Act, 1962 reported by about 30 local authorities not having separate record offices or joint arrangements with county record offices, six authorities report that one effect of this action has been the addition of an archivist to the staff. One authority to have appointed an archivist following this Act says that users have benefited because it has been possible to make available for study and research many official records which otherwise would have remained largely inaccessible.

Many librarians and archivists have commented on the changes in emphasis that have taken place in local studies in recent years and a comment from Plymouth perhaps expresses best what others have also noticed, namely that: 'The pattern of use too has altered, there being considerably more "in depth" enquiries from students. Far more emphasis is now placed on geographical and interpretative approaches.' This change has certainly brought about a livelier attitude to the collection of suitable material and has also prompted many librarians to acquire copies of theses written by students pursuing local studies in depth.

A detailed investigation into the use of local history collections and record offices would probably yield many surprising results, but it would unquestionably confirm a need for many more full-time staff to be employed upon this most rewarding aspect of public and county library activity.

Chapter 3

Printed Records

In many municipal libraries the local collection has a long history, having developed as an integral part of its parent library from the earliest days. It may indeed be said to antedate their foundation, for the claims of local history as an indispensable part of public libraries were referred to by William Ewart when introducing the first Public Libraries Bill into the House of Commons on 14 February 1850, while in Manchester the first librarian, that same Edward Edwards who had done so much to bring public libraries into being, emphasised this aspect of his work in his preliminary report to the Committee.[1] London's Guildhall Library has collected and preserved local records since 1824 and the origin of Warrington's local history library can be traced to the first accessions register which commenced in 1848, and manuscripts and archives of local interest are entered therein from January 1849 onwards.[2] Liverpool's Thomas Binns Collection, acquired in 1854, became the nucleus of its local library and several others commenced in these early days.

Indeed, for some seventy-five years the public library laboured almost alone in trying to bring together materials for the study of local history, and many thousands of records would have been lost to posterity during this period but for the efforts of many librarians, working alone and with funds hopelessly inadequate to allow competition with the private collector or

1. See the *Manchester Review*, 1946. p. 185.
2. G. A. Carter. 'Libraries and Local History'. *The Librarian and Book World*, August 1956. p. 131.

even the pulping mill, and lacking any sort of lead from the government or other national body.

Many library local collections owe their origin to the acquisition, by purchase or bequest, of the private library of some well-known collector or antiquary, and even today the opportunity to secure a collection occasionally presents itself, such as the naval history library acquired by Plymouth in 1962 and housed in a room next to the Plymouth local history library, and the Colman Collection presented to Norwich City Library in 1954. The William Jackson Collection presented to the city of Carlisle in 1890, the Charles Skidmore Collection presented to the city of Wakefield in 1906, and the Alexander C. Lamb Library, presented to Dundee by Edward Cox in 1901, still form the basis of their respective public library collections. Bedford Public Library is remarkable in having inherited a number of older collections from institutions which preceded the public service, notably the Old Bedford Library founded in 1700, the Bedfordshire General Library (1830) and the Bedford Literary and Scientific Institute (1846). It also received by bequest in 1956 the collection of historical material of Mr W. N. Henman, who had been a collector for sixty years.[3]

Economic considerations sometimes preclude the presentation of private collections to the library as a gift today, but it is usually possible to stimulate local patriotism and pride to the extent of raising a fund for its purchase. Derby's extensive local collection commenced in 1876, when the library was but six years old, with the presentation by the 7th Duke of Devonshire of his Derbyshire books, supplemented by many local books from the magnificent library at Chatsworth. In expressing their thanks to the donor the Library Committee announced their intention to make the topography and literature of the county a cardinal feature of the library service, and the collection was greatly augmented by the Bemrose Library, built up over many years by Sir Henry Bemrose and his two librarians, John Tilley and E. E. Taylor, which was purchased by public subscription in 1914, following the personal intervention of Lord Curzon of Kedleston.

Sometimes the library may have the opportunity to acquire a local parochial library, which parish churches are finding

3. See *The Library Story*. Bedford Public Library, 1958.

difficult to maintain in these days. These libraries which, for various reasons, cannot be kept properly in the parish present a problem and in some areas county and borough librarians have been asked to help. A collection of such libraries in Shropshire County Library is described in Chapter 10. The matter is of moment here because they often contain books, and occasionally even manuscripts, of local interest; at least one may expect to find a file of the local parish magazine and perhaps sermons and tracts by former clergy. For the rest they will consist mainly of theological and philosophical works, with a sprinkling of literature. They should, ideally, be kept together as a collection, a condition which does not always appeal to the modern library, invariably short of space.[4]

It is desirable that a definite sum should be allocated in the annual estimates for the purchase of local material and particularly for the special, and often expensive, items which come into the market from time to time. Some libraries have a special fund for the acquisition of important items of this kind, which it is possible to carry forward if unspent at the end of the year. In this way a sizeable reserve can be built up against the day when a special collection is offered. Such a fund for the equipment and maintenance of the collection is important, serving to remind the local authority and the library committee of its existence. It should be administered not by the committee but by the chairman, since local items must often be secured at short notice and in the face of competition and will be lost if committee sanction has to be awaited.

Haphazard methods of selection and overmuch reliance on gifts can only result in incomplete files, gaps in series and the lack of important books. 'No amount of organisation will make a good library out of badly selected material.' This remark of F. A. Sharr is as true of the local collection as of any other, for it is not merely a matter of diligent searching of the current output of publishers and wide reading of reviews, but requires a constant awareness of the opportunities which may present themselves, often in devious and outlandish ways.

Each library will have its own search routines for tracing out-of-the-way local books, adapted to the circumstances of its

4. Neil R. Ker (ed.). *The Parochial Libraries of the Church of England*. The Faith Press, London, 1959.

own collection and of the district and carried out with varying degrees of thoroughness and enthusiasm. Each, too, has its criteria which govern the material that goes into the collection and we can do no more than suggest a few rewarding avenues of approach which have been found useful by librarians in their quest for local items.

The basis of the selection of local material, as for normal book selection, should be the regular and unrelenting inspection of the British National Bibliography and similar lists of the bibliographical output of British and foreign publishers. It is true that much local material evades the long arm of the Copyright Office on which the BNB is based, but all kinds of odd and unusual items *do* feature in its weekly lists. Local studies are making increasing use of new printing and publishing techniques such as the mimeograph, multilith and the varieties of microprint, and the location and acquisition of the specialist material is often not easy. For material not included in BNB constant vigilance is needed, but if the local collection has been fully and correctly publicised over the years, much of this will come in unsolicited, though regular reminders are often essential to keep up-to-date. In this respect the knowledge and abilities of members of the library staff, who may be connected with local organisations, and even of friends and members of the library, can be utilised. This is particularly useful in county libraries where branch librarians should be encouraged to look for items relating to their own locality.

A well-tried and usually most effective method is the circular letter sent periodically to local societies and other bodies, business firms, solicitors, estate agents, clerks of district and parish councils, asking for information concerning their publications. Similar letters may be sent to local incumbents requesting details of guides to their churches, parochial magazines and other publications. For important material of this kind a personal signed letter should be sent. Guides to churches, buildings of historic or architectural interest, country houses open to the public and archaeological sites can be obtained by personal visits, and this applies to theatres, sports and social meetings. Local newspaper and printing offices should be asked to supply lists or details of their publications, however slight and apparently unimportant – a personal visit and acquaintance with the proprietor will help here too. Local BBC and press agency offices often receive local publications for review and any organisation which has a public relations officer provides an obvious and amenable avenue of approach. Finally the columns of local newspapers and periodicals should be screened regularly by the staff for reviews and notices of books and other materials.

The advisability of attending auctions is arguable. Better results can often be obtained by making friends with a local dealer or even paying him a small commission to execute bids for the library. The librarian should, of course, keep an eye on all local sales, especially of country houses and estates, and he should, where possible, view the lots prior to the sale, either personally or through an agent. It is dangerous to bid without examination of the lots, since catalogue entries can be notoriously misleading and material cannot be returned. The library can often acquire collections by private treaty prior to sale, and for important collections this is often desirable to prevent them being sold piecemeal.

National sales such as those of Messrs. Sotheby, Christie, etc., should be carefully watched, especially for local manuscripts. Catalogues can be ordered at moderate charges, and auctioneers will usually give advice on the approximate value of items or execute bids on behalf of the library, but this is advisable mainly for items where prices are not expected to be high.

An agreement was reached in 1969 between the Association of Municipal Corporations and the British Railways Board concerning the sale of railway plans not covered by Section 144 of the Transport Act, 1968 but which are likely to be of interest to the public. As a result of this agreement the Board advises the AMC and the Society of Archivists when documents relating to a particular railway are available for sale and states when they will be available for inspection in order that this information can be passed to members of the Association and the Society. An opportunity is given, therefore, to local authorities to make offers for these plans before they reach the auction room.

The framework of the local collection will be the general literature about the area, whether it be a county, city, town or rural district. General historical works written about the locality or any part of it will be accompanied by social, economic, political or military histories; guidebooks, road books and topographical works will be augmented by books on natural history, customs and folklore, and by monographs on geology, land utilisation, soil science, etc. The religious history of the area will embrace all sects and denominations and its educational history will include schools of all kinds from the early Bell, Lancasterian and endowed schools to public schools and the modern 'comprehensive'. There will be books and articles, too, on ancient crafts and modern industries, on sports and games, and on the arts – music, the theatre, painting and architecture.

The class of material is extensive and will constitute the bulk of the collection. The smallest handbook, guide or almanac should not be despised and much of the material will consist of ephemeral items such as pamphlets, posters, programmes and leaflets, which are easily destroyed unless vigilance is constantly employed. Books and pamphlets should be sought in each variant edition, since these may contain important changes or corrections which are not always apparent on cursory inspection.

Another important section is the imaginative literature, both past and present, pertaining to the locality. The alert librarian will find it a simple matter to collect novels, essays, poems and plays by local residents and natives, but the literature with a local setting, whether based on historical fact, presenting an authentic picture of local life, or merely romance in a regional background, is usually less obvious. Some libraries, in addition to collecting the printed works of local imaginative writers, have tried to build up collections of their manuscripts. Norwich paid £75 for the MS. of part of R. H. Mottram's famous war series, *The Spanish Farm Trilogy*. A tactful approach usually finds authors willing to present their original manuscripts to the library. Stories and articles in the local dialect should be sought as well as local word-books and studies in phonology.

Most local books published before the last war are now out-of-print and few will ever be reprinted. Hence the necessity for diligent searching in second-hand bookshops and booksellers' catalogues, and the need to form a reserve of duplicate copies against the day when the originals wear out. Many popular books need to be duplicated in other departments of the library,

but first copies of all books about the area should be allocated
to the local history library.

Local works have always been, to a large degree, printed in
the locality and the local bookshop is usually the best place to
seek them; albeit often the worst as regards the price! Where a
firm of long standing still exists their attics and storerooms will
often bring to light many of the firm's productions. On the
other hand local books can often be picked up quite cheaply in
bookshops at the other end of the country, and many a librarian
has enlivened a dull annual conference and made it more
profitable by discoveries in the venue's antiquarian bookshops,
to say nothing of the annual pilgrimages to Charing Cross
Road! There is room for closer co-operation between librarians
in searching and reporting on local literature.

Apart from books, periodical articles are an extremely
important item in any comprehensive local collection. In no
other country are local societies so numerous, or so active in
transcribing and publishing local records, as in Britain, and
their publications have great value for the historical worker.
Full sets of the journals or proceedings of any archaeological,
historical, record and parish register societies active in the
neighbourhood are therefore invaluable, and they should be
duplicated for lending purposes wherever possible. Publications
of natural history societies and field clubs should be similarly
sought. Many of these societies have extensive libraries of their
own. Some have been deposited in public libraries with mutual
benefit, as at Gloucester where the city library houses the
libraries of the Bristol and Gloucestershire Archaeological
Society and the Cotteswold Naturalists' Field Club. *A Guide to
the Historical and Archaeological Publications of Societies in England
and Wales, 1901–1933* (University of London, The Athlone
Press, 1968), compiled for the Institute of Historical Research
by E. L. C. Mullins, contains 30,000 entries, fully indexed, to
the publications bearing upon the history and archaeology of
England and Wales, the Isle of Man and the Channel Islands,
of more than 400 local and national societies located within
these areas and issued by them between 1901 and 1933. It is
complementary to *Writings on British History 1901–1933* (5 vols.
in 7 separate books in progress of publication by Jonathan Cape
for the Royal Historical Society) and is continued in *Writings*

on British History, 1934 also compiled for the Royal Historical
Society and published by Cape annually until 1939. Two
further volumes cover the years 1940–1945 and later volumes
are being prepared at the Institute of Historical Research.

The nature and extent of local serial publications varies
greatly from area to area. Some consist entirely of record series,
such as parish registers, handlists of documents of local
authorities, facsimile reproductions, texts and calendars; others
publish chiefly secondary material in the form of articles on
local history, archaeology and kindred topics. In some counties
one society fulfils all these functions; in others the work of the
archaeological or historical society is supplemented by parish
register or record societies. R. Somerville's *Handlist of Record
Publications* (British Records Association, London, 1951), has
been brought up to date from time to time in *Archives* and
William Kellaway's 'Record Publications of Societies' (*Archives*,
vol. 7, no. 20, 1965, pp. 46–9), contained a further supplement
that gives a fair conspectus of the recent publishing activity of
record societies.

Tracing current periodical articles relating to any particular
locality has become much more difficult since the *Regional
Lists* that were issued from 1954 until 1966 by the Library
Association ceased publication. These lists contained material
conveniently arranged from the *Subject Index to Periodicals* and
later the *British Humanities Index*. The local history librarian,
therefore, must now search each issue of *British Humanities
Index* for this material. Publications of the Council for British
Archaeology are also helpful, especially the *Archaeological
Bibliography for Great Britain and Ireland* which is published
annually, is arranged by counties, and interpreting the term
'archaeological' very widely, its lists include references to
history, architecture and industrial archaeology up to 1600.
Where a county collection is maintained it should be noted
that journals issued in adjacent counties occasionally contain
articles of interest. Offprints of these can often be obtained
through the 'offprints scheme' organised by the Council for
British Archaeology which publishes half-yearly *Current and
Forthcoming Offprints on Archaeology in Great Britain and Ireland*
as well as an annual *British Archaeological Abstracts*. A useful
review of the periodical literature and occasional publications

relating to the six northern counties of England has been published annually in *Northern History* since 1966 and periodical articles relating to Northern Ireland are now listed in *Northern Ireland Local History*, which is issued bi-monthly from Belfast Public Libraries to a group of contributing libraries in Northern Ireland. A number of the fourteen regional groups of the Council for British Archaeology issue bulletins, newsletters, etc. periodically. The material of these often overlaps into the fields of local and industrial history, as well as that of conventional archaeology. Some cite newspaper articles and other ephemeral material. Most include brief or interim reports of local excavations, fieldwork, etc., which concern either projects which have not reached the stage of a full final report, or minor projects which may not warrant a fuller report.

The more fugitive publications of many smaller societies active in the area must also be sought. These include cultural, charitable and sporting organisations of all kinds. Such material is naturally particularly important in a town or city collection and Birmingham receives more than 1,000 annual reports each year from organisations as diverse as churches, hospitals, charitable institutions, rambling and sports clubs, dramatic, operatic, political, scientific, educational, artistic, photographic and religious societies.

Material which emanates with regularity from the departments of the county or municipal authority must be assiduously collected and, surprisingly, many libraries find their local government colleagues less responsive than outside bodies to requests for regular distribution, and a periodic check-up is necessary. Council minutes, estimates, official diaries and the annual reports of the various departments invariably reach the library in due course, but a keen watch needs to be kept on the less regular material, which includes by-laws, programmes of civic events such as official openings of new buildings and amenities, visits of important personages, and publicity material of any kind. The Local Government (Records) Act, 1962, has given an opportunity to all local authorities in England and Wales to provide an adequate system for the periodic review of all local records in order that a suitable collection of these records should be made for retention, and it was envisaged that such a selection should include 'a sample of case histories and other documents of the council's detailed work'. Although this Act has been implemented by some local authorities and some local libraries and record offices have become the repository for such records, there appear to be few instances so far of the operation of any detailed plans for the systematic review of local records which could be made to include important printed material such as development plans authorised under various Town and Country Planning Acts as well as under the New Town Acts.

Many publications of the central government have a local significance, and HMSO lists should be regularly scanned for them. Matters affecting local boundaries, mines, trade and agriculture, public health, water supply, geology and land utilisation are frequently discussed in government publications, in addition to the Acts of Parliament and statutory instruments. Local acts are by no means as numerous today as they formerly were, when they dealt with a variety of topics from agriculture to water. They were found to be necessary to meet a variety of special or pressing problems in the eighteenth and nineteenth centuries, such as the regulation of local courts, manorial and other; inclosing, dividing and allotting common lands; the making and maintenance of turnpike roads, building of bridges, etc.; for cutting canals and later for the construction of railways; for town improvements, drainage, sanitation, lighting, etc., and for the recovery of debts. Many *ad hoc* authorities were established for these and other purposes, and their records, printed and manuscript, have occasionally survived.

The early reports of the charity commissioners shed light on our old parish charities, while the minutes of evidence taken before parliamentary committees or at local inquiries are useful basic source material. In Spring 1970 the Irish University Press published a *Short Title Catalogue of the First 520 Titles* of its Series of British Parliamentary Papers ('Blue Books'), published with the active co-operation of Southampton University Press, which when complete will contain 1,000 volumes of these Papers. The chief editorial advisers of the project are Professor P. Ford and Mrs G. Ford.

The best general guide to Acts of Parliament is the *Index to Statutes in Force, 1235–1968* (HMSO, London, 1969). The town clerk or clerk to the county council can usually supply a list of recent statutes affecting his own authority, but in county districts each parish may have its own special acts. A large number of these are still in print. Nowadays numerous statutory orders affect local government, and the librarian must keep up-to-date on these by examining the monthly lists. Other guides and finding-aids for Acts of Parliament are dealt with by M. F. Bond in *Guide to the Records of Parliament* (HMSO, London, 1971).

Private acts are generally more difficult both to trace and to obtain, being older, yet they are important in throwing light upon the social aspects of history. They deal with such matters as the settlement of disputes relating to estates, legacies and entails; separation orders; lunacy; divorce (obtainable only by Act of Parliament before 1857); questions of citizenship and change of name. Acts since the year 1801 are included in the *Index to Local and Personal Acts, 1801-1947* (HMSO, London, 1949). The best guides to earlier private acts are Vardon's *Index to Local and Personal and Private Acts, 1798-1839* (London, 1840) and Bramwell's *Analytical Table of Private Statutes* (2 vols., London, 1813). For some areas lists of local Acts have been compiled and published, such as *Acts of Parliament Concerning Wales, 1714-1901*, edited by T. I. Jeffreys-Jones (University of Wales Press, Cardiff, 1959), *Lancashire Acts of Parliament, 1266-1957*, compiled by Sidney Horrocks (Joint Committee on the Lancashire Bibliography, Manchester, 1969), and *Acts of Parliament and Proclamations Relating to the East Riding of Yorkshire and Kingston upon Hull, 1529-1800*, edited by K. A. MacMahon (University of Hull, 1961).

Some libraries have built up or acquired extensive collections of printed material dealing with local industries, sometimes forming a library in its own right. High Wycombe has a collection relating to furniture; Macclesfield a silk library; Walsall and Yeovil a collection on leather; Warrington a collection on tanning and wire; Stourbridge and Guildford on glass; Darlington and Swindon on railways; Douglas, Isle of Man, on the T.T. Races; both South Shields and Lowestoft have good collections of photographs relating to shipping, and shipping material is also collected at Sunderland and Tower Hamlets. Derbyshire County, Whitehaven, Barrow and Truro all have material relating to mining; whilst a collection relating to spas and mineral waters at Harrogate contains material dating from 1572 onwards. Lincoln's Exley Collection of MSS. and photographs relates to Lincoln Inns, Lincoln and Lincolnshire watch and clock-makers and Lincolnshire windmills, and Norwich has a collection on East Anglian windmills.

Records of local business and industrial firms are often ignored and it is only recently that their value in economic history has been appreciated. We shall not deal here with collections of business records as such, since we are considering printed materials at the moment. Most libraries receive copies of any printed histories of local firms which are produced. They are usually lavish productions proudly issued in connection with jubilee or centenary celebrations. We are indeed frequently consulted during the preparation of these and such historical details as they contain have often been unearthed in the library. The Guildhall Library has built up over the years an extensive collection of London business house histories, which comprises 900 items, mostly privately issued, relating to London firms or to firms having close association with the city.

Other material, such as trade catalogues and pattern books may be even more important. They are the source of much reliable data and successive editions over a period will illustrate the development of a firm as no other record can. Advertising and publicity material is not so readily forthcoming, but the eighteenth- and nineteenth-century trading cards, handbills, catalogues and bill-heads of local tradesmen should be assiduously collected. For current material the co-operation of the local chamber of commerce is important, but individual requests to firms remain the only sure way of gathering in a substantial part of it. In large libraries, too, the commercial library will be asked to transfer data relating to local firms to the local history department when its immediate usefulness has ended.

The house organs or magazines issued by many large industrial enterprises or company groups may be worth retaining if they relate mainly to local firms, but often today they contain little of interest or merit, consisting of personalities and gossip and details of sporting events. Occasionally, however, articles on the history or development of the firm appear and they may provide biographical details not otherwise known. Sheffield has issued an excellent duplicated list of

'House Histories and Magazines of Manufacturing and Commercial Firms in the Department of Local History and Archives' (Local History Leaflet, no. 8, 1966). The importance of patent specifications in industrial development is frequently overlooked. They are filed only in the largest libraries, but copies of specific patents taken out by local firms of individuals can easily be obtained.

Sale catalogues are acquired fairly easily by asking local auctioneers and estate agents to place the library on their mailing lists, or by inspecting the advertisement columns of local newspapers regularly. The older catalogues of houses and estates were usually accompanied by valuable plans, and even a brief outline history of the house and family, and some of these can still be secured from the older firms. The Estate Exchange in London has a huge collection of the catalogues of important estates, arranged by counties. Printing costs today preclude lavish presentation, and most of the larger estates have already wilted beneath the auctioneer's hammer. Smaller catalogues of the contents of houses have a slighter historical appeal but are not without interest as showing the condition of the property at the time of sale, while the fact that valuable local books, prints and pictures often appear in them constitutes an argument for obtaining them which no librarian should ignore. The help of the local museum curator who usually receives these catalogues is invaluable in this connection.

Many libraries possess material, which is often unique, relating to the history of the theatre in their own locality. Special collections of playbills, programmes, handbills, newspaper cuttings, letters and papers, photographs and pictorial material, as well as plans, drawings and portraits, have often been made by enthusiasts and eventually come to the library. A special collection on Sadler's Wells is housed at Finsbury Library which is now administered by the London borough of Islington; Bristol has the Richard Smith Collection, which includes manuscripts, relating to the theatre in Bristol. Leeds has Alfred Mattinson's manuscript 'Chronicle of the Leeds Stage', in addition to a large collection of playbills, while York possesses Tate Wilkinson's account books and Norwich the Bolingbroke and other collections. Brighton, Leicester, Nottingham, Scarborough, Sunderland and Tynemouth all have large collections of playbills. A collection on theatres at Richmond upon Thames includes material on the Theatre Royal once managed by Edmund Keen and the Guildhall Library and Westminster both have large collections (Westminster's exceeds 18,000 items) relating to theatres throughout the metropolis.

These library collections contain material not only on the famous theatres and companies such as the Old Vic at Lambeth and Sadler's Wells at Finsbury, but also on the Victorian music halls and even on their forerunners, the concert rooms attached to public houses. Most provincial libraries have at least nucleus collections of playbills of their local theatres. The resources of the metropolitan libraries in this field are detailed by R. L. Collison in *Theatre Collections: A Symposium*, edited by A. M. C. Kahn (Library Resources of the Greater London Area, no. 4. South-Eastern Group of the Reference and Special Libraries Section of the Library Association, London, 1955).[5]

Naturally any special events in music and drama, such as centenaries and festivals, will be thoroughly covered and often a special volume is made up for these. Edinburgh keeps a detailed record of its Annual Festival of Music and Drama. Since 1947 all programmes, exhibition catalogues and news cuttings containing description and criticism of the various activities are made up annually and bound into quarto volumes. Leeds now holds a complete set of programmes for the Leeds Musical Festivals, which have been held since 1858 and Norwich has an almost complete set of its programmes for the triennial festival which commenced in 1824. Lowestoft has a Benjamin Britten Collection containing all published scores with some manuscripts and letters as well as programmes of first performances, and Blackburn has a Kathleen Ferrier Collection. Box offices are not particularly interested in the preservation of such items and often the surest way is for the librarian to attend and present his own copy to the library. Collections relating to art and artists are less numerous in libraries, being more usually attached to museums, but there are exceptions such as Islington's W. R. Sickert Collection

5. Collections outside the metropolitan area are covered in Dr Alfred Loewenburg's *Theatre of the British Isles, excluding London: A Bibliography* (Society for Theatre Research, London, 1950), while the international field is dealt with in *Theatre Collections in Libraries and Museums: An International Handbook*, by Rosamund Gilder and G. Freedley (Stevens and Brown, London, 1936).

and a collection of drawings and paintings by L. S. Lowry at Swinton and Pendlebury. Weymouth received a fine collection of local paintings and prints as a gift in 1967. A cyclostyled catalogue of this collection, known as the Ernest Bussell Collection, issued in 1968 contains entries relating to 239 items.

The political history of an area is represented mainly in the squibs and cartoons, election addresses and the many pamphlets and broadsides issued by the protagonists in the days when, contrary to popular opinion, there was much more partisan and party feeling in local elections than there is today. While older material of this kind is collected by most libraries when opportunity beckons, it would seem that few make a concerted effort to acquire the literature of modern elections, and the party organizations appear to make little attempt to keep their own material. An exception is Birmingham which writes to every candidate on nomination day preceding every election, parliamentary or municipal, requesting a complete set of the circulars he has issued, and by this means claims to receive the bulk of the available literature. Its files of election literature are fairly complete from 1874 for general elections and from 1901 for municipal elections. South Shields has a unique collection representative of both local and parliamentary elections from the first borough election of 1832.

Two writers refer to the value of election addresses as historical material, pointing out that 'they are not documents which find their way into the great libraries of deposit. They are indeed the most fleeting and ephemeral of political testaments . . .' and suggesting that 'university libraries and any other bodies concerned with inquiry into the political life of the nation should in future make every effort to preserve such material. It costs nothing except the postage of sending for it and it occupies very little space in the library itself.'[6] Municipal election addresses are unfortunately often standardised and repetitive today and the library can be selective.

Many writers have commented on the value of directories in dealing with a wide range of inquiries within the period during which local directories have been published. They

6. R. B. McCallum and Alison Readman. 'The Election Addresses' in *The British General Election of 1945*, edited by Geoffrey Cumberlege. Oxford University Press, London, 1947. pp. 88–91.

began to appear generally in the late eighteenth century and the directories containing the fullest information were published between the 1830s and 1930s. Although warnings have been given by many historians concerning the accuracy of the information in some directories, they are often regarded with printed maps and newspapers, as 'original sources'. This valuable section should be as complete as the most diligent search can make it because directories, like other classes of material, derive added value from being part of a complete series. Photocopies can often be obtained today when the originals cannot. Libraries such as the British Museum, the Bodleian Library, the Guildhall Library, London, and the Society of Genealogists contain many local poll books and directories. The local section of early national directories such as Barfoot and Wilkes's *Universal British Directory*, c. 1790, or the Enumerators' Returns for the Censuses of 1841, 1851, 1861 and 1871 at the Public Record Office are vital records of this kind which can be obtained on microfilm.

An invaluable bibliography of local directories is Miss Jane E. Norton's *Guide to the National and Provincial Directories of England and Wales, Excluding London, Published before 1856*, issued by the Royal Historical Society in 1950. A comprehensive list of *Lancashire Directories 1684–1957*, compiled by G. H. Tupling was revised, enlarged and edited by Sidney Horrocks and published in 1968 as the first part of a Lancashire Bibliography. Fuller reference to the Lancashire Bibliography is made in Chapter 15. A second copy of all modern directories should be purchased for the collection since reference copies are subject to extensive wear. Copies of the electoral roll and earlier lists of voters and poll books are also valuable as supplying lists of inhabitants at various times and thus supplementing local directories. For earlier periods the roll of burgesses or freemen, subsidy rolls and hearth and poll tax records, where printed, meet a similar need.

Newspapers published in the area have long been recognised as valuable sources of historical information of many kinds and most librarians file and bind at least one local paper, usually a weekly edition. Few today can afford to bind a daily paper. Binding costs and the doubtful permanence of modern newsprint account for the increasing popularity of microfilming for newspapers in recent years. The eighteenth-century newspaper was made of pure rag stock and the very fact of its survival in readable condition is eloquent testimony to its enduring qualities, but even so where storage space is at a premium files are today being put on to film.

Happy the library which possesses a complete file of its local newspaper from its commencement, for few have survived the ravages of time and the political and parliamentary history of the past two centuries cannot be fully written in their absence. Edinburgh's file starts in 1705 and has very few gaps: Northampton has a complete set of the *Northampton Mercury* from 1720 to the present-day and Derby of the *Derby Mercury* from its commencement in 1732. Such files are in great demand and not only, of course, for local inquiries, and a local newspaper file becomes a tool of the greatest value when equipped with an index. Few libraries have so far attempted to index local newspapers in detail, although York possesses an index of York newspapers 1728–1878 and from 1899 to date and work is also in progress to fill the gap. A card index to the *Nottingham Journal* is in process of compilation following an advertisement for volunteers in 1963. So far an index covering persons, places and subjects has been made for the years 1801–20 and some of the original volunteers are still working on this index. A single voluntary worker in Ealing has just completed an index to the local newspaper after ten years' work. At Chester the library staff have produced a selective index to three Chester newspapers for the years 1955–59, published in 1964 and now out of print and a further index covering the period 1960–64 was published in 1970. Opportunities for acquiring newspaper files are limited but microfilming programmes of recent years undertaken by libraries and newspaper offices have filled many gaps.

Papers which are not filed for permanent preservation are usually examined regularly for cuttings, and a well-selected clippings file will eventually have a positive value. Birmingham binds its mounted clippings into volumes covering broad topics, such as streets, elections, railways and biography. At Edinburgh, where the collection of news cuttings consists of 50,000 items and 415 bound volumes, the cuttings are mounted on standard-size sheets of cartridge, classed and indexed, then stored in boxes. When there is enough material on a subject the sheets are bound into a volume which is shelved in a special sequence of press cutting volumes. *The Triennial Report 1964–1967* of the Norwich Public Libraries stated that

The collection of mounted press cuttings has increased by some 15,000 items in the last three years. . . . Press cutting collections take time to accumulate, but they supply the answers to approximately one-quarter of all requests received, and are often the only source of information on recent Norfolk events frequently needed by such various enquirers as local authorities, authors, television programme planners, and press agencies (p. 7).

The collection of books printed or published in the locality, but not otherwise pertaining to it, should be approached with care, and money should not be wasted upon books whose local value is confined to the title-page. Books which contribute materially to the history of local printing and allied trades may be bought, and any gifts will naturally be retained. Some librarians prescribe a definite date and collect only books published earlier, but there are occasionally modern imprints of special interest, fine or rare editions, and in some areas, of course, special presses whose productions are worthy acquisitions. Edinburgh collects nothing of this nature later than 1700 and it has some rare examples of the work of the Holyrood Press, a Jesuit printing press set up in the precincts of Holyrood from 1686 to 1688 and destroyed by a mob after the accession of William III. Glasgow's collection covers books produced in the city prior to 1800: it also includes an outstanding selection of Foulis Press books, said to be more complete than that in the British Museum. Hounslow has a large collection of the products of the Chiswick Press, operated by the Whittinghams at Chiswick from 1809 to 1852; Hammersmith collects works of the Kelmscott, Dove and Eragny Presses; Reading possesses a collection of Golden Cockerell Press books published in Berkshire 1921–33; Warrington's collection of books printed by William Eyres, Lancashire's most outstanding eighteenth-century printer,[7] from 1760 to 1802, contains many books printed for scholars, scientists and philanthropists associated

7. Arthur John Hawkes. *Lancashire Printed Books: A Bibliography of All the Books Printed in Lancashire down to the Year 1800.* Printed for the Public Libraries Committee by J. Starr & Sons, Wigan, 1925. pp. xxii–xxiv.

with the Warrington Academy; Bristol's Sabin Collection is of local fine and private printing, while Montgomeryshire County has an interesting collection of Gregynog Press books. Two of Sheffield's local history leaflets are concerned with books printed in Sheffield: *Books Printed at Sheffield in the Eighteenth Century* (Local History Leaflet, no. 12, 1967) and *Books Printed by John Garnet, Sheffield's First Known Printer* (Local History Leaflet, no. 13, 1969).

Magazines published locally should be filed permanently, except in the larger publishing centres such as London. Even when their contents have no direct value for local history, they may be interesting as examples of printing and they may contain early and comparatively unknown works of local writers who may later achieve fame. This applies with special force to school magazines, such as the early poem by A. E. Housman in *The Bromsgrovian* for 1882, only a single copy of which could be found when the Housman Centenary Exhibition was organized in 1959, or *The Granthamian*, to which Frederick Rolfe (Baron Corvo) contributed a poem while serving as assistant master between 1884 and 1886 and for which a biographer sought in vain in 1960.[8]

Every figure in the history of literature and letters, and in other walks of life, should have his special collection, as complete as possible, in some publicly accessible library, preferably in the area in which he lived and worked. Here should be gathered every book written by him, in all editions, so that the keen bibliographer can compare them all in one place, and critical and biographical material about him. With early, well-known or voluminous writers it may not be possible to secure each variant edition in book form, but microfilm faculties will assist this today. It is worthwhile compiling a bibliography of local writers, listing every edition, with the location of copies.

Some of these collections in libraries are so extensive as to form special collections in their own right. Pre-eminent is the monumental Shakespeare Memorial Library in Birmingham Reference Library, which consists of over 40,000 volumes in 74 languages.[9]

8. See *Notes and Queries*, September 1960. p. 347.
9. See W. R. N. Payne. 'The Special Collection: Some Present Day Problems'. *Library Association Record*, vol. 52, July 1950. pp. 231–2.

The Tennyson Research Centre at the Lincoln Central Library containing material deposited there by Lord Tennyson and members of the Tennyson family contains, *inter alia,* 4,000 volumes from the poet's own library, family papers, letters, household books and publishers' accounts; a *Catalogue of the Wordsworth Collection* (Carlisle Public Libraries, 1970) extends to fifty pages; and Miss Lucy I. Edwards, Local History Librarian of Nottingham City Library, has compiled a most useful guide entitled *D. H. Lawrence: A Finding List [Showing] Holdings in the City, County and University Libraries of Nottingham* (Nottinghamshire County Council, Nottingham, 1968) which extends to 125 pages. A catalogue has also been published by Northampton of the John Clare Collection which contains MSS. of some 1,350 poems, autograph letters and Clare's personal library of about 400 volumes with portraits and other items. There is also a John Clare Collection at Peterborough. Enfield has a Charles Lamb Collection and Ealing the Selborne Society Library of material on Gilbert White. There are George Eliot collections at Nuneaton and Coventry; and collections on: John Bunyan at Bedford; Robert Burns at Glasgow; Walter Scott, R. L. Stevenson and Conan Doyle at Edinburgh; the Brontës at Keighley; Byron at Nottingham; Thomas Hardy at Dorset County; Samuel Johnson at Lichfield; Francis Thompson at Preston; the Sitwells at Scarborough; H. G. Wells and Walter de la Mare at Bromley; Keats at Camden; Sir Richard Burton at Richmond; William Morris at Waltham Forest; Winifred Holtby at Bridlington and Hull; William Blake at Lambeth and Westminster and G. B. Shaw at Luton.

The simplest way to compile a list of local worthies is to check the *Dictionary of National Biography* or its Epitome, but this will not be exhaustive. There has always been a great divergence of opinion as to what constitutes a 'local' author. The controversy may be studied in the literature and will not be entered into here, except to say that the author would prefer a definition which insists that, to qualify, the writer should have contributed something significant to the life of the area, not merely lived for a time within its boundaries. Such a restriction is essential in the large city and metropolitan libraries, whose lists would otherwise be formidable, and most libraries limit their collections to people with real and well-established local affiliations, not merely several years' residence.

It is clearly impossible for the libraries of the London boroughs to attempt complete coverage of the many writers who have at one time or another lived in various parts of the metropolis. Nevertheless, there are substantial collections on a few outstanding writers to be found in some London boroughs as has just been indicated and it is of interest that Bromley's H. G. Wells Collection which started in 1952 was augmented by the purchase of a large collection from Heffers in 1958. In 1966 it became the basis of a large centenary exhibition and was used by the producers of radio and television programmes on Wells, and a catalogue of this collection is to be published. It is also intended to build the Walter de la Mare Collection, started in 1967, in a similar manner. The Sir Arthur Conan Doyle Memorial Collection presented by the Sherlock Holmes Society of London is housed in the Marylebone District Library of the City of Westminster and the City also came into possession of the Preston Blake Library in 1967 through the generosity of its owner and creator, Mr Kerrison Preston, himself a Blake scholar. This collection will be developed as new books and material on William Blake appear, since Blake was born and spent most of his life in the City.

Outside the metropolis Southport has attempted perfection in a comprehensive collection of local authors, but Birkenhead states that 'local authors are no longer collected'. Manchester, on the other hand, in addition to its collection of printed works of all local authors, houses the library of the Lancashire Authors' Association.

Literature relating to the foremost figures in English literary history is often collected by the national and university libraries, and it is difficult and unnecessary for local libraries to compete, at any rate on the same level of intensity. It is not surprising, therefore, to find that the authors collected by libraries form a heterogeneous list, and include many fiction and even juvenile writers, such as Kathleen Fidler (Wigan), Angela Brazil (Coventry), Reginald Maddock (Warrington), Edna Lyall (Herefordshire), Hesba Stretton (Shrewsbury) and Daisy Ashford (Norwich). In Scotland authors are allocated on a local basis under the Scottish Fiction Reserve Scheme which theoretically (and increasingly in practice) ensures the systematic collection and preservation of the works of Scottish novelists, both major and minor. It is being planned on a basis of regional associations with libraries being responsible for authors within their area or closely connected with it.

A list of authors included in the scheme, compiled by Dr W. R. Aitken, formerly County Librarian of Ayrshire, was published by the Scottish Library Association in 1955.

While the imaginative writers, poets, novelists and play-wrights, are important, the factual writers must not be neglected. When such an author is an accepted authority on his chosen subject his works may be placed in the general collections, but they should appear in the local catalogue and be earmarked for eventual transfer when their general usefulness has ended. There are also notabilities in various walks of life, scientists, clerics, political figures, social reformers, inventors, indus-trialists, who have written little or nothing but about whom a substantial literature has grown. Newcastle-upon-Tyne's special collections include the Cowen Collection dealing with the nineteenth-century Reform movement, and the Bewick Collection, commemorating Thomas Bewick, the naturalist and engraver. S. Roscoe's bibliography of Bewick, published in 1953, was largely based on the latter. Haringey's postal history collection includes manuscripts of Rowland Hill, originator of the Penny Post. Sheffield's material relating to Edmund Burke (part of the vast Wentworth-Woodhouse Muniments) has been sufficiently extensive to cause Professor Thomas Copeland of the University of Massachusetts to work in the Sheffield City Libraries on and off for twenty years as Editor-in-Chief of *The Correspondence of Edmund Burke* (to be published in ten volumes by the Cambridge University Press and the Chicago University Press of which 9 volumes, 1958–1970, have so far appeared). Probably one of the greatest works of scholarship ever produced in any public library in this country, the facilities have resulted in the agreement of Professor Copeland and his fellow editors to deposit in Sheffield all microfilms and other copies of Burke material which are housed elsewhere. The collection of material relating to James Nasmyth at Eccles shows how photocopies can make a small collection almost complete. Occasionally the collection consists chiefly of the personal library built up by the personality. York has the library of the late Sir John Marriott, historian and M.P. for the city. Kensington owns the greater part of Sir Richard Burton's collection, but this is now situated at the Royal Anthropological Institute and is for public use there, whilst Southwark has the Faraday Memorial Library.

Family histories and genealogies are closely allied to biography and akin to both are heraldry, parish registers, marriage licences, wills, epitaphs and monumental inscriptions. Many standard works of this kind will be found in G. W. Marshall's *The Genealogist's Guide*, 1903 (reprinted by the Genealogical Publishing Co., New York, 1967) supplemented by T. R. Thomson's *A Catalogue of British Family Histories* (Oxford University Press, London, 2nd ed. 1935) and in the Subject Catalogue of the Manchester Reference Library, Section 929, Genealogy, Parts 1–3 (1956–58), while in Scotland Miss Joan P. S. Ferguson's *Scottish Family Histories Held in Scottish Libraries* (Scottish Central Library, Edinburgh, 1960) is valuable. There are, however, many more family histories and pedigrees, privately printed for circulation amongst members of the family; some merely typed in a limited edition, others remaining in a single manuscript copy. It is often possible, when work is being done on such compilations in the library, to request or invite the author to place a copy of the finished work in the local collection, even to the extent of offering assistance, clerical or financial, towards the production of the finished article. Authors usually respond willingly to this, though there is the occasional person who feels that notes compiled for the delectation of the family should not be exposed to public view and criticism. The librarian must often be prepared to agree to restriction placed on the use of such volumes, if they are presented. A descriptive guide to *Genealogical Manuscripts in British Libraries* (Magna Charta Book Co., Baltimore, Maryland, 1967) has been compiled by Marion J. Kaminkow who has also compiled *A New Bibliography of British Genealogy with Notes* (Magna Charta Book Co., Baltimore, Maryland, 1965) which contains 1,783 numbered items arranged in eight main groups.

Public awareness of the importance of thesis literature has increased during recent years: many important local studies

3

submitted for degrees or teaching diplomas are never published and have a very limited availability in university and college libraries. Yet in these can be found some of the most valuable original research work done upon the area, especially in such fields as geology and the related sciences of geomorphology and petrology; economic and industrial history; agriculture and soil science (pedology); phonology and dialects; and the history of education. *The Index to Theses Accepted for Higher Degrees in the Universities of Great Britain and Ireland* published annually by Aslib (vol. 17, 1966–67, edited by G. M. Patterson, Aslib, London, 1969) illustrates the wide variety of topics selected as subjects for theses and also gives details of the standards drawn up by SCONUL concerning the use of thesis literature, and gives a list of British universities showing the present position concerning the borrowing and copying of theses at each university listed. A further guide to theses is published annually by the Institute of Historical Research in two parts – 'Theses in Progress' and 'Theses Completed' under the general title of *Historical Research for University Degrees in the United Kingdom.*

Maps, photographs, prints, drawings, broadsides and other visual material can assist the study of local history at many points and, unless there is agreement with the museum or other institution they should be acquired as diligently and as systematically as other printed material. In some libraries collections of this material approximate to completeness or at least give a representative picture of the situation; in others they are incomplete and unrepresentative, oddments acquired by accident or fortune rather than by design. The Dryden Collection of drawings, plans and notes on churches, houses and various archaeological matters in the Northampton Public Library is of national importance in so far as it covers almost every county in England. This material, left by Sir Henry Dryden, now contains about 3,000 items and has been described in a printed catalogue as well as having been given special mention by W. G. Hoskins in his *Local History of England* (p. 34). In 1957 the Council for British Archaeology undertook the compilation of a guide to the collections of topographical drawings and similar material in public libraries, museums, record offices and in the libraries of antiquarian societies throughout Britain. The information collected by the CBA is being up-dated by M. W. Barley at Nottingham University and is now (1972) nearing completion.

Maps and plans, both printed and manuscript, are extremely important as ancillary records, and the coverage of the area should be as complete as possible. Most counties have a long series of 'county' maps from the days of Saxton and Speed to the modern directory maps, and a collection of printed maps can be built up gradually by purchase from dealers' catalogues, supplemented by gifts. Many of the early county and town maps made their initial appearance in historical and topographical works such as Christopher Saxton's *Atlas* (1579), William Camden's *Britannia* (1586) and John Speed's *Theatre of Great Britain* (1611), and a useful guide to these is Thomas Chubb's *The Printed Maps in the Atlases of Great Britain and Ireland: A Bibliography, 1519–1870* (reprinted by Dawson, London, 1966).

A useful guide to the Ordnance Survey of Great Britain was prepared by J. B. Harley and C. W. Phillips for a series of articles in the *Amateur Historian* and subsequently reprinted by the Standing Conference for Local History as *The Historian's Guide to Ordnance Survey Maps* (National Council of Social Service, London, 1964). Outline maps of England, Wales and Scotland in this publication indicate the dates of publication of the various editions of Ordnance Survey Maps from 1805 onwards. The manuscript surveyors' drawings of these early 1 in. Ordnance Survey maps, to scales of 2 in., 3 in., and 6 in. to the mile, have been deposited in the British Museum whence photocopies may be purchased.

Manuscript maps can help the local historian to a greater extent than printed maps since they often cover a more limited area in greater detail. Many are found amongst family papers, estate and business records, and printed sale catalogues often include valuable plans. Smaller plans of individual properties are frequently annexed to old deeds of conveyance. Most important of all are tithe maps, with the accompanying apportionments and the village enclosure awards, but where these have survived they are usually in official custody. Plans of local developments for drainage and land reclamation, communications such as roads, canals and railways, surveys of mineral rights, modern town planning and aerial surveys all contribute to the picture of local history presented in maps.

Professor Simmons has commented upon the disappointingly incomplete collections of maps and plans of towns in local libraries.[10] He suggests that these collections could, and should, be strengthened by purchase or by the acquisition of photostats or photographs of manuscript plans in public and private archive collections. Hamilton in Scotland has reproduced manuscript plans of the town from 1699 to 1812 from the muniments of the Duke of Hamilton, and Lancaster has secured copies of early maps from the Lancashire Record Office. Libraries that have issued separate catalogues and lists of maps in their collections include Edinburgh, Manchester and Stockport; whilst the collection of local maps and plans in the Leeds Public Libraries was the basis of a publication of the Thoresby Society (vol. 47) by J. Bonser and H. Nichols, *Printed Maps and Plans of Leeds, 1711–1900* (Leeds, 1960). Leeds also has sets of four printed maps of early Leeds on sale to the public and held an exhibition of manuscript and printed maps in 1961. The photographic reproduction of maps and plans for loan or sale to teachers and students is a considerable aid in the teaching of local history and a recent publication of the Public Record Office, *Maps and Plans in the Public Record Office. 1. British Isles, c. 1410–1860* (HMSO, London, 1967), is of obvious importance to all libraries anxious to ensure that their collection of maps is as complete as possible.

One final question remains to be considered. How pervasive should be our search for local material and how absolute our retention of it when it has been collected? In this respect much depends upon the extent of the area covered by the collection. One limited to a single town can obviously attain greater completeness and aspire to perfection with more justification and hope than a regional collection, but in a large city staffing problems might impose a limit on the collection of ephemeral items such as posters, notices and programmes which appear regularly, however desirable in theory the dictum 'collect

10. Jack Simmons. 'Reference and Special Libraries: A Reader's View' in *Proceedings of the 7th Annual Conference of the Reference and Special Libraries and Information Bureaux, Held at Leicester, April 1959.* Library Association, London, 1960. pp. 5–14.

everything' might appear. This question touches the acquisition of current material more than the older items, since it may be assumed that we shall be very chary of discarding the most trifling item which has already successfully withstood the ravages of time.

When we think of the amassing of modern items such as showbills, programmes of theatrical, musical and other entertainments, we must be sure that the results, even to future historians, are commensurate with the effort involved. Birmingham adds to its Shakespeare Collection each year programmes and playbills of performances of Shakespeare's plays which have taken place all over the world, and takes pride in maintaining this collection as nearly complete as it is humanly possible to make it. This is a special case which few librarians can emulate. Future needs are perhaps adequately met by preserving a selection of such material, and a limited amount does find its way to the library without solicitation. Microcopying may aid us here by enabling us to film and destroy much of this ephemeral material as it is produced, but even so a selection of the originals should be retained. The record of the musical and artistic life of the community is bound up in an intimate way with this kind of material, and the eventual history of a theatre or society may depend largely on its existence. I well recall the delight of a secretary of a local musical society, faced with the task of writing its history, on finding a complete set of its reports and programmes which the society had not troubled to save, in the library.

In conclusion, then, if we support the study of the history of the past we should logically proceed to make possible the *future* writing of history, particularly that section of it for which we have a unique and solitary commitment – that of our own locality. Unless a comprehensive and coherent plan for acquiring these materials is pursued, the history of our present times will not be written by future scholars, at any rate with full knowledge of the facts, and the blame for this will inevitably be laid at our door, even as we blame our predecessors for their sins of omission. The logic and inevitability of this would appear to escape many librarians and most councils, for rarely is there evidence that such a policy operates.

It may be convenient for students if the main headings of

material referred to in this chapter which should be collected in the average local collection are summarised. They are:

1. General literature about the area: history, geography, natural history, etc.
2. Religious and educational history of the area.
3. Imaginative literature: poetry, fiction, drama.
4. Periodical and magazine literature.
5. Material produced by local societies and organizations.
6. Local government material.
7. The relevant government publications, local acts, etc.
8. Industrial and commercial literature, patents and sale catalogues.
9. Theatrical, musical and other material on the fine arts.
10. Political history, election and trade union records.
11. Directories, poll books and other lists.
12. Newspapers and news cuttings.
13. Books printed or published locally.
14. Books by local authors.
15. Material relating to local people (biographical).
16. Family history, genealogy and pedigrees.
17. Thesis literature.
18. Maps and plans, and other visual material.
19. Ephemera.

Chapter 4

Manuscript Records

Although many library local collections consist almost entirely of printed materials, there are also many which have extensive and valuable collections of manuscripts, and these have often been built up slowly over the whole period of the library's history, perhaps a century or more in time. Before the establishment of public libraries, material available for the study of local history was limited and was concentrated in the hands of a few private individuals and historical societies. For seventy odd years after the passing of the first Public Libraries Act the position was substantially unaltered except that libraries were, so far as extremely limited funds allowed, collecting local records and had attracted many valuable gifts and bequests, and by 1900 many libraries had fairly substantial collections.

Private archives, at this time, were often carefully kept and preserved for their legal value as title to the family estates, and it was only the introduction of short title coupled with the abolition of copyhold tenure in the 1920s which freed large quantities of local archives which are today finding their way into record offices and libraries. This development gave a great impetus to the establishment of county record offices which, set up primarily to care for the official county and parochial records, soon began to collect also private archives pertaining to their areas. It also led directly to the formation of the Manorial Documents Committee, through which the Master of the Rolls originally exercised his functions under the Law of Property Act, 1922 (section 144A, sub-section 7) and to the approval of many libraries as depositories for manorial records under this Act.

It may be noted that a library is not precluded from accepting manorial documents in an emergency because it has not yet been recognised as a manorial repository by the Master of the Rolls. Any library which holds, or intends to hold, manorial documents should however apply for this recognition. In either event the library is under a statutory obligation to preserve them in accordance with the Manorial Document Rules, revised in September, 1959 (Statutory Instruments, 1959, no. 1399) to which amendments were made in 1963 (Statutory Instruments, 1963, no. 976) and in 1967 (Statutory Instruments, 1967, no. 963) and to report any such acquisitions to the Secretary of the Historical Manuscripts Commission for inclusion in the Manorial Documents Register. Repositories should note that the particulars now required are somewhat fuller than under the 1926 Rules, but where lists are supplied for the National Register of Archives these will be accepted for the Manorial Documents Register, provided that manorial documents are readily distinguished and that the details required by the schedule to the 1959 Rules are provided. Application for recognition of a library as a repository for manorial documents should be made by the controlling authority to the Master of the Rolls via the Historical Manuscripts Commission. The Master of the Rolls will then order an inspection of the repository to be made and base his decision upon the results of that inspection.

Many extensive series of manorial records have been placed in libraries and close contact should be kept with the lords of the manors in the neighbourhood, since many still remain in private hands or in those of family solicitors. Manorial records include court rolls and presentments, 'compoti' or accounts, custumals detailing the customs of the manor, maps, surveys and terriers, and books and documents relating to the bounds, wastes, franchises and courts of the manor. Conveyances and deeds relating to the title of the manor, though often found with them, are not manorial documents in the strict legal sense.

Many important land-owning families carefully preserved not only their manorial records but large accumulations of private archives, such as deeds of title, leases, agreements, estate surveys, rentals and terriers, account books and personal material such as diaries, letters and wills. If they went into business there may also be commercial correspondence, minutes and account books. Such records are still to be found in private muniment rooms, in the attic or basement of private houses or in the offices of the family solicitor. They no longer have a legal value, and there is no statutory provision for the safety of the non-manorial records, and lawyers and owners often destroy them without consulting anyone, but the alert librarian and archivist can often save them and encourage their deposit in suitable custody. Heirs and trustees often look upon family papers with misgiving and suspicion, fearing that skeletons may be exposed to view if the papers are allowed to leave their possession. Solicitors are, by the nature of their calling, particularly prone to such anxieties and they feel they have a duty to their clients not to risk unauthorised access to them. It is in these circumstances that records are often destroyed and the removal of such fears and prejudice is often the major step to securing their custody. These fears are not unnatural and the archivist must respect them and consider, within reason, the susceptibilities of interested persons other than the donors who may be affected by them. Where conditions regarding public access *are* imposed, we must honour them, while seeking to limit these to an essential minimum.

Periodical approaches to owners, firms and solicitors, inviting them to give their records to the library or to place them on loan often have good results. Such approaches, either personal or by letter, should stress the value of official custody, the safe conditions in which they would be kept, the benefit to historians and students, and the fact that they will be properly listed and calendared. A copy of the calendar will be presented to the depositor. The British Records Association has made a comprehensive survey of and continues to approach all solicitors in the Greater London area, and it has persuaded many to present their older records for distribution to the appropriate repositories in various parts of the country. Many metropolitan libraries have been the recipients of collections from the Records Preservation Section of the BRA under this scheme. While few accessions are on the scale of the Wentworth-Woodhouse archives deposited in Sheffield City Library or the Newcastle papers from Clumber now in the library of

Nottingham University, many smaller collections are annually being transferred to safe custody by their owners.

In building up its National Register of Archives, the Historical Manuscripts Commission found it useful to list the following normal types of record commonly found amongst private archives, while pointing out that, in addition, all kinds of official documents, both secular and ecclesiastical, often accumulate in such collections due to the original owners having held various official appointments. Archives of this nature should be specially noted.

List of Normal Types of Private Archives

1. Manorial records, e.g. court rolls; rentals; accounts and vouchers.
2. Muniments of title, e.g. charters and deeds; cartularies; abstracts of title; marriage settlements; wills.
3. Records of estate management, e.g. surveys; maps; accounts and vouchers; development schemes; related correspondence.
4. Records of household management, e.g. accounts; inventories; plans; manuscript recipe books and other memoranda.
5. Personal papers, e.g. Letter books and original correspondence; certificates of birth, marriage and death; wills; commissions, grants, licences and passports; diaries and commonplace books; notes of family history, pedigrees and genealogical memoranda; old printed broadsheets, tracts and pamphlets.
6. Legal papers, e.g. opinions; correspondence with solicitors; precedent books.
7. Business archives, e.g. minutes; accounts and vouchers; ledgers, journals, and other books with related correspondence.
8. Miscellaneous, e.g. manuscript service books; newsletters; chronicles; literary manuscripts including poetry, notes on local history, and unpublished treatises.

County councils succeeded to the administrative duties of the courts of quarter sessions under the Local Government Act, 1888, and the modern records generated by them fall outside the scope of this book. However, as an extension of responsibility for the care of the records of quarter sessions, they have established record offices in which the extensive records relating to the county are to be found. These records include the main record of the court, in sessions books and files, dealing not only with criminal cases, gaols and houses of correction, but also with the administration of the poor law, support of maimed soldiers, repair of county bridges, oversight of highways. In addition the clerk of the peace was responsible for the custody of officially deposited records, such as hearth tax lists, land tax assessments (1745–1832), electoral register (1832 onwards), deposited plans relating to public utilities (1792 onwards), enclosure awards, oath rolls and enrolled deeds. These records do not usually survive before the mid-sixteenth century. For an appreciation of the quantity and variety of these records, reference should be made to the excellent guides to county and local record offices which have been compiled by archivists, such as those of Kent, Berkshire, Lancashire and Essex.

The first inquiry expressly directed at discovering the state of local records was that of the Select Committee of 1800, but this was primarily concerned with the public records. Questionnaires were, however, sent out to all clerks of the peace, and those who replied revealed the current attitude of their councils towards historical documents, not, as a rule, an encouraging one. More extensive inquiries resulted from the efforts of the Record Commissioners of 1831, but the replies elicited revealed no marked improvement during the intervening years. As public interest in record preservation grew several counties did review their records during the later decades of the nineteenth century and some began the process of printing the principal classes, notably the rolls of quarter sessions. After the First World War, Bedfordshire, led by Dr Herbert Fowler, and Essex were the first counties to take full and proper steps for the better preservation of their records by developing record offices as centres for historical research. This movement, which has grown apace since Dr Fowler's valuable pioneer work, has revolutionised the work of local record preservation in England and Wales by establishing it upon a firm official basis.

The county record office today has attracted to its custody numerous local records of all kinds. The local librarian should be prepared to work closely with the archivist of his own and neighbouring counties: he should know the contents of their offices intimately so that he can guide or refer students to relevant material in them and there should, if possible, be an exchange of calendars and lists. A general conspectus of county records will be found in *County Records* by F. G. Emmison and I. Gray (Historical Association, London, 1967) and in *Local Records: their Nature and Care*, edited by Lilian J. Redstone and

Francis W. Steer (Society of Local Archivists, London, 1953).

A great many municipal boroughs have a corporate history going back over many centuries and have record accumulations in various states of completeness from the early middle ages. Their survival has been in large measure fortuitous and results from their intrinsic value to the body corporate rather than to any statutory provision for their care and safety. The charters particularly were preserved with care, since on them rested the privileges and even the existence of the Corporation in medieval times.

Although descriptions of the records of selected boroughs and of the conditions in which they were kept in the nineteenth century may be found in the Reports on Public Records of 1835–39, and the Reports of the Committee on Municipal Corporations, 1876–80, it was the work of the Historical Manuscripts Commission which first drew the attention of scholars to the wealth of material available in this class of record. The Commission examined and reported on the records of several boroughs and printed brief inventories of them. Elsewhere local antiquaries, members of local archaeological and historical societies, sometimes librarians and archivists, sorted, arranged and calendared the records, but some are still largely unsorted and inaccessible.

In some towns the borough records are preserved in a local record office which may be a separate department or may form part of the local history collection at the library. Elsewhere they will be in the custody of the town clerk at the town hall but it is evident that the implementation of the Local Government (Records) Act, 1962, has resulted in the transfer of borough records from the town hall to the library in some instances and has also resulted in the appointment of archivists. The implementation of this Act in many more towns would be a service to scholarship but in the meantime F. G. Emmison states that: 'County archivists are becoming more and more involved with borough records, especially those of the smaller boroughs without an archivist, and their records are now being deposited in increasing numbers in county record offices, e.g. Berkshire, Sussex and Kent; the last has also been entrusted with the important Cinque Port archives.'[1]

1. F. G. Emmison. *Archives and Local History*. Methuen, London, 1966. p. 36.

Municipal records generally fall into two main classes – the legal and the administrative. Of greatest value are the charters and letters patent and many towns have an unbroken sequence of these from the reign of King John. The basis of the Corporation's rights and privileges, they were jealously guarded and scrupulously preserved.

'Many ancient boroughs were legal centres of considerable importance developing an unusually varied and comprehensive system for the administration of justice.'[2] They often exercised the rights of manorial courts, holding a court leet, a court baron and view of frank-pledge. There was also the Mayor's Court, sometimes called the Borough or Town Court, and often a Court of Record, and a Court of Conscience or Requests. If the town were an important market centre there might be a Court of Piepowder (Piepoudre), a court of summary jurisdiction at markets and fairs; while ports might have an Admiralty Court or Staple Court. Many boroughs, too, had the right to hold quarter sessions independently of the county, and these records include a variety of papers, since from the sixteenth century onwards the justices had increasing powers conferred on them in such matters as the repair of highways and bridges, poor law administration, licensing alehouses, etc. The judicial records will include indictments and presentments, recognisances, oaths of allegiance, lists of justices or juries and calendars of prisoners. Occasionally material relating to local cases which appeared before superior courts, such as the Court of Chancery, is found amongst the local judicial records.

In towns which were important trading centres in the middle ages, the early rolls of the Gild Merchant will be found, and later there are records of the trading guilds or companies which grew out of the Gild Merchant. These are often important for genealogy and family history no less than for economic history, as is the Freemen's Roll, or the records of the admissions of burgesses and apprentices. Gild records include the original grant or charter, ordinances of the Gild, indentures of apprentices, minute books and accounts, etc. The Guildhall Library has acquired by gift or deposit the archives of seventy city livery companies, though some of the larger guilds still retain their own.

2. Redstone and Steer (eds.). *Local Records.* p. 158.

Other important records include the Assembly Books of the Common Council, containing details of the election of bailiffs, coroners and other officials; the 'Remembrance' Book, which listed the by-laws and ordinances affecting the work of the Council, and the Minute Books, recording details of the actions taken by the Corporation.

The financial records include subsidy rolls, often found in series from early dates, poll tax records and assessments for pavage, murage and tallage and, later, house and window tax records. The numbers and names of accounting officers vary from town to town, but chamberlain, mayor, steward or bailiff are the more usual. With their accounts are often filed details of the town's income and rentals of corporate property. Various other accounts may also be included such as for coroners, overseers of the poor, surveyors of highways, churchwardens and constables, many of these being the records of the parish officials.

Military papers, such as muster rolls, levies and assessments may be found and there may also be records of schools for which the Corporation may have been trustees, or of local charities vested in the Corporation or passed over to them. A wide variety of other papers may be found amongst the official records, typical examples being documents of title to town property; petitions to the mayor or bailiffs, records of horse and cattle fairs, election records, prison records, minutes of the street commissioners and turnpike trusts. Since the town clerk was often a practising solicitor stray records from his private practice are sometimes found amongst the borough records, but unfortunately the converse is more often the case and official records occasionally come to light in the hands of his descendants. A large quantity of the Chichester borough archives, which had been retained by the lawyer who acted as part-time town clerk in the nineteenth century, were found in a local solicitor's office in 1947 by the county archivist and have been restored to their rightful custody. Archives are found in the most unexpected places. An 'Inspeximus' of 1646, a copy of Leeds' first charter of 1626, was found in a Canterbury bookshop in 1952, identified by the city archivist and restored to Leeds Corporation. In some instances the medieval records of boroughs may be in other ownership; the early documents relating to the manor and borough of Leeds are amongst the records of the Duchy of Lancaster.

The following basis for a classification for borough archives has been worked out in the Berkshire Record Office and is printed by permission of the former County Archivist, Mr Peter Walne, M.A. It will serve not only as a guide to the arrangement of records but as an indication of the types of archive habitually found amongst municipal records, although nearly every borough will exhibit minor peculiarities of administration which will produce exceptional and distinct archive groups. Reference should also be made to the introduction to the *Inventory of Borough Records* (Surrey County Council, Kingston on Thames, 1929) where problems of classification of this class of record are discussed at length.

A–*Administrative Archives*
- B   Bridges
- C   Council minutes *(a)* pre-1835; *(b)* post-1835
- E   Elections *(b)* borough; *(p)* parliamentary
- M   Markets and Fairs
- O   Officers' appointments, etc.
- P   Parochial and Poor Law (i.e. the Corporation or its officers acting in a capacity normally covered by parochial officers)
- Q   Charity (i.e. charities administered by the Corporation)
- T   Properties
- U   Undertakings *(e)* electricity; *(g)* gas; *(w)* water
- W   Watch Committee
- Z   Miscellaneous

F–*Financial Records*
- A   Accounts (differentiated according to officer responsible viz: *(b)* bailiff; *(c)* constable or chamberlain; *(m)* mayor; *(t)* treasurer)
- B   Bridge accounts and tolls
- P   Parochial and Poor Law
- Q   Charity
- R   Rentals and Rates
- T   Mortgages of Tolls
- V   Bills and Vouchers
- Z   Miscellaneous

G–*Gild Records*
  A Administrative archives
  F Financial archives
  z Miscellaneous

I–*Incorporation and Privileges*
(derived from Central Administration)
  c Royal Charters of Incorporation
  F Fee Farm rent
  z Miscellaneous

J–*Judicial Records*
  B Borough Court of Record
  c Coroner
  J 'Custodes pacis'
  M Clerk of the Market
  Q Quarter Sessions

L–*Legal Records and Law Suits*

M–*Manorial Archives*
  T Title to Manor

R–*Enrolment and Deposit*
  A Apprenticeship indentures (not relating to a municipal charity)
  E Electoral rolls *(b)* burgesses; *(p)* parliamentary
  M Markets and Fairs
  o Oaths *(f)* freemen; *(d)* declarations; *(j)* justices; *(s)* sacraments
  T Deposited and enrolled deeds *(a)* medieval; *(b)* modern; *(l)* leases
  z Miscellaneous

T–*Title to Town Properties*
  c Medieval charters
  L Leases
  Q Charity

z–*Miscellaneous*
  B Burghal
  c Special Commissions
  P Parochial
  Q Charity

Sometimes a local authority will have acquired the civil records of parishes which have been absorbed within the borough, and these are often deposited in the library. Stoke-on-Trent library thus secured the records of those local authorities which were amalgamated in 1910 to form the county borough. The possibility of future boundary changes in our heavily populated conurbations may give rise to similar problems or opportunities.

Parochial records have great significance for the study of both the secular and religious history of a community, providing the best available data for a true estimate of the social and economic lives of our ancestors. Few parishes, if any, have a complete series of their civil and ecclesiastical records from the sixteenth century and this class of record has suffered, more than any other, from the perils of inadequate custody. Certain categories, such as churchwardens' and overseers' accounts, and vestry minutes, have been particularly liable to pass into private custody, whence they may occasionally be recovered into public ownership.

The reports of the Treasury Committee of 1900 and of the Records Commission of 1910, and the works of the Webbs and others all testify to the neglect to which these and other ecclesiastical and semi-public records were subject. The Local Government Act of 1894 gave county councils power and authority to take steps for the proper listing and preservation of civil parish records, but little was done, although Shropshire in 1895 appointed a committee to review its parish records and eventually published a detailed list under parishes. This list (now kept up-to-date in manuscript by the county archivist) is now incomplete to the extent that some of the records listed have disappeared during the intervening period, eloquent testimony to the dangers which still beset them in their present semi-official custody.

The Parochial Registers and Records Measure, 1929, empowers diocesan bishops to establish diocesan record offices or to appoint and recognise one or more repositories within their dioceses as appropriate places in which they may direct incumbents, churchwardens or parochial church councils to place registers and parish records for which they have no proper means of custody. The diocesan authority has the power under this measure to inspect registers and other records and to order their transfer to a recognised repository if they are in danger. Many record offices and libraries have been approved by bishops, either for the diocese as a whole or in part.

An important preliminary step is to discover the extent to which these records have survived, and to examine and list the records of parishes within the purview of the library or record office. In the diocese of Sheffield the city library shortly before the last war sponsored the formation of a record society to make a detailed survey of the parochial records in the diocese, and to compile lists which are kept at the central library. Since 1964 this library has been the official repository for parish records in the diocese. A similar *Inventory of Parochial Documents in the Diocese of Bath and Wells* (Somerset County Council, Taunton, 1938), edited by J. E. King, was based on the results of a questionnaire circulated to parish councils, a method much inferior to that of personal visits. Several other counties have instituted similar surveys, and the lists are in process of inclusion in the National Register of Archives, so that the whole country may eventually be covered.

Better protection is usually afforded in churches today to the principal records, especially the parish registers, and where this is so, there are strong arguments for retaining them in the care of the incumbents, subject to periodical inspection by the diocesan authority. In view of the uniqueness and importance of the registers, there have been many efforts to make transcripts or photocopies for local libraries in recent years. Several libraries have transcribed and in some cases indexed their own local registers, while the Society of Genealogists has, with the collaboration of its members, done a great deal to encourage the transcription and distribution of typewritten copies, in addition to publishing two indexes, one of its own holdings and another *National Index of Parish Register Copies* (London, 1939). Elsewhere parish register societies have been printing registers, but are often finding costs prohibitive for extensive ventures today. Sometimes their unprinted transcripts are available in libraries, such as those of the Shropshire Parish Register Society at Shrewsbury Borough Library. Southwark has the Bishop's transcripts of registers belonging to the former Archdeaconry of Surrey and the archives department of Leeds City Libraries holds the Bishop's transcripts for the Yorkshire deaneries of the Archdeaconry of Richmond.

Manchester and Birmingham were pioneers in preparing photocopies of local parish registers. Manchester has almost completed an extensive programme of microfilming the registers and other surviving parochial records of all pre-1837 churches in the diocese of Manchester and is doing the same for the eastern part of the diocese of Chester. These films, with the existing fine collection of printed and transcript registers, make the library one of the most comprehensive in this particular field.

Apart from making the information available to students the deposit of copies in libraries does ensure its survival should anything happen to the original. Newcastle-upon-Tyne has nearly 500 volumes containing the transcripts of about 160 parish registers and other genealogical material and Kidderminster has microfilms of the parish registers of Kidderminster and Wolverley, 1539 to date. The early registers of Hanwood, Salop, were destroyed by a fire which consumed the rectory some years ago, but fortunately a copy from 1559 to 1763 is preserved in Shrewsbury Public Library. Parish registers lend themselves readily to microfilming, and several schemes for filming registers are under way. In some instances library staffs have indexed their local registers to facilitate reference to them.

Other classes of ecclesiastical parish record include vestry books, churchwardens' accounts, church rate books, tithe maps and apportionments, and records of parochial charities and church schools. The parish vestry had authority to levy its own poor rate, to elect overseers and parish constables, and its church wardens, the oldest lay office in the church, had considerable local authority and responsibility. The Guildhall Library, London, has a large collection of documents of its churches and is providing excellent guides to these, including handlists of vestry minutes, churchwarden's accounts, inhabitants lists and non-parochial registers.

The Historical Manuscripts Commission has identified the following principal types of ecclesiastical parish archives, likely to be found in the custody of the clergy:

1. General administration.
2. Service of the church.
3. Fabric of the church and of other church buildings.
4. Churchyard.
5. Property and income of the Benefice.
6. Parish lands and boundaries.
7. Churchwardens' and vestry papers.
8. Chantry records.
9. Fraternities, guilds and societies.
10. Parish charities.
11. Church schools.
12. Miscellaneous.

Records of the civil parish, not always coterminous with the ecclesiastical parish, form a distinct class, although they are often found along with the religious records of the parish. The most important are the enclosure acts and awards; maps, rentals and surveys; parish rate books and the records and accounts of old-time parish officers such as the constable, the overseers for the poor and the highway overseer. Valuation lists, rate and account books formerly held by parish councils were, under the Rating and Valuation Act, 1925 (section 52) transferred to the custody of the rating authorities (borough and district councils). They may be deposited in such custody as the authority may direct and many have been placed in local libraries. Birmingham has a large collection of manuscript rate books dating from 1736 to 1870.

The remainder of the older records of the civil parish may still be in the custody of the parish clerk, or in the parish chest, but this class has suffered greatly from the vicissitudes attendant upon their custody by a long succession of unpaid officers and full series are rare.

Provision for the custody of the more general ecclesiastical records, as a class, has given historians much more cause for anxiety in the past, but the authorities responsible are now more mindful of their duty to ensure their protection and preservation, stimulated in the main by the greater attention given to record preservation generally and by the increasing use of the records by students. The Pilgrim Trust carried out a survey of ecclesiastical archives in 1950–51, covering capitular, diocesan and archidiaconal records. Copies of the typescript of this survey were deposited with the Historical Manuscripts Commission and at the British Museum, Lambeth Palace Library, the Bodleian Library, the University Library of Cambridge and for each diocese at the Diocesan Record Office. Full catalogues have subsequently been published for some collections of episcopal and capitular records which are noted in Dorothy M. Owen's *The Records of the Established Church in England Excluding Parochial Records* (Archives and The User, no. 1, British Records Association, London, 1970). This guide describes this class of archives and gives the present location of such ecclesiastical records as are regularly available to searchers.

Probate records, consisting principally of wills, inventories and letters of administration have long been recognised as vital records by genealogists and students of family history, and are now coming into their own as important sources for the economic historian, but even today they are not easily accessible. 'Sacks full of inventories lie at Somerset House and at other probate registries waiting to be indexed and made available', wrote Francis W. Steer and added, 'This historical value of inventories cannot be too strongly emphasised, because these documents tell us precisely what goods a person had at the time of his death and what they were worth; they help, even more than the manorial records, to determine the social positions of members of a community, and they supplement the evidence of past ages as shown in painting, literature, correspondence and manuscripts.'[3]

Prior to the Court of Probate Act, 1857, all wills were proved in ecclesiastical courts. Hence some probate records are still to be found with diocesan and capitular records. However, that Act transferred the responsibility for probate records to the President of the Probate Division of the High Court of Justice and the records were in consequence transferred to the principal and district probate registries. Subsequently under the Public Records Act, 1958, all pre-1858 probate records were scheduled as public records. In consequence the records of the Prerogative Court of Canterbury which were recently at

3. F. W. Steer. *Farm and Cottage Inventories of Mid-Essex, 1635–1749*. Essex Record Office Publications, no. 8, Chelmsford, 1950.
See also Owen Ashmore. 'Inventories as a Source of Local History'. *Amateur Historian*, vol. 4, nos 4–5, 1959. pp. 157–66 and 186–95.

Somerset House, are now in the Public Record Office. But the pre-1858 records from the district registries have now all been transferred to local record repositories and an indispensable guide is A. J. Camp's *Wills and Their Whereabouts* (Society of Genealogists, London, 1963). Shrewsbury Public Library possesses the original wills proved in the Manorial Court of Ruyton-XI-towns in Shropshire, together with two manuscript volumes of wills and administrations from 1666–1816 and two manuscripts containing copies of wills and inventories from 1765 to 1783.[4] The Sedgley probate inventories from 1614 to 1787 in the Dudley Central Library have been transcribed by John S. Roper and published.[5] Bootle has obtained photocopies of all local wills registered from 1553 to 1825 with transcripts and indices of names, places and archaic terms.

The National Library of Wales includes all Welsh probate records and those of the dioceses of Hereford and St Asaph, while the Bodleian Library is the approved diocesan record office for the entire diocese of Oxford. Gloucester City Library has acquired the contents of the city diocesan registry, together with cognate material from Somerset House and the probate records of the diocese from 1541. It has also obtained microfilms of parish registers and proceedings of the Peculiar Courts.[6] The record office in the Norwich City Library houses the records of the Norfolk portion of the ancient diocese. The probate records of Lichfield are kept at Lichfield Public Library in a depository jointly administered by the county and city councils in accordance with an agreed scheme.

There are, too, records of many semi-public or statutory authorities, such as those of turnpike trusts, poor law guardians and foundling hospitals, commissioners for improvements, commissioners for sewers, and early records of infirmaries, schools, etc. which may occasionally find their way to the library. Though now abolished, many of these formerly exercised considerable authority locally and were indeed a vital part of English local government. Some of their records have passed into the hands of county and borough councils; others

4. A calendar of these was printed in *Transactions of the Shropshire Archaeological Society*, vol. 52, 1948. pp. 116–18.
5. *Sedgley Probate Inventories*. Privately printed, Woolsetton, Worcs., 1960.
6. See *Archives*, vol. 4, no. 21, 1959. p. 59.

remain in private ownership or in the possession of solicitors whose firms formerly acted for the trusts. Some have almost acquired the status of 'official' records, due to the transfer of powers to local authorities. Those of the various units of poor-law administration have in many cases joined the county records, those of municipal guilds are happily often in official custody, though many have been lost. This applies to many of the old charities, since the administration of many charitable trusts passed into the hands of local councils.[7] Many miscellaneous records of this nature have found their way into libraries. A large accumulation of land drainage records relating to West Norfolk, found in a shed in King's Lynn Docks, have been deposited in the record office in the Norwich City Library;[8] Barrow in Furness has the business papers and records of a typical lakeland farm from 1623 to 1896; Boston has manuscript maps relating to navigation and drainage of the Fens; Bournemouth has the poor law records of the Bournemouth and Christchurch Union from 1729 to 1948; Shrewsbury the minute books and records of the Bridgnorth and Black Brook turnpike trust and Warrington the minute books of the Warrington improvement commissioners from 1813 to 1847.

Records of public and endowed schools have generally been preserved by the school authority, although occasionally they have strayed. Rarely do the records of such bodies fall into the hands of public libraries, but sometimes those of an endowed school, usually incomplete, come to light. Stray documents from such sources are by no means uncommon amongst private archives. Where such records can be traced it is often possible today to obtain microfilms. Warrington has filmed the minutes of its Bluecoat School from 1832 and is seeking the whereabouts of the earlier records.

Many a library which disdains the collection of 'archives' has accepted the custody of the minute books and other material relating to local societies. These are archives in the best accepted sense of the term and should be preserved according to the recognised principles of archive science. The organisations may be cultural, such as the art club or historical society; social

7. Hubert Hall. *Repertory of British Archives*. Historical Society of Great Britain, London, 1920. pp. 103–7.
8. See *Bulletin of the National Register of Archives*, no. 10, 1959. pp. 26–8.

such as the Yorkshire Society or Burns Club; charitable such as
the Red Cross or the Discharged Prisoners' Aid Society; or
relate to business organisations such as the Law Society, the
Institute of Bankers or the Chamber of Commerce, or to
religious bodies and youth organisations. The librarian who is
in close touch with his community and what is happening
within it, will find many opportunities of accepting records of
this kind. Shrewsbury library has secured the records of such
widely different bodies as the local Boy Scouts Association; a
defunct literary and debating society; the Yorkshire Society,
also defunct; the local branch of the WEA; a local field club,
and a church men's society, etc. Newark has all the records of
its local cricket club.

Records of this nature have been discussed in two interesting
articles by Colonel Le Hardy,[9] then a former county archivist
of Middlesex and by Mr J. F. W. Bryon,[10] then borough librarian
of Eccles. An excellent opportunity arises when these associations
are dissolved, but even where they are flourishing there can be
no objection to the older and non-current papers being deposited in the library for safe-keeping. It is often an advantage if
the librarian or a member of his staff assumes the title of
Honorary Librarian or custodian of the society's records. Those
of older associations such as Co-operative and Friendly
Societies, Savings Clubs, societies for the Suppression of Crime
or the Prosecution of Felons, Masonic lodges, educational
bodies, Mechanics' Institutes, circulating libraries, are all
contributory sources for the cultural history of a locality and,
where they have been preserved, the continuance of such safety
should be ensured. The extent and preservation of the records
of Friendly Societies was the subject of a report published in
Archives by R. L. M. James.[11]

Records of trade union branches are not easy to acquire.
An approach through the local trades council or local branch
secretaries is sometimes productive, though the fear of confidential information being made public has also to be con-
tended with. This is a pity for these records, though they have

9. William Le Hardy. 'Records of Clubs and Societies'. *Archives*, vol. 1, no. 3,
1950. pp. 29–39.

10. J. F. W. Bryon. 'Records of Local Societies'. *Library Association Record*, vol.
63, November 1961. pp. 372–5.

11. 'Friendly Society Records'. *Archives*, vol. 6, no. 32, 1964. pp. 223–4.

rarely been properly kept owing to lack of continuity over the years and to a succession of part-time officers, are a rich source for the economic and social history of the last two hundred years, and they deserve more attention than they have received hitherto. A session at the Annual Conference of the British Records Association was devoted to a paper on these records by Dr E. J. Hobsbawm.[12] As a result of this, interest in affording better protection to both centralised union records and those of branches has been shown on a national scale by the Trades Union Congress.

Finally, an important class of independent records must be mentioned – those of commercial and industrial firms. They are important not only to the understanding of the development of the particular firm, but also as providing comparative data for the social and economic historian to consider and work upon.[13] Their value in this latter connection has long been recognised, and it is significant that the Business Archives Council, formerly the Council for the Preservation of Business Archives, received its initial impetus from the London School of Economics. Similarly in the United States the Business Historical Society, founded in 1925, is closely linked with the Harvard School of Business Administration.

Businessmen are not, as a rule, very co-operative as regards placing their records in the safe custody of libraries and record offices. Many fear that confidential information may be contained even in older ledgers and account books, while others are too preoccupied with current business problems. Some have little or no interest in their older records and are only too anxious to dispose of them, in the unlikely event that they have so far escaped distribution for salvage. Firms surrendering their records may therefore wish to place restrictions on their use, but they should be persuaded to make these as lenient as possible and, in any event, to place a time limit on their duration. To avoid misunderstanding they should be included in a written agreement between the company and the repository.

12. 'Records of the Trade Union Movement'. *Archives*, vol. 4, no. 23, 1960. pp. 129–37.

13. W. H. Chaloner. 'Business Records as a Source of Economic History with Special Reference to their Selective Preservation in Libraries'. *Journal of Documentation*, vol. 4, no. 2, June 1948. pp. 5–13.

Although masses of such records have been pulped and destroyed and many went for salvage during the war, there are still many old-established industrial firms and companies which are proud of their long history and which treat their records with the utmost care and consideration. Such independent companies are getting fewer year by year as they are swallowed up by big combines. Firms being thus 'merged' or going out of existence give the librarian his best opportunity of asking for the records. Archives of small businesses may sometimes be found amongst family and estate papers. Such collections of business records may, on the other hand, be extremely large, such as the extensive series of Boulton and Watt papers in the Birmingham Reference Library; the Fairbank collection of surveyors' plans and account books at Sheffield, and the Stannary Court mining records at Truro Public Library, which consist of the ledgers, journals, cash books, etc. of some three hundred mines in Devon and Cornwall, from 1703 to 1800. Two articles published in *Archives*,[14] review the records of the brewing industry.

In most towns there are small family businesses whose origins can be traced back to the early nineteenth century and even to the eighteenth century and beyond, and personal contact with the present proprietors will often result in the deposit of such early records as have survived. In this respect the co-operation of the local Chamber of Commerce or the Rotary Club is of value. The Guildhall Library's holdings of business records have increased considerably in recent years. They include account and letter books of several seventeenth- and eighteenth-century London merchants and merchant bankers and the historic archives of large and still-flourishing City-based companies and insurance companies. Records of banking firms are of special importance; they were often founded in the eighteenth century by country solicitors as an adjunct or support to their mortgage activities. A comprehensive survey of banking records is currently (1972) being undertaken by the Business Archives Council. Apart from their intrinsic importance the records of old-established solicitors often yield the business records of bankrupt or deceased clients.

14. Peter Mathias. 'Historical Records of the Brewing Industry'. *Archives*, vol. 7, no. 33, 1965. pp. 2–10. R. L. M. James. 'Brewing Records: Inquiry and Its Lessons'. *Archives*, vol. 7, no. 36, 1966. pp. 215–20.

In recent years many standard histories of firms have appeared which are based almost exclusively on extant records of the firm. The third part of the *Lancashire Bibliography*, published in 1971, records many such business histories dealing with a multiplicity of Lancashire firms.

Business records which the library may not wish to retain for any reason may be passed on to the Business Archives Council which has established a library of published histories of firms and collects information about business archives and records accessible to students. Information concerning business records may be obtained from the Secretary, Business Archives Council, Dominion House, 37–45 Tooley Street, London Bridge, London, s.e.i.

We have already stated that many important local records are to be found in national repositories. Some of these have been printed in the calendars of State Papers and in local record series, but for all areas there is a vast amount of material virtually untouched and unexamined by historians. Some researchers have worked on certain classes of this material and even transcribed some of it, and their notes and transcripts are occasionally presented to libraries by grateful scholars when their work has been completed. A. L. Humphreys, the historian, presented a large collection of his notes to the Reading Public Library. They can be extremely useful, although of course absolute accuracy cannot be guaranteed and they do not invalidate reference to the originals.

Much of the material we have been discussing, particularly that at the Public Record Office, is not easily microfilmed, for too much preliminary work would be necessary to search out the local references in long series of public records which are not arranged topographically. Hammersmith, in a novel experiment, appointed a research assistant temporarily to copy such material relating to the borough and, as a result, a large amount of manuscript material has been added to the local collection. Where the records were too long to copy or to photograph with reasonable economy, a précis of the record was made and filed at the appropriate point. This is a venture which could usefully be adopted by other libraries, especially where local source material is sparse.

There are, finally, a host of miscellaneous manuscripts of

various kinds – diaries and correspondence of individuals, literary manuscripts of local writers, historic notes, pedigrees, drafts and scrap-books and other material collected or written by historians and genealogists which never got into print. Such 'made' collections often represent a life-time's work on the part of the collector, and they can be extremely valuable sources of original or secondary material. Many such collections of early local antiquaries passed into the national collections of the British Museum and the university libraries during the nineteenth century, and can now be acquired only through photocopies. Others remained in private ownership and sometimes become available or they may be traced to the possession of surviving relatives, while many already repose in library local collections.

Anxiety has recently been expressed in literary circles concerning the loss of scholarship in this country through the migration to the United States of the manuscripts of modern British writers, and the growing practice of some American libraries in approaching British authors for their MSS. and working papers during their life-time. It is considered that there should be a much more dynamic approach to this question by British librarians who may well imitate the pertinacity of their American confrères. Some libraries do make a point of collecting the manuscripts of living local writers, and find that a courteous approach often brings in a collection of their works in manuscript form. The author may deprecatingly say that his manuscripts are too 'untidy', not realising that the untidy manuscript throws far more light on his working methods and the development of his thought than the final immaculate typewritten copy specially prepared for the publisher which is, in truth, no better than the printed book. Note and memoranda books are even more valuable, but the writer will rarely surrender these while he, or she, is still working.

The remarks made in the previous chapter concerning the collection of printed material relating to local 'worthies' is also applicable to any manuscript material which may be easily and economically obtained. But perhaps a warning is necessary here. There is nothing so unremunerative as collecting odd autograph letters of the famous. In themselves and divorced from relative papers they are rarely interesting and contribute little to our knowledge of the man, yet they often command fantastic prices. Let the autograph hunter have them!

Source material relating to national figures in history or literature is widely sought by national and academic libraries on both sides of the Atlantic, and local libraries cannot normally compete. The papers of well-known political, military or naval personalities inspected by the Historical Manuscripts Commission are, if the owner wishes to dispose of them, usually offered to one of the national libraries. Charles Darwin was born in Shrewsbury, but its library would not be justified in trying to build up a collection of his manuscripts, letters and papers. Neither would it be wise to collect the manuscript materials relating to A. E. Housman, author of *The Shropshire Lad*, many of which, including his poetical notebooks, have in any event found their way to the United States.

To the librarian there should be no greater intrinsic merit in the manuscript than the printed book; he should be concerned mainly with the information it contains, and the urge to spend large sums on manuscripts of little merit should be resisted. Nowadays a few trivial words in the hand of a Nelson or Napoleon will fetch a price ranging into three figures, but the association value needs to be great before the librarian is justified in entering the market.

Chapter 5

Local Records: The Present Position

Britain is extremely fortunate in the number and variety of its local records and also in the extent to which these have survived considering that, until recently, they had no recognised place of deposit and little legislative authority as regards their custody. While this fortunate position must be ascribed mainly to our comparative freedom from war and revolution, our system of local and of national government did tend to ensure that records, both of a public and private nature, were retained because of their legal and practical value. Most public records have remained in official custody since they were produced and preservation was motivated by the practical consideration that they were regarded as essential to the smooth functioning of the government departments.

The manorial system ensured the safety of court rolls and related records, while families and corporate bodies kept their records intact since they constituted the visible proofs of their title to lands and privileges. In the counties the 'Custos Rotulorum' was, from the fourteenth century onwards, charged with responsibility for keeping the records of the quarter sessions, although the duty actually devolved upon the clerk of the peace.

During the sixteenth and seventeenth centuries many famous savants were collecting literary and documentary remains, amongst them Bale, Leland, Dodsworth, Sir Robert Bruce Cotton and Sir Hans Sloane, and their collections usually found their way into a national or university library, though some, like the later library of Sir Thomas Phillipps, were split up and sold. This was an age, too, rich in competent antiquaries of the calibre of Camden, Dugdale and Speed, who first demonstrated the value and importance of local records as primary sources. From the eighteenth century onwards many aristocratic families assembled fine libraries, in which special emphasis was often laid upon local antiquities. Many local historical works were published under the patronage of the nobility – indeed this or the issuing of a subscription list were the only ways a poor writer could get into print. The nineteenth century saw a strenuous effort to place documentary materials at the disposal of scholars, a movement which, originating in the national records, spread later to administrative and local records of every kind.

The deliberations of a Select Committee of the Commons, appointed in 1800, and of the Records Commission of 1830, led eventually to the first Public Records Act of 1838. Lord Langdale, the first Master of the Rolls under this Act, who was given comprehensive powers, devoted himself to his new duties energetically, and in due course the national archives were collected together in the Public Record Office.

Apart from the legal and official records, there had been no attempt, save on the part of a few local antiquaries, to collect and preserve local material. The only bodies interested were a few archaeological and antiquarian societies, to whom this country owes a great debt for their assistance in promoting the collection of this material and the encouragement of local libraries and museums. The establishment of these institutions, from 1850 onwards, encouraged the hope that the position would be remedied, but progress was hampered by the limited funds available and by the absence of the necessary legislation.

A major step forward was the appointment in 1869 of the Historical Manuscripts Commission, whose extremely valuable reports served to focus attention on the vast amount of un-calendared and unlisted manuscripts in the possession of private families, institutions and local authorities, and upon the neglected state in which many collections were found. Public awareness of this situation stimulated the appointment of a Local Records Committee of the Treasury, following public agitation, in 1900, and the Royal Commission on Local Records which met from 1910 to 1919 and visited many provincial centres to collect evidence.

Meanwhile the local history collection had grown to be a prominent feature of many libraries and their suitability as repositories for manuscript records found many champions who urged these claims to the Treasury committee. If one may point to any particular weakness in the case put forward by librarians at this time, it is that they showed no recognition of the fact that archive administration is a profession quite distinct from librarianship, requiring special training and different techniques, but archive science was then in its infancy and such obliquity was not confined to librarians. Although the committee's report, published in 1902, revealed the total inadequacy of existing measures to safeguard local records, it contained no mention of the efforts, unostentatious but nevertheless far-reaching in view of the limiting factors to which we have referred, which public libraries had been exerting towards their conservation. The essence of its case against libraries as record repositories is given on page 46 of the report, which proceeded to recommend the establishment of local record offices in the custody of town clerks and clerks of the county councils. No legislative action was forthcoming, however, and in the absence of compulsion few local authorities took any active steps in the matter.

Following the publication, in 1923, of Dr G. H. Fowler's *The Care of County Muniments*, several county councils interested themselves in the custody and preservation of records and since that date the movement has grown apace, particularly since the last war, and there are now very few English and Welsh counties without a county record office.

In the towns municipal authorities still looked to their libraries as the natural centre for both printed and manuscript material relating to their areas, and in many places the librarian was entrusted with the care of the official records of the Corporation. Many libraries, too, had received notable accessions of private and business records and had shown a proper appreciation of the obligations attendant upon such custody by making adequate provision for their safety and for public access to them. There was, unfortunately, no lead nationally and no organised policy to guide the Library Association or its membership. Too much was left to the enthusiasm, or lack of it, of individual librarians. Had more libraries established muniment rooms and taken a positive interest in archive science and their own local records during the formative period of the twenties and thirties there might have been a very different story to tell today.

The abolition of copyhold tenure under the Law of Property Act of 1922, by depriving manorial records of their legal value, gave added impetus to this matter. Fortunately the danger was recognised and an Amending Act of 1924 placed these records in the charge of the Master of the Rolls who, mindful of his duties, encouraged the establishment of a central repository in each county for the preservation, not only of manorial documents, but of records of every description relating to that area. Surprisingly, it proved no simple matter to find a suitable repository in each county and many libraries were thus approved since other bodies were not inclined to fulfil the obligations imposed by the acceptance of manorial documents. The first list of approved repositories issued in 1926 included 18 libraries, while that of 1934 included 10 county record offices, 26 municipal libraries, one county and 13 special libraries. It is apparent, therefore, that at this time public libraries *were* alive to their responsibilities in the matter of local record preservation, especially considering that many libraries were refused recognition under the rule which prescribed that only one repository should be approved for a given area. Manchester Public Library, in spite of its vast collections relating to the city and the county of Lancashire, was refused because the John Rylands Library had been accepted for Lancashire and Cheshire. Liverpool, Plymouth, Newcastle and Leeds were similarly not approved although they had large collections of manuscript and manorial records and qualified staff to deal with them.

The establishment for the first time of 'official' repositories provided a stimulus to the collection, not only of manorial records, but of all records of a private nature and many collections which might otherwise have been dispersed or lost found their way into safe custody. The British Records Association, inaugurated in 1932, had, by the outbreak of war in 1939, succeeded in facilitating the transfer of many thousands of documents from private to public ownership by co-operating with lords of the manors, solicitors, parish clerks and others.

4

During and since the war, with the movement for better preservation of records and the establishment of county record offices growing apace, there was an unannounced, yet significant change of policy on the part of the Master of the Rolls. The 'one area – one repository' rule was no longer applied, and the policy became instead to recognise each new county record office as it was established as *the* appropriate repository for each county. Where an existing library or other body had previously been an accredited repository it continued to function as an *additional* repository, but it no longer was regarded as the primary repository for the area, however well it had fulfilled its obligations in this respect in the past. This decision, of course, was only relevant in so far as documents deposited by direction of the Master of the Rolls were concerned, since there is nothing to prevent any library not officially recognised from collecting manorial records providing it henceforth preserves them according to the conditions laid down in the Manorial Documents Rules.[1] It was agreed, too, that where an existing repository owned or had custody of the records of a particular manor, further records relating to that manor would be sent there. The redirection of records to the newer repositories did, however, jeopardise the comprehensiveness of some library collections, and there were instances of manorial records being divided in this manner between two repositories, thus confounding the principle of the sanctity of the archive group.

Deeply concerned with the need for a plan to preserve local records other than manorial documents, the British Records Association made representations to the Master of the Rolls in 1943 proposing the creation of a National Register of Archives. A committee was then appointed by the Master of the Rolls to consider the question of the protection of English archives as a whole. It included representatives of the Public Record Office, the British Museum, the Historical Manuscripts Commission, the British Records Association, the County Councils Association, the Association of Municipal Corporations, and the Church of England, and the first action of this committee was the formation of a National Register of Archives

1. Manorial Documents Rules, revised September 1959. Statutory Instruments, 1959, no. 1399; 1963, no. 976; and 1967, no. 963.

which commenced work in 1945 under the direction of the Historical Manuscripts Commission. A leading part was played by the Register in founding several local record offices and interest in local records was stimulated through the county organisations of the Register.

Following the passing of the Public Records Act of 1958, which implemented the recommendations of the Grigg Report on Departmental Records of the Government, the direction of the Public Record Office was transferred from the Master of the Rolls to a Minister of the Crown, the Lord Chancellor. The Master of the Rolls, who had exercised his responsibilities for manorial and tithe documents through the Public Record Office, decided after the passing of the Public Records Act, 1958, to use instead the Historical Manuscripts Commission, and a new Royal Warrant in 1959 reconstituted the Commission with extended terms of reference. This resulted in both the Historical Manuscripts Commission and the National Register of Archives moving from the Public Record Office to independent accommodation at Quality Court, Chancery Lane, London, WC2A 1HP. Subsequent reorganisation has integrated the Register more closely with the work of the Commission as a whole so that the Register is now more clearly seen as a function of the Commission rather than as a separate department.

Whilst the responsibility for the custody and care of manorial documents thus remains with the Master of the Rolls who exercises this function through the Historical Manuscripts Commission, certain other local records have become Public Records as a result of the Public Records Act, 1958, and are now subject to control by the Lord Chancellor through the Keeper of the Public Records. The Lord Chancellor has power to appoint a special place of deposit other than the Public Record Office for such records and in order to enable the records of quarter sessions, petty sessions, coroners and hospitals and probate records to be kept in local repositories a number of places of deposit have been approved by the Lord Chancellor where the facilities for the preservation of these records is not lower than that hitherto required by the Master of the Rolls for manorial documents.

Even before the Public Records Act, 1958, had passed to the

Statute Book, however, the safe keeping, use and the general care of modern local government records were being considered by a committee of the British Records Association, whilst in 1950 the newly formed Archives Committee of the Library Association was also concerned with the preservation of local records in libraries. The concern of the various bodies interested in the care of archives eventually led to the drafting of a bill on Local Government Records by the Ministry of Housing and Local Government so that in 1961 a Member of Parliament, the Hon. Nicholas Ridley, who had been successful in the ballot for private members bills in that year, decided to pilot the Bill through Parliament.[2] The resulting Local Government (Records) Act, 1962, was primarily concerned with the preservation and use of local records. Local authorities in England and Wales were given additional powers to make records in their possession available for study, to contribute towards the expenses of persons looking after local records and in the case of the county and county borough councils, to purchase local records, accept them as gifts or accept deposit of them by their owners. A very clearly expressed Circular explaining the effects of this Act was sent to all the local authorities concerned in 1962 and this Ministry of Housing Circular no. 44/62 is reproduced as an Appendix to the present work. Although the implementation of the 1962 Act by local authorities other than county councils has resulted in the transfer of local records to the local public library in about thirty instances, mostly to public libraries already recognised by the Master of the Rolls or by the Lord Chancellor, it is clear that local authorities have so far given insufficient attention to the fourth paragraph of this circular which called for 'an adequate system to be established to ensure that records are reviewed after a suitable period, and a selection made for retention'. As a result of this Act some local authorities have transferred records to the local library or other suitable repository, where better facilities for the care and study of the records are provided than in the often inconvenient storage arrangements prevailing in many town halls and council offices, and these transfers have also resulted in the appointment

2. Nicholas Ridley. 'The Local Government (Records) Act, 1962: its Passage to the Statute Book'. *Journal of the Society of Archivists*, vol. 2, no. 7, 1963. pp. 288–92.

of archivists in a small number of instances. There is a need, however, for many more local authorities to take more positive steps to ensure that the powers given by this Act are properly applied, not only for the benefit of present and future research workers, but also for the smoother working of the local authority itself where matters involving the consultation of the oldest records are concerned.

Since 1956 the Archives Committee of the Library Association has functioned as a sub-committee of the then Library Research Committee, now the Research and Development Committee, and has held a watching brief on behalf of the Association on all matters pertaining to archive administration. Representatives of the Society of Archivists, the Historical Manuscripts Commission, the British Records Association and the Business Archives Council have sat on this sub-committee, so that the Library Association has established useful links with these bodies and has thereby helped considerably to obtain a wider recognition of the valuable work of public libraries in relation to local archives. Recognition of the services rendered by the Chairman of the Archives Sub-Committee, Mr H. M. Cashmore, Emeritus City Librarian of Birmingham, was shown in 1965 when the British Records Association elected Mr Cashmore as a vice-president. The general policy of the Library Association on archive matters was outlined in 1957 and revised in 1967 and this revised statement of policy on *The Place of Archives and Manuscripts in the Field of Librarianship* is printed as an Appendix to the present work. The Association has also published Philip Hepworth's pamphlet *Archives and Manuscripts in Libraries* (Library Association Pamphlet, no. 18, 2nd ed. 1964) an admirable record of the achievements of libraries of all kinds in the conservation and use of archives and manuscripts. The sub-committee has compiled a 'Register of Biographical Manuscripts in British Repositories', issued as an L.A. Research Publication under the title *Select Biographical Sources: the Library Association Manuscripts Survey*, edited by Philip Hepworth (Library Association, London, 1971). It has also issued a statement of views on the Report of the Committee on Legal Records which was sent to all professors of history at British universities; and has been concerned quite recently with the problems connected with the export of manuscripts to other countries as well as the collection of manuscripts of living authors.

Following a survey carried out by Philip Hepworth on 'Archives and Manuscripts in Libraries – 1961' (*Library Association Record*, vol. 64, August, 1962, pp. 269–83) which showed that 73 municipal libraries possessed substantial to very large collections of documents (i.e. from 1,000 to over 75,000 documents) many public libraries that had not previously been listed in the *List of Record Repositories in Great Britain* (British Records Association, London, 1956) were included in the subsequent editions of this publication so that in the fourth edition, 1971, prepared by the staff of the Historical Manuscripts Commission, the total number of repositories listed has increased to 321 from the 155 listed in 1956.

Although the London Government Act, 1963, and other reorganisations of the local government structure has reduced the number of local authorities in recent years, there were in 1970 still more than seventy municipal authorities with substantial to very large collections of documents and about half of them employ archivists. As a result of the London Government Act, 1963, the Middlesex County Record Office and the County of London Record Office became together the Greater London Record Office under the new Greater London Council although each continues to be housed separately. Of the thirty-two new London boroughs, twenty-two appear to maintain collections of archives in their public libraries and although as yet the number of archivists employed in these libraries is no greater than in provincial municipal libraries with similar collections (about half of the libraries concerned both in London and in the provinces employ archivists) it would appear that the reorganisation of the London boroughs has resulted in the appointment of a small number of archivists. It has also resulted in the reorganisation of some archive services, notably in the City of Westminster where the Paddington and St Marylebone archives have been brought together at the former Marylebone Town Hall, giving these records greater accessibility; and in the transfer of a large number of borough archives from town halls and local government offices to the libraries of the new boroughs. It is also evident that as new central libraries and other buildings are erected by London boroughs further reorganisation and centralisation of archive collections will take place and such projects are envisaged at Bromley, Ealing, Hackney, Hammersmith and Waltham Forest. The City of London has a fine collection of records divided between the Guildhall Library, where the deposited records are kept including the archives of the City companies or guilds and many parish registers relating to the City,[3] and the Corporation of London Records Office housing the judicial and administrative records, all on the same site.

The varieties of record offices maintained by local authorities have already been described in Chapter 2. Details of existing record repositories will be found in the Historical Manuscripts Commission's *Record Repositories in Great Britain* (HMSO, London, 4th ed. 1971), whilst a useful guide to these repositories as well as to the use of archives generally is contained in F. G. Emmison's *Archives and Local History* (Methuen, London, 1966).

It has been observed that record repositories in England exist 'at a greater average density than in any other country in the world except Belgium and Switzerland, but with individual contents of correspondingly smaller average bulk' and the possibility of reform in the interest of service to the historian that 'will make the task of the historian in finding his way around even more difficult than it has already become, as a result of repeated overlaying of one pattern of repositories by another' was a thought expressed in this article.[4] The proliferation of repositories has been deprecated both by the Library Association and the British Records Association and schemes to reduce the number of repositories have been proposed by various bodies and individuals[5] but perhaps the real concern of the historian is not so much with the number of record repositories that exist as with the lack of really detailed information that is available concerning their contents. The Library Association's

3. See P. E. Jones and Raymond Smith. *A Guide to the Records in the Corporation of London Records Office and the Guildhall Library Muniments Room.* English Universities Press, London, 1951.

4. G. R. C. Davis. 'Some Home Thoughts for the English Archivist from Abroad?' *Archives*, vol. 4, no. 23, 1960. pp. 176–7.

5. See, for example, Derek Charman. 'On the Need for a New Local Archives Service for England'. *Journal of the Society of Archivists*, vol. 3, no. 7, April 1968. pp. 341–7.

Archives and Manuscripts Sub-Committee considered in 1967 that: 'An important requirement in the compilation of directories of archival resources is for as full a description as possible of the materials recorded. Descriptions in a number of existing sources are too general to be of any use to a serious enquirer.' The sub-committee also considered that: 'The recording of archival collections is an operation which . . . could lend itself to mechanised methods. An important preliminary requirement is national agreement amongst archivists as to the descriptive symbols for computer use.'[6]

A list of printed guides to archive collections appears in Philip Hepworth's *Archives and Manuscripts in Libraries* (Library Association Pamphlet, no. 18, 2nd ed. 1964) and although printed guides to archive collections containing reasonably detailed information concerning the separate parts of the collection, such as the Gateshead Public Libraries' publication *Gateshead Archives: A Guide*, 1968, the Sheffield City Libraries' *Catalogue of the Arundel Castle Manuscripts*, 1965, and other guides that have appeared subsequently, it still remains an unfortunate truth that there are not a sufficient number of detailed guides to archive collections to satisfy the needs of research workers.

Information to scholars, however, has always been a primary function of the Historical Manuscripts Commission and in describing 'The National Register of Archives, 1945–1969', Felicity Ranger said: 'It is therefore not surprising that the most spectacular change in the Register over 24 years has been its development as an information service. We have no National Union Catalogue of archives in this country, and this is a deficiency. Instead there is the National Register of Archives which does not claim the comprehensiveness of a union catalogue but does incorporate a good deal more detail than any union catalogue can possibly do.'[7]

From a modest beginning in 1945 as little more than a directory of archive collections in public and private hands, the National Register of Archives now contains information relating to some 15,000 archive accumulations mainly in the form of typescript lists which are reproduced by the Com-

6. 'Access to Archival Material'. *Library Association Record*, vol. 69, no. 6, June 1967. pp. 213–15.

7. *Journal of the Society of Archivists*, vol. 3, no. 9, April 1969. pp. 452–62.

mission's Reproduction Section for the copyright libraries and appropriate local centres. A complete set of these reports is kept at the Search Room of the Commission, open to all researchers without formality. The Search Room contained 14,600 lists in December 1970 with additions being received at the annual rate of about 1,000. A small library of published guides to the contents of record offices is also maintained in the Search Room together with indexes to the lists. A *Central Index* gives a short title and number of each list together with the last known location and the entries are filed alphabetically under the names of owners or custodians. Three additional indexes cover the contents of the reports: an *Index of Persons*, a *Subject Index* and a *Topographical Index*. The *Index of Persons* contained 21,000 entries and the *Subject Index*, 45,900 entries by October 1968, and details concerning these indexes as well as of the Manorial Documents Register were given in an article in the *Journal of the Society of Archivists*, vol. 3, no. 9, April 1969, pp. 462–6, entitled 'The Use of the Resources of the Historical Manuscripts Commission' by H. M. G. Baillie. The history and work of the Historical Manuscripts Commission 1869–1969 was described in general by Roger H. Ellis in two articles appearing in the *Journal of the Society of Archivists*, vol. 2, no. 6, October 1962, pp. 233–42 and vol. 3, no. 9, April 1969, pp. 441–52, and in the introduction to the catalogue of the Centenary Exhibition of the Commission at the National Portrait Gallery in 1969 (*Manuscripts and Men*, HMSO, London, 1969). The current work of the Commission is reviewed annually in the reports of the Secretary to the Commissioners (*Report of the Secretary to the Commissioners 1968–1969*, HMSO, London, 1969, and *Report of the Secretary to the Commissioners 1969–1970*, HMSO, London, 1970). Another important service of the Historical Manuscripts Commission is the editing and publication of the *List of Accessions to Repositories*. This function was taken over from the Institute of Historical Research in 1954 and this *List of Accessions*, though recognised as containing only brief and summary descriptions nevertheless gives information relating to the recent accessions of some 140 repositories in Great Britain. Libraries should co-operate with the work of the Commission by submitting annual returns of their manuscript accessions, and by sending lists of calendars of archive collections to the

Commission. At the local level many librarians have taken an active part in the work of the local NRA committees and in some counties are acting as area secretaries. The South Yorkshire NRA Committee, which is based on Sheffield City Library, employs one part-time archivist together with a part-time typist to list accumulations for the Commission, and the West Riding Northern Committee, working from Leeds, has done the same with the help of local authorities.

That the field of local record preservation is too large to be fully catered for by one particular form of depository; that there are records of such a peculiarly local character that they should be preserved locally and not deposited in a central office; that in many cases printed and manuscript materials go together hand-in-hand; these are facts which would readily be admitted by any realistic archivist or librarian. 'In the world of this decade, no single institution, whether record office or library, is a suitable place in which to store all the records of a county; safety lies in dispersal, within reason.'[8]

We end this chapter, therefore, with a plea for co-operation between libraries and record offices and for forbearance, recognising that each has its part to play in conserving local historical materials and that they are partners in adding to the sum of human knowledge. There is no room for parochialism or insularity in librarianship or record preservation and every effort should be made to ensure the maximum of co-operation and good feeling at local and at higher levels. Not only must the twin professions of librarian and archivist respect each other, but there must be understanding on the part of the local authorities and of their national associations.

Unfortunately political speculation and vacillation over the future of local government, especially its areas and boundaries, has created a climate in which the different kinds of local authority find it difficult to co-operate with each other, even in non-political issues such as libraries, archives and museums. Such liaison as does exist, and we have shown it to be no small amount, is due to the goodwill existing between the officials concerned rather than to directives from above.

Civic pride, a sense of tradition and a desire to perpetuate these on the part of small authorities should be regarded as virtues

8. Redstone and Steer (eds.). *Local Records.* pp. 39–40.

and not with derision, for they are, in essence, those virtues on which the past we are trying to preserve was essentially based. County authorities should remember this in their relations with boroughs and county districts within their areas. The county borough, too, should limit its objectives. In the past many county towns have taken the whole county as their sphere of influence and large cities have tended to collect for an extensive regional area. With the advent of county record offices these horizons are becoming more limited. It is often better to leave records which are purely local in the areas to which they properly relate, than to build up large accumulations in the county town or city, and this policy could be adopted as far as the sanctity of the archive group allows. On this basis rivalry gives way to friendly co-operation to the mutual advantage of all.

The conservation of local source materials is a task which, notwithstanding the great strides forward taken in recent years, still requires energetic action by all corporate bodies and individuals who are interested. Rivalry, either locally or nationally, can only be detrimental to the interests of students and of the records themselves. The co-operative spirit engendered during the war, when the support of librarians was welcomed in the primary task of rescuing records from destruction did, to a considerable extent, pave the way for this necessary development. Continued today this same spirit will facilitate the development of a comprehensive programme of archive administration, which will infinitely extend the range of our cultural resources.

Chapter 6

The Care and Treatment of Archives

Archives were defined by the Master of the Rolls Archives Committee as 'all documents (except documents to which the Public Record Office Acts and the Probate Acts apply), accumulated and preserved by a natural process in the course of the conduct of affairs of any kind, public or private, at any date, and surviving in the keeping of the persons responsible for the business *or their successors*.'[1] The final phrase is important and the word 'successor' needs careful definition in such a way as to include libraries and other institutions which have acquired such natural accumulations of archives, solicitors or estate agents and even the families of bygone clerks of the peace who may have retained official records in their private possession. Records do not lose their archival quality when they are transferred 'as a whole' into the custody of a library or other repository. Printed material may, in certain circumstances, be or become archival in character, e.g. a series of annual reports, statements of accounts, sale catalogues, or published government documents.

The official or legal nature of archives is all-important. Their value lies largely in the fact that they are essentially a product of their time and of conditions which can never be reproduced. They have accumulated naturally in offices to serve the practical purposes of administration and for no other reason. As that doyen of archivists, Sir Hilary Jenkinson, has stated – 'Fundamental is the organic unity of the documents, expressing the life of the organisation which created them.' Archive science

1. In *Heads of Proposals for the Preservation of Local Archives*. Master of the Rolls, Archives Committee, London, 1951.

is, in the main, a matter of adherence to certain simple fundamental and time-honoured precepts, but the practical matters
relating to their conservation have hardly been standardised at
all, which is scarcely surprising in a comparatively new
profession.

One of the chief objections to libraries as local record
repositories has been that their outlook and training is fundamentally different from that of the archivist, and it is true, of
course, that, at the turn of the century, librarians of that period
showed little appreciation or knowledge of archive techniques,
although probably the first local archivist in the country was
attached to the Birmingham City Library before 1900. It would
be equally true to point out, in extenuation, that these techniques had not then been evolved by Fowler, Jenkinson and
others, and old-time librarians might therefore be forgiven for
seeking to adapt the principles of Cutter and Dewey to their
comparatively small record collections. This does not, however,
excuse the librarian of today who makes the same mistakes
or absolve him from an awareness of the differences of technique
and treatment involved in the care of archives as opposed to
books. Amongst librarians there has not been a proper
appreciation of the fact that the professions of archivist and
librarian are separate and distinct. The relationships between
the two professions, and differences in holdings and in methods
which obtain in their institutions are discussed by Dr
Schellenberg.[2]

While eminent and successful archivists have been trained in
libraries and several librarians have become successful county
archivists, the wider and more general training available today
should be accepted as the norm for archivists in charge of substantial record collections. It is to the credit of the Library
Association that it was the first body to commence, in 1921,
training in palaeography and archive science, and the suitability
of its papers in these subjects in the current (1972) Syllabus as a
qualification for a librarian working with archivists are given
in the Library Association's statement of policy: *The Place of
Archives and Manuscripts in the Field of Librarianship* (Appendix I).

There has, perhaps, been too rigid an insistence amongst

2. T. R. Schellenberg. *Modern Archives: Principles and Techniques.* F. W. Cheshire,
Melbourne, 1956.

archivists upon the uniqueness of archives and their attendant science, and not enough understanding or appreciation of the fact that many libraries, museums, firms, societies and local authorities possess small or insubstantial collections of archives. It is often as impossible to insist on such bodies employing a qualified archivist as it would be to expect that a county repository should place its often large library of printed material in the charge of a trained and qualified librarian.

In this respect it would be helpful if there were more scope for archivists in libraries (and there are many libraries where the appointment of an archivist *ought* to be considered) and more movement of archivists between libraries and other record repositories. The mutual understanding of one another's problems could not but be beneficial.

Librarians in charge of archive collections, however small, should endeavour to keep abreast of professional developments in the archive world, and acquaint themselves with the professional publications and activities of archivists. Archivists working in libraries should be encouraged to join the professional organisation, the Society of Archivists, and to attend its meetings and conferences. The Library Association has expressed the view that there should be complete mobility between libraries, record offices and other employing bodies, and it urges equal respect for all kinds of archivists. Co-operation and consultation between the Library Association and the Society of Archivists should be closer, and within libraries archivists and librarians should work in closer contact. The largest libraries should class their archive collections as record offices, as Dr Chandler has done at Liverpool. The more dignified status is necessary if staff of high quality are to be secured.

One thing *must* be said. It is that librarians, however competent and well trained, should not be allowed to deal with extensive archival collections without special training. The methods employed by well-meaning and enthusiastic librarians in the past to deal with archives have tended to bring librarianship into disrepute and to widen unnecessarily the gap between archival and library practice. Faulty methods of storage or arrangement can cause endless trouble. The odd paper or document, once misplaced, may be lost far more incalculably than a book in a library. Our predecessors certainly had the excuse that archive science had not then been formulated, but there are today well-established codes of practice for accessioning, listing and calendaring records which every record repository should observe in its essentials. Some librarians, such as Miss Mary Walton at Sheffield and Mr Sargeant at Birmingham, did indeed play their part in helping to formulate and standardise these procedures.

The aim of any process of arrangement applied to archives should be to correlate the groups or series of papers, and to show their inter-relationships, and there should be no attempt to fit them into a predetermined schedule or to rearrange them in chronological or other order. Their collective value as a group far exceeds that which they would have when broken up, however perfect the system by which they were rearranged. The individual paper, unless it possesses some unique significance, is not indicated in this process, though it will be in the listing. Archives are classed, not by subject as in the case of books, but according to the agency or body which originated them, and a careful survey of each collection is a necessary preliminary to any scheme of arrangement.

Archive classification,[3] then, is based only on groups and series, according to the originative agency, but this does not mean that each series is to be a conglomerate mass of unrelated documents. On the contrary, it is essential that there should be some logical internal order, based on detailed examination of the documents and their history. The fundamental principle of the sanctity of the archive group, known to archivists as *respect des fonds*, is the guiding principle of archive arrangement based on their administrative origin.

When a large collection enters the library the first step is to enter the details of date of receipt, quantity and depositor and kind of deposit (gift, loan, purchase) into an accessions register. The accession number allocated will then identify the

3. Dr Hubert Hall attempted a structural classification of British archives many years ago in his *Repertory of British Archives*, and several have been made since, notably in the report of the British Records Association Committee on *The Classification of English Archives* (General report of a committee of English archives, London, 1936) and the class lists prepared by the National Register of Archives. These are schemes of arrangement of the various kinds of administrative bodies which give rise to archives and are intended as nothing more.

source of the collection. The archivist will make a preliminary survey of the whole with a view to ascertaining if there is any readily discernible order in the manner in which it is arranged. If so this will be maintained as far as possible in the subsequent arrangement of the records. This done, the documents can be examined more carefully, cleaned, stamped with the ownership stamp and given a temporary number. Some archivists eschew this preliminary sorting and accession the documents in the often rather fortuitous order in which they reach the repository, but a certain amount of rearrangement is usually considered necessary. It should, however, at this stage be kept to a minimum. The stamp should be placed on a readily visible part of the document: in the margin if both sides bear writing.

A simple accessions list, giving brief details, can then be prepared. For this one needs to master the technique of rapid analysis, of selecting and extracting the salient facts from a welter of words and papers, a process which is greatly facilitated by familiarity with local family and place-names. Following this preliminary listing the collection may be stored away, unless final arrangement and cataloguing are contemplated immediately, which depends upon the pressure of work on hand at the time. The records are, however, now available for public inspection if need be.

The collection then awaits the more leisurely processes of calendaring and indexing, and it must never be thought that the initial listing absolves the librarian or archivist from any fuller treatment of his records. It is indeed desirable that the next stage should be attended to as soon as possible, while the 'bird's eye' view of the collection can be retained in the mind. The whole collection will be considered integrally, with a view to deciding the best arrangement of its many parts. In this internal arrangement the archivist is seeking to reproduce, as far as possible, the original order and purpose of the documents and to find out how they fit into the general pattern. 'Always regard provenance as the guiding principle, the essential problem is the reason behind the presence of a document or bundle in the collection.'[4]

It will now be appreciated that many problems are involved in the treatment of archives, for which it is impossible to lay

4. Redstone and Steer (eds.). *Local Records*. p. 78.

down rules, and the reader must stand referred to the textbooks on archive practice for details of these. There are, however, one or two special points of which the librarian in charge of archives should make note because they may conflict with his library training. Firstly, every archivist draws a distinction between 'official' and 'unofficial' records, and keeps them separate in practice. Many library collections, of course, contain no official records, but where the records of the municipality are in his care they should be rigidly separated from the remainder, even to being kept in their own storage or strong room, where this is feasible. Secondly, printed material, maps, plans and drawings forming part of a collection of archives should not, as a rule, be removed from the collection though they may have to be stored separately for convenience. There was, in all probability, a reason for its placement there, and it is on this association that its archival value depends. The librarian may believe, quite rightly, that the item would be of much more value if it was extracted and placed with cognate material, but we reiterate that such 'classification' is indefensible with archive material. There are occasionally obvious 'strays' to be met with, or duplicate items, and sometimes large maps or rolls are removed from a series in the interests of safer storage, but in such cases it is imperative to make a note detailing what has happened and why, giving the date and the new location.

Shrewsbury Public Library received the minute books and papers of the Iron Bridge Trust as a deposited collection, and it was noticed that the first minute book, covering the period 1774–98, was missing. It was found in a collection of papers of a local family, one member of which had acted as Secretary of the Trust in its early years, and since there were no further related papers in this collection, the volume was restored to the Trust records to complete the series. The question as to how often such stray records should be replaced in their proper place is one for consideration on the merits of each particular case. There is the occasional 'made-up' collection, perhaps the gathering of a local collector or antiquary, which defies the normal principles of archival arrangement, but even these should not be split up, apart from restoring items which obviously belong to other series.

We may sum up the principles of archive arrangement by quoting three simple rules which Charles Johnson suggests archivists should observe when sorting records:

1. The original grouping of the documents must be preserved.
2. No scheme of arrangement can be fixed until the whole group of documents has been examined, and its original arrangement understood.
3. No original volume, file or bundle must be broken up until its nature and principle of arrangement is understood and recorded.[5]

These rules are elaborated by the author in his *Care of Documents*. To them may be added another, postulated by the authors of *Local Records* to the effect that 'Every collection must be dealt with according to its nature, and the contents of no two will be alike; what has worked in one instance may not apply to the next.'[6]

The basic arrangement of a collection being settled, the next step, that of cataloguing, can be faced. The ultimate aim in every library or repository should be the compilation of a full calendar of each collection, but the volume of accessions to many repositories in recent years and the limited number of staff available to deal with them, has reduced the opportunities of providing such detailed treatment. It is more usual, therefore, to compile a summary catalogue or inventory, which gives a conspectus of the whole collection and is of some value to the student as a guide to what he may expect to find in it. A description of the preparation of such a catalogue, with an example, is given in *Local Records* by Redstone and Steer, pp. 80–1.

These inventories, usually typed on folio sheets, may be kept in loose-leaf binders, but those of the more important and well-used collections should be bound for convenience of use by both reader and office staff. Such inventories are invariably limited in the amount of detail given. Entries describing title deeds, for instance, may be confined to a brief description of the property and the covering dates, and rarely include details of personal names, field and other minor place-names which give such documents their principal value to the modern

5. Charles Johnson. *The Care of Documents and Management of Archives*. S.P.C.K., London, 1919. pp. 11, 13, 17.
6. Redstone and Steer (eds.). *Local Records*. p. 77.

student. It is worthwhile, therefore, where time allows, to compile a full calendar and the following form of entry for calendaring deeds is taken from *Local Records*, which usefully covers the care and treatment of local archives.

Date in full.

Type of deed, with a note of consideration, rent and term.

Names of parties, with full details of status and abode.

Property (indented) with full details as given in the original deed, all place-names and names of fields; with parish names underlined for ease of recognition.

Notes regarding special covenants and the like.

Witnesses in medieval charters.

Note on endorsements, signatures and seals, and any other special matter, i.e. the language in which it is written.

Early charters deserve fuller treatment which consists of a careful transcript of the document, a summary in English, and notes on style, seals, former ownership, material, size and other features such as illuminated initials or endorsements.

This form is adaptable to most documents and papers which are separate in themselves. Good calendaring depends to a large extent upon an adequate knowledge of legal forms and formulae. There is no really good guide to these and the student must rely upon a reading of general books fortified by actual experience gained in reading documents. For early deeds a study of the facsimiles to be found in Andrew Wright's *Court Hand Restored* (London, 1867), Johnson and Jenkinson's *English Court Hand, A.D. 1066–1500* (2 vols., Clarendon Press, Oxford, 1915) and Jenkinson's *The Later Court Hands in England* (2 vols., Cambridge University Press, London, 1927) is necessary. These can be supplemented by the publications of the Essex Record Office, especially Miss Hilda Grieve's *Examples of English Handwriting, 1150–1750*, 2nd ed., 1959) and by L. C. Hector's *The Handwriting of English Documents* (E. Arnold, London, 1958).

For the more official records, including manorial, a slightly simpler form may be adopted, the main part of the calendar entry consisting of a summary of the record with all the personal and place-names which may be recorded. For elucidating the nature and form of such records some of the printed volumes, and especially their introductions, are valuable. Many local authorities and county archaeological societies have published volumes of borough, county and parish records, which are invariably compiled by experts and these have much to teach the learner.

The beginner should confine his initial attempts at calendaring to later deeds in modern English, not Stuart deeds which are often extremely elaborate and prolix. Then, when he is thoroughly familiar with the form of the more typical classes of document, he may proceed to Latin, Middle-English and Norman-French deeds, confident of finding some points of familiarity to guide him. Alternatively, having first learnt palaeography, he may start on the medieval deeds which, because of their extremely simple form, present few difficulties apart from the textual. It is not usually difficult, if the hand can be mastered, to make a short abstract for early deeds, embodying the essential details, but after 1500 they increase in size and complexity, and contain much historically irrelevant, however legally necessary, verbiage from which the salient points have to be disentangled. Palaeographical skill, it has been well said, 'is the product of constant practice and infinite attention to detail' (G. Barraclough).

Access to the *Medieval Latin Word-list from British and Irish Sources*, revised by R. E. Latham (Oxford University Press, London, 1965) is essential, and the most useful dictionary of abbreviations and contractions is Adriano Cappelli's *Lexicon abbreviaturarum. Dizionario di abbreviature latine ed italiane* (6th ed., Hoepli, Milan, 1961). This has been supplemented by A. Pelzer's *Abréviations latine médiévales* (2nd ed., Béatrice – Nauwelaerts, Paris, 1966). Charles T. Martin's *The Record Interpreter* Stevens, London, (2nd ed. 1910, repr. 1967) based on English material is still useful for the beginner in research. For the elucidation of saints' days, regnal years and other dating problems F. M. Powicke's *Handbook of British Chronology* (Royal Historical Society, London, 2nd ed. 1961) is the most useful reference work.

The final stage of calendaring is the preparation of detailed indexes to the calendars and handlists. Only when this is done can the collection be regarded as fully ready for public use, but in many repositories the pressure of work has meant the postponement, at least temporarily, of the preparation of such aids. Essex County Record Office has shown that the largest office can, with adequate staffing, and the will, attend to the preparation of these essential aids. In addition to its lists and calendars of individual collections it has compiled three detailed indexes to help students. These are references to parishes, personal names and subjects, the latter being arranged under 1,200 headings.

We are aware, of course, that such detailed treatment as has been recommended here is a counsel of perfection which is not always capable of realisation in a busy archive repository or library and that some have, through sheer pressure of accumulating work, been forced to discontinue or suspend detailed cataloguing in favour of listing or other more summary treatment. In some the brief inventory is the only public aid provided, while elsewhere this is dispensed with and a catalogue ranging between a full calendar and a summary list is made for each collection, the degree of fullness in the entries depending upon the nature and importance of the specific series.

Libraries can often attend to the cataloguing and listing of deposited documents more rapidly and in greater detail since they generally have larger staffs and are also free of the necessity of giving priority to their local authority records, while indexing can be entrusted to suitably qualified library staff. In the smaller collections of public libraries the complete calendar of the records, fully indexed for personal and place-names and subject matter is a practical possibility, a fact which perhaps constitutes an argument against building up collections so vast that they cannot receive full treatment. In the large archive repository this is in many cases illusory: to deal fully with all collections will take many years, and a simpler form of treatment has to be adopted to make the material available to the public with the minimum of delay.

'The important thing', said Miss Mary Renshaw, writing of the problems of the large repository, 'is to get a collection in working order; to get it cleaned and sorted, and for the archivist at least to have some idea of its contents, to be able to answer queries, and to bring material to the notice of students.'[7] It is essential that information concerning archives

7. Mary Renshaw, 'A University Archive Repository'. *Library Association Record*, vol. 56, March 1954. p. 79.

should be disseminated amongst scholars and students as rapidly as possible, and this is achieved in the best and most efficient manner through the National Register of Archives.

The storage and packing of records does not call for lengthy treatment here. It must be remembered that many collections will remain on the shelves for years with few requests for their contents. Hence, for the majority, a simple, inexpensive form of storage may be used. Some record series, on the other hand, will be in fairly constant use and here methods must be such as will withstand this handling, and more expense is justified. Brown paper parcels are to be eschewed (Jenkinson) and ordinary container board boxes of a uniform size, punched at each end to allow air to circulate, are the best solution. The technical committee of the Society of Archivists has given attention to the suitable materials and specification for document storage boxes. The U.S. National Archives has developed a useful box of cardboard covered with aluminium foil which is claimed to be as fire resistant as the old-fashioned metal deed box, which has no place in a modern strong room. A hinge at one side of the box is a concession to easier access to the contents. Very long rolls require special accommodation in files or racks.

In some repositories loose papers are fastened together and guarded or they may be kept loose in boxes flatter than those used for deeds, in which case they may first be placed in manilla folders or tied between sheets of stiff board. Economical binders for the preservation of loose papers or the rebinding of manuscript volumes have been developed at the Public Record Office and the U.S. National Archives. In the Public Record Office single documents are attached to guards which are pierced and laced together through the holes. The U.S. National Archives uses buckram or canvas-covered binders, in which the pages are held by means of semi-permanent steel posts, which permits rearrangement, removal or reinsertion of pages. This binder, it is claimed, costs less than one-third of the cost of the conventional binding process.

Rebinding of records which are in volume form is a matter to be done warily. Questions of the value of the original binding and of continuous custody arise. When it is necessary, the original covers should be conserved as far as possible, and detailed instructions should accompany the volume. If the existing binding can be strengthened this should be done. Where rebinding is involved, the old covers and anything which might help the expert in dating or identifying the manuscript ought to be preserved. The folding of paper documents should be minimised and smaller papers stored flat. Metal fasteners, paper clips, rubber bands and string should not be used; a good quality lawyer's tape is the best fastening material.

Repair work on records is a skilled operation requiring special abilities and training which should not be attempted by untrained staff. Nor should the archivist, except in a very small repository be expected to do repairs, although it is desirable that he should have had some training in this work. His qualifications are better utilised on the technical tasks and repairs left to assistants who have been specially trained. Many libraries would find it useful to have at least one assistant trained in the repair not only of books but in the more difficult work of repairing manuscripts and documents. Even skilled book repairers should not, as a rule, work on archives without special training. The reverse does not generally apply, and a records repairer can be of considerable assistance in the problems of repairing valuable books for the reference library and local collection, especially those whose absence from the library will impair its efficiency. Sheffield's document repairers spent much time dealing with nineteenth-century directories, yearbooks and similar printed works in heavy demand which were in poor condition after being heavily guarded and oversewn many years ago.

Any library which can afford the appointment and the necessary equipment should press for the establishment of a small repair shop or laboratory. Norwich's may be cited as a good example and it is housed in the record office. Qualified repairers are rare and it is usually best to appoint a trained bookbinder, who can take a course in document repair, either at a neighbouring record office or one of the courses arranged by the Society of Archivists.

The Society of Archivists has set up a committee to give technical advice on problems of repair and preservation and since the subject is also fully covered in the archive textbooks, in works such as Sydney M. Cockerell's *The Repairing of Books*

(Sheppard Press, London, 2nd ed. 1960), W. H. Langwell's
The Conservation of Books and Documents (Pitman, London, 1957),
and D. B. Wardle's *Document Repairs* (Society of Archivists,
London, 1971), little need be said of it here. Save for urgent
matters, repairing should not be attempted piecemeal, but
should be a systematic process undertaken collection by collection. A cardinal rule is that documents should be repaired with
the material of which they are made, although in view of the
expense, substitutes for backing parchment have been used with
only moderate success. The selection of suitable adhesives is of
prime importance; a good-quality flour paste is satisfactory in
most cases. Treatment may, to a certain degree, vary according
to the value or permanence of the record.

Lamination, a process by which paper documents are
placed between two sheets of transparent acetate foil, which
melts into the document when heat and pressure are applied, is
the accepted treatment today in some large depositories,
including the Library of Congress, and U.S. National Archives
and the India Office Records in this country. It strengthens
the records considerably and renders them impervious to heat,
water and further decay, and it is preferred in the United
States on the grounds of its adaptability for various kinds of
record, its efficiency and economy, but there have been
suggestions that it has increased the scholar's difficulty in
deciphering manuscript texts. An essential preliminary for this
process is the de-acidification of the document, which is
provided for in the materials used in the Postlip lamination
process.[8]

Lamination is a comparatively rapid process, simpler than
the skilled methods which require craftsmen, but some lamina-
ting processes have not proved entirely satisfactory, and they
do not have the flexibility of repairs using paper and silk gauze.
Dr H. J. Plenderleith and Dr A. Werner[9] of the British Museum
Research Laboratory contend that silk gauze has a life of not
more than twenty-five years, when it needs replacing, but
Roger Ellis contests this assertion from his wide experience

8. W. H. Langwell. 'The Postlip Duplex Lamination Processes'. *Journal of the Society of Archivists*, vol. 2, 1964, pp. 471–6; and vol. 3, 1968, pp. 360–1.
9. 'Technical Notes on the Conservation of Documents'. *Journal of the Society of Archivists*, vol. 1, 1959. pp. 195–220.

with this material at the Public Record Office. He concludes that 'lamination is a repair process with great possibilities, and it is hoped that the uncertainties at present attending its use will in due course be resolved . . . but to archivists working in this country [it] still offers only a partial solution.'[10]

The care and treatment of seals presents a difficult problem and one which few repositories have the technical staff or the materials to deal with adequately. When repairs are called for application should be made to the repairing department of the Public Record Office or reference made to the standard archive manuals. At the Public Record Office the repairing process does not attempt to complete or fake a broken design, and in order that the renovation shall be clearly apparent wax of a different colour is used.[11]

The care of seals is, however, a different matter and the adoption of simple rules will eliminate the need for many repairs. While small, unimportant seals may safely be folded inside the document, it is generally desirable to prevent friction between the seal and the parchment. Documents with large pendant seals, such as royal seals, should have these encased in a suitable receptacle, preferably a linen or buckram bag. Cellulose wadding with polythene covering should be used for protection, and too much handling is to be avoided. Seals affixed to the parchment or paper may not, in a small repository, need further protection than that provided by the folds of the documents, but any of special value or interest should have the exposed surface protected.

The identification of seals is very much a matter for the expert, but in a full calendar of records armorial seals, at least, should be described in detail. Many can be identified by reference to W. de Gray Birch's great work *A Catalogue of Seals in the British Museum* (6 vols. London, 1887–1900), while the standard work of reference on royal seals is A. B. and Allan Wyon's *The Great Seals of England* (London, 1887), although it contains a number of inaccuracies. *The Guide to the Seals in the Public Record Office* (HMSO, London, 2nd ed. 1968) has a useful

10. 'An Archivist's Note on the Conservation of Documents'. *Journal of the Society of Archivists*. vol. 1, 1959. pp. 252–4.

11. Sir Hilary Jenkinson. 'Some Notes on the Preservation, Moulding and Casting of Seals', *Antiquaries Journal*, vol. 4, 1924. pp. 388–403.

introduction by Sir Hilary Jenkinson. The number of seals on a document should be noted and their size and shape. Circular seals should be measured by diameter; pointed or oval seals by the length and maximum breadth. The colour should also be given – natural, red and green are the usual. The lettering on the seal should be transcribed precisely. It commences as a rule with a star or cross, followed by 's' or 'sig' (Sigillum) and then by the name. Occasionally there is a short verse, usually of a religious nature.

Libraries and record offices which have responsibility for modern administrative records may have to face the question of the weeding or disposal of surplus or unimportant files. Consultation with the town clerk or the clerk of the peace is essential here – a scheme should be worked out, erring on the side of retaining too much initially, but with provision for a periodical review at intervals of, say, ten and twenty-five years. This elimination should be part of a continuous process, *not* a radical operation under the stress of suddenly finding that accommodation is full and overcrowded. Most record offices now have a logical programme of records administration, including arrangements for the controlled disposal of records and the elimination of ephemeral material, which is essential if storage facilities are not to be hopelessly cluttered up with unimportant files.

Chapter 7

Extension of Service

Library extension activities are principally concerned with persuading those who do not use the library service to do so, as well as with informing those who only use a part of any library service that it might be beneficial for them to consider the use of the other aspects which they may have overlooked previously through ignorance of the availability of all that is provided. All extension activity is based on the belief that a service provided by the community as a whole should be used by the widest spectrum of individuals comprising that community and that successful extension activities increase demands. Demands for some aspects of the services provided by local history libraries and record offices in recent years, however, have tended to embarrass some librarians and archivists to the extent that restrictions on the unfair use of staff for time-consuming genealogical research, or on the indiscriminate use of original material for educational exercises of sometimes doubtful value have had to be imposed in order to protect both staff and material alike. Are extension activities for the local collection, therefore, really necessary?

It should be observed at once that if one or two sections of a community make demands that prove embarrassing, appropriate remedial action can be taken should these demands result in an abuse of the service provided. Certainly such an excess on the part of sections of a community does not mean that others who could make use of a service should not be informed of the facilities available. Indeed, it is much more necessary to inform all sections of a community about the existence, purpose and nature of a local collection than of any other part of a library service. This is because the acquisition of the full range of material needed to build and maintain a local collection in a useful condition depends very largely on the supply of printed, written and photographic items not usually available by purchase and certainly not listed in any way. It is only through the co-operation of those who are aware of the needs of the local history collection that much of the appropriate material can be acquired and these needs must be made known to both users and non-users of the collection. Extension activities applied to the local collection therefore, should result not only in an increase in demands but also in an increasing flow of useful material.

In the introduction to *Public Library Extension Activities* by Harold Jolliffe, the author says: 'It seems hardly necessary to mention that all extension work must be supported by an adequate library service, which means a first-class book stock served by a good staff in at least reasonable accommodation.'[1]

Thought given to accommodation is a useful starting point. Do we consider the convenience and comfort of readers in our local rooms as we should? Do we aim to remove all sources of distraction as far as possible? Do we provide the comfortable furniture which makes prolonged study more bearable? Do we provide the miscellaneous items of equipment which will help the student to study the material in reasonable comfort, such as reading stands for heavy books, weights or rules to hold maps or documents in position? Do we not make our newspaper files unnecessarily bulky and heavy by binding too many issues in a single volume? There are countless ways in which a thoughtful library staff can assist the comfort of their patrons, and in this department, where the reader often spends a considerable time at each visit, everything possible should be done.

There are various means by which the staff can exploit both their stock and their personal knowledge to encourage people to make greater use of the available facilities. The basis of most useful extension work is the personal contact between the librarian and reader, which is invariably greater in this department than in most others. The local librarian will be

1. 2nd ed., Library Association, London, 1968.

dealing to a large extent with specialists and people of more-than-average intellectual attainments, and he must be able to meet and converse with them on a not-unequal footing. Such users of the library rightly expect intelligent service and only assistants trained in both scholarship and technical knowledge should be permitted to administer to their needs. One of the most effective contacts that can be established between librarian and reader is a system of informing readers of material likely to be of interest to them. Cambridge Public Library, for example, operates a Selective Dissemination of Information scheme whereby users complete a form and their interests are entered on coloured catalogue cards which are filed at all appropriate headings in the catalogue. When cards for new material are added to the catalogue the reader is notified. Readers find this a useful service and the collection also derives benefit from those who pass back information as a mark of appreciation.

If publicity and exploitation of material has been properly directed to reach all local residents, however, there will be a much greater use made of the local collection by a large number of untrained historians and casual enquirers than by expert historians.

The collection will be extensively used by young students and novices, many of whom will need help and advice and much of the librarian's time will be devoted to rendering personal assistance. Much detailed knowledge of the contents of books and manuscripts, accumulated over long periods of service or through the intense study necessary for calendaring and indexing records, reposes in the mind and memory of the librarian, and it should be freely accessible to all who seek it. In the light of his knowledge and experience he will be able to evaluate the printed books relating to the locality, to guide readers to the best authority for their particular purpose and, in certain circumstances, to warn them of inaccuracies or bias in certain books. How far such estimating of the relative value of historical sources may be taken is at the discretion of the librarian and it is, of course, essential that if he does offer such advice it should be absolutely impartial and free from personal bias.

For basic source material, such as archives, this evaluative process is neither necessary nor desirable. It is sufficient for the librarian or archivist to be able to describe the contents of collections and series in general terms, and to say whether they are likely to contain material of interest to the student. True, the unskilled researcher may require help in the transcription of documents, matters of dating, chronology and regnal years, or the use of the more complicated catalogues, handlists and indexes needed for manuscript materials. The amateur historian is often dismayed by the mere sight of a manuscript, and it is sometimes said that unskilled students should not be allowed to use this material. Some record offices insist that students must be 'accredited', that is recommended by some proper authority before being allowed to study archives. However necessary this may be in national repositories, it is quite foreign to library, or at least to public library, tradition and, subject to the usual precautions, students should be encouraged to use them, unless obviously incompetent to do so.

University staff and trained historians can use large accumulations of research materials without assistance; the undergraduate and the trainee may need the skill and expert advice of the librarian. The scholar needs access to large library collections of original material in producing the research work or theses usually expected of him today. In addition to the use of archives by trained and responsible historians, it must be remembered that they also serve as a training-ground for students in historical and various other studies. Many such students from our training colleges and universities work on these collections, producing written work for their tutors without any intention of the results ever being printed. Many local history librarians have become increasingly aware, however, of the usefulness of acquiring copies of reasonably executed exercises and theses as additions to the collection. The friendly contact often established between librarian and reader pursuing research in such exercises is usually sufficient to ensure that a copy of the completed original work is presented to the library on request.

The study of local history and of local records is still far too superficial, despite what has been done in recent years to make original sources more widely and more easily available: this fact must have impressed itself upon many of the librarians in charge of our reference and local collections. Students are disinclined to study original records, preferring to rewrite items which have already appeared in print, sometimes giving it a new slant. It is the job of the library and the muniment room to encourage and assist the scientific reader, to provide the source materials where possible and beyond this to provide handlists or details of the scope and location of other records in the vicinity or relating to the area.

Even where the library takes no part in the actual preservation of records, due to the presence of an active record office in its area, or some other circumstance, it should at least be prepared to play its part in publicity and advice, and be equipped to give guidance about sources. The local librarian should know the contents of other libraries and record offices in the vicinity and should collect their published handlists and catalogues of manuscript materials.

The library staff should further be prepared to assist and encourage students by publishing the facilities which exist both for the study of local history and for publishing local studies. In most areas universities and other adult educational bodies regularly organise courses of various kinds relating to the many branches of this subject. These are often publicised in the *Local Historian*, the *Bulletin of the Standing Conference for Local History* or the *C.B.A. Calendar of Events*. London University's extension programme includes advanced courses leading to a diploma in history and courses for amateur students, both with tutors of high academic standing. The Borthwick Institute at York arranges courses at a similar high academic level.

Leicester University offers, through its department of English local history, special facilities to qualified persons who wish to do research in their spare-time and not as part of undergraduate or post-graduate studies. They may use the department's large collection of material and obtain advice on their problems from the staff. It also publishes occasional papers giving the results of original research in local history and offers annually the John Nichols Prize (value £25) for an essay on some topic of English local history. Candidates need not be members of a university but the subject must have prior approval. The essay must be based on original and genuine research, and the possibility of publication is offered. Some local authorities have also tried to encourage more serious study at a local level by awarding prizes or a trophy for essays and photographs. In 1970 Bath invited essays of not less than 1,500 words in a scheme of 'Local History Research Awards'. A premier award of £20 was offered for the best contribution and all entries became the property of Bath Municipal Libraries. These are noteworthy efforts to diminish the gap and break down the barrier between the professional and amateur historian by placing some of the aids of the former at the disposal of the latter.

It is natural that the library which acquires much original source material will find this producing enquiries from many people who cannot visit the library owing to the distance or expense involved. Hence postal enquiries assume greater importance in the duties of the local librarian and the archivist, and they can take up an inordinate amount of his or her working time. Inasmuch as this correspondence is a legitimate service, we should seek to extend it and common courtesy, as well as the bonds of international fellowship, enjoin that that which comes from overseas, most often from the United States or the Commonwealth, is dealt with as fully and as faithfully as possible. Limits none the less have to be placed on the time taken over these researches, particularly those of American friends seeking to complete their family 'trees', and it is useful to have the names and addresses of professional searchers and genealogists in the vicinity, to whom we can refer these enquiries.

For postal enquiries from this country, research by the library staff should be limited to brief searches, the checking of specific points, consulting catalogues and indexes, supplying where possible bibliographies and references, and the limited transcription of specific items. The essential point which the writer usually wishes to establish is whether the library possesses sufficient potentially useful material to make a personal visit worthwhile, and it is incumbent upon the librarian to provide this information as accurately as possible. There is nothing so exasperating to a research worker as to visit a distant library only to find that there is nothing to interest him, especially if he has made a preliminary enquiry. Where the enquirer seeks to go much beyond this and to have his research done for him he must be politely, but firmly, dissuaded and referred to professional workers. It is no part of the archivist's duty to undertake researches of an extensive nature: he can only indicate collections or items where relevant material *may* be found, but his intimate knowledge of these will frequently help him in this. The local librarian is similarly situated with regard to printed materials.

The above remarks embody a counsel of perfection, and the readiness of librarians and archivists to go beyond their official duties, even in their spare-time, to help genuine students and scholars is proverbial and will remain so until all enthusiasm for their work has gone. All we can do is to suggest that the librarian does not let this enthusiasm run away with him to the extent that he may neglect his primary duties of preserving his records and his wider obligations to scholarship as a whole in the interests of a few. There is a not-unnatural tendency to take more trouble for well-known personalities and writers, but this should be resisted. The librarian is not always competent to judge the merits of an enquiry, and a seemingly frivolous query may be extremely important to the writer.

Lectures to the public are a legitimate and well-recognised method of publicising libraries and one which is particularly apposite to the requirements of the local collection since the wide interest in local history creates a great demand for talks on the subject. A good local collection is regarded with pride as a civic possession, its manuscript material in particular bestowing honour and dignity on the town. Civic groups welcome talks drawing attention to this material and its potentialities, and these can have both an educational and a publicity value. They have a missionary value, too, encouraging others to preserve or present material.

Subjects for such talks are almost unlimited, and organisations such as Rotary, Inner Wheel, Soroptimists, the Business and Professional Women's League, Women's Institutes, Townswomen's Guilds, archaeological, historical and natural history societies and business groups such as the Law Society, church organisations and a host of others are ever eager for interesting talks with a local angle. It is often possible to supplement the talk by a visit to the local history room to inspect some of its treasures, and an inspection of the muniment or strong room, with a sight of original records, such as early charters or estate maps, or a demonstration of repair work, greatly enhances the interest of these visits and impresses them on the memory,

5

particularly of children. The lecture must be suited to its audience.
A branch of the Historical Association or the local archaeological society may require a straight talk on the records; a youth
club or Townswomen's Guild will need a simpler talk on local
history to which local records appear merely as a background.

The sponsoring of local history societies by libraries as well
as the independent formation of others has relieved many
librarians of the necessity of organising courses of lectures in
local history. Many local societies now hold their meetings in
central libraries and members of the library staff are often
involved with these societies as officers or members. As a result,
the typescripts of lectures given to local societies are often
acquired by the library for addition to the local collection and
occasionally tape-recordings of lectures are also made. Where a
local society has an archaeological section the results of fieldwork and carefully executed excavations together with maps
showing Roman roads and other sites of local archaeological
interest, are also compiled and presented to the library.

When the librarian has established a reputation as a speaker,
he may be called upon to act as tutor to local history courses,
but outside speakers should be encouraged and helped as far
as possible with loans of material. There is an urgent need, as
Professor Hoskins has pointed out, for more teachers and tutors
capable of effectively guiding local history studies. The library
can further assist by building up collections of visual aids, such
as lantern slides, transparencies, film-strips and photographs
which lecturers can borrow, and by providing equipment such
as projectors, screens, blackboards, lecterns and other desirable
apparatus.

An increasing number of local history courses, both weekend
and longer, are now organised throughout the country by universities, national societies, local education authorities, rural
community and local history councils and other bodies, and
help in the form of booklists, loans of books and publicity
material should be offered. In sponsoring or supporting lectures
it is desirable that the library should, through co-operation with
the WEA and other bodies, seek to encourage those courses
requiring more sustained study, such as tutorial classes, and
should give preference to those likely to stimulate further study
rather than the popular lecture which is listened to and

promptly forgotten. Various schemes for compiling scrapbooks or present-day records of villages or for recording contemporary local history utilising a system of local correspondents are in operation in some parts of the country. They may operate through county local history committees, schools or Women's Institutes and similar organisations and there is not always any arrangement for the permanent retention of the results in a local library. In some areas village history and scrapbook competitions have been organised and help here may ultimately bring the deposit of the completed work.

Educational opportunities in particular should not be neglected and the local librarian should feel a special responsibility towards the schoolchildren in his locality and a desire to inculcate in them a love for the past, for they are his students and historians of the future. For reasons we have explained in Chapter 1 local history lessons are amongst the most popular in the curriculum and schools should be encouraged to bring classes to the library regularly for instruction. This applies specially to groups working on local projects and to senior students who may be encouraged to undertake research in the library during holidays. An effective method of publicity is to invite school-leavers, particularly those proceeding to universities or training colleges, to the library for instruction and explanation as to the ways in which the library can assist their future academic careers. Local studies loom large amongst the subjects selected for theses and essays, and the resources of this department need to be particularly impressed upon the young student.

'School studies', writes Mr Shercliff, former librarian of Manchester's local history library, 'which inevitably include the quaffing of large draughts of second-hand opinion, can be balanced by occasional inspiring drinks at the fountainhead, the actual records of the past.'[2] He instances four types of school visit to the local history library which are organised in co-operation with teachers in schools in Manchester and district. The first, and most successful, is a programme of weekly visits by a class engaged in a special project or studying a particular theme, previously agreed between the teacher, who knows the

2. W. H. Shercliff. 'The School and the Local History Library'. *Manchester Review*, vol. 9, summer 1960. pp. 33–8.

varying abilities of the children, and the librarian, who knows the materials available. The second type of visit comes from classes studying a special period or a part of national history. Here the reality is brought home to the children by having selected appropriate local records, both printed and manuscript, shown and explained to them. The third type encourages older children to visit the library on their own account to make use of the library's resources; the fourth is that arranged with a school society which comes to pursue its own special interest.

This applies equally at a higher level to students at teachers' training colleges, adult residential colleges, field study centres and the like, to whom the fullest facilities of the library as well as training in its resources and in research methods should be offered. Students at training colleges are the teachers of the future and a knowledge of the library's resources inculcated during their college days can be passed on to successive generations of pupils down the years of active teaching. The Dudley College of Education, for example, includes environmental studies as an important part of courses for all students, who make heavy use of the Dudley local collection in consequence. The duplication of items in the collection by xerography has thus been necessary, not only to avoid wear but also to enable larger numbers of students to use the collection at any given time.

The problems of co-operation between the library and the school have exercised the minds of many librarians and the need for this increases as schools build up their own libraries and facilities. The initial contacts are hard to make and it may well be that through local projects the basis of such co-operation will be laid and fostered. Help can be given in all manner of studies relating to the locality – local government and affairs, field studies, topography, social and industrial surveys, the history of the school and its eminent scholars – and the library may hope to benefit by the acquisition of the best results of such work.

The study of original records in schools and colleges has prompted the Department of Education and Science to produce a pamphlet *Archives and Education* in which it is stated 'that no student should complete a course of education without being made aware of what sources exist and being given at least a

limited opportunity of using them'.[3] This in turn has encouraged the increased production of a variety of archive
teaching units. In Dudley a project known as 'Resources for
Learning' has been led by Mr John West, a Senior Inspector of
Education. It consists of building a 'data-bank' of electro-
stencils of material which can be duplicated for classroom use
when required. Although the coverage of the scheme is not
limited to local history topics, as a result of Mr West's own
experience and interest and the co-operation offered by the
library, a large part of the material used so far, and the most
interesting and significant results, have been obtained in this
field. Many documents in the archives collection have been
copied in part or in full and teaching notes and appropriate
commentary added. Electro-stencils are prepared from the
photocopies supplied by the library. An incidental benefit to
the library is the duplication of otherwise unique records and,
sometimes, the provision of indexes or other aids to their use.
An example is the apprentice book of a local workhouse which
was copied in full, indexed, and explanatory notes added. This
is now in use in several primary and secondary schools in
Dudley not only for local history purposes but also in teaching
other subjects such as arithmetic by the compilation of totals,
preparing elementary statistical tables and graphs. This
project goes beyond the concept of producing folders of facsimiles for class use such as are usually contained in an archive
wallet of the 'Jackdaw' pattern. Archive Teaching Units have
been produced by a number of authorities including the
Department of Education of the University of Newcastle-upon-
Tyne, and by the Sheffield City Libraries. County record
offices have also produced such units and a series of travelling
exhibitions of 'Jackdaw' material is being built up by the
Westmorland County Library where the services to teachers
are explained in a leaflet entitled *Local Studies, the Teacher and
the Westmorland Library.*

Visual aids are being used to an increasing extent in schools
and libraries to further the interest in local history. Film-strips
consisting of local views, maps, photographs and material
objects can be made in conjunction with photographic societies,
teachers' groups, the county film officer or with the help of

3. Education Pamphlet no. 54. HMSO, London, 1968.

enthusiastic amateurs. Accompanied by teacher's notes prepared by the library or by a local historian, they are an excellent
means of bringing local history to life for children and adult
groups. Some libraries have prepared a series of strips illustrating the development of the area from prehistoric to modern
times. The local collection and the museum could provide
illustrative material for most local studies, but they might need
to be supplemented by drawings, plans or imaginative representations to fill gaps in the picture.

Prints, maps and slides can be made up into suitable groups
for loan and tape-recorded talks accompanying such selections
add considerably to their effectiveness. Some libraries make
available for use in schools duplicate material such as photographs, engravings, posters, playbills, prints and coins, and
even mount small topical or subject displays on peg-board
screens to assist educational projects. Photostat copies to spare
the originals may be made of particularly important records,
including those not in the library's custody, such as the borough
charters, and these can be freely used to illustrate lectures.
Swinton and Pendlebury has compiled several sets of a local
history unit of printed and duplicated material for distribution
to local schools, and hopes to organise further sets at intervals.

Cinefilm records of current events can be used to build up a
permanent visual record of the cavalcade of our times, and tape-
recordings enable a fuller account to be made. Swansea
combines film and tape-recordings of civic events and now has
50,000 feet of 16 mm. film in colour and black and white. Bootle
also has made cinefilm records of local area development and
events since 1961. A number of libraries have recorded reminis-
cences of inhabitants on tape and such recordings are a particularly useful method of acquiring information about crafts
and industries that are dying. Old songs and ballads, mumming plays and other customs, and children's rhymes and
games can be recorded, although it is desirable that they
should also be committed to paper. Local dialect and dialect
stories can be similarly treated. Fieldworkers for the Survey of
English Dialects sponsored by the Institute of Dialect and Folk
Life Studies at the University of Leeds, which is compiling a
linguistic atlas of England, are now trying to record local
dialects systematically. The older residents who speak and are

familiar with the natural dialect of the area are getting fewer year by year and it is important that as many examples as possible should be obtained before they disappear.

The closest association will naturally be maintained with established county archaeological and historical societies and with local branches of the Historical Association. Very often the librarian serves on the council or committee or acts as honorary librarian to the society, which usually means that its collections can be deposited in the library and can be used, by agreement, by students, although care must be taken not to abuse the position. Close co-operation of this kind can often be beneficial to the library in several ways and has resulted in the enrichment of many local collections in the past. Perhaps the best example of mutual assistance is that afforded by the amity between the Sheffield City Libraries and the Hunter Archaeological Society, but the collections of many libraries have been augmented by the support, both collective and individual, of members of these societies which have, in this country, played a unique part in furthering local history in all its aspects. Co-operation is specially desirable in those areas where the local society has built up an extensive library of local literature for the benefit of its members. The Surrey Archaeological Society maintains an extensive library and museum which is open daily at Castle Arch, Guildford, and the Sussex Archaeological Society has similar collections at the Barbican House, Lewes. Wiltshire Archaeological Society has an extensive library at Devizes, while the Dorset County Museum at Dorchester, which has a large manuscript collection, is controlled by the Dorset Natural History and Archaeological Society.

This co-operation with local societies can be mutually beneficial in many ways. Local queries are frequently directed at the secretaries which could in many cases be dealt with more adequately by trained library staff, but the latter may often need to call upon the specialised knowledge possessed by officers and members of the old-established antiquarian societies. One or two fortunate libraries have found good friends amongst the local historians to trace useful information and records, to transcribe local records or to compile indexes for the library. Those with leisure and an interest in historical studies may be prevailed upon to index local newspapers and other sources,

thus creating a tool of permanent value for succeeding generations. At Folkestone a worker has typed and indexed transcripts
of many manuscript sources, including all surviving local
government records between 1515 and 1835, and parish
registers, while another has transcribed the local churchwardens' accounts. Conversely librarians can help the societies
in various ways: for example by caring for their libraries, or
by editing or indexing their publications. Miss D. M. Norris,
formerly Birmingham's local librarian, compiled an index to
the first sixty-nine volumes of the *Transactions and Proceedings
of the Birmingham Archaeological Society*, which was published in
1954, and in Montgomeryshire a member of the county library
staff has indexed the first fifty-four volumes of the transactions
of the Powysland Club.

The Selbourne Society in 1958 presented its library, including a valuable collection of the works of Gilbert White, on
permanent loan to the Ealing Borough Library. A special
exhibition was arranged to coincide with the official handing-
over ceremony, and a printed catalogue of the collection was
produced. Opportunities of this nature for effective publicity
should never be neglected.

The local history collection can be of value to other departments of the Corporation. The mayor and the town clerk
receive many letters and requests for information which can be
answered from its shelves or files, and which should be passed
on to the librarian for reply. The highways department can be
encouraged to use suitable historical names for new streets and
estates, based on local field and other minor names, instead of
the trite, unimaginative names usually selected. To facilitate
this Beddington and Wallington (when it was an independent
library) indexed its 1840 tithe map and equated its field-names
with present-day streets and features as far as possible. Plymouth has encouraged the use of extinct local heraldic devices
as the basis of badges for new schools which have been built on
the site of old manor houses or landed estates: another interesting and desirable example of securing continuity of local history
in a practical form.

A civic or local information service forms part of the facilities
of some libraries and where this is so the resources of the local
collection are brought into play extensively to support its

activities. Holiday resorts usually have a separate department for this purpose but others give the responsibility to the library, so much so that the additional title of Information Officer is added to that of Librarian. Similarly in one or two towns of great historical importance, which attract many tourists and visitors, a voluntary guide service operates from the library. At York the Association of Voluntary Guides has the city librarian as its honorary secretary and enquiries for the services of guides are dealt with by the library staff. The members have studied and been trained in the history and topography of the city and are given badges bearing the civic coat of arms, which indicate to the visitor that they are accredited guides whose knowledge and ability may be relied upon. In summer there are daily tours, but at all times special tours are arranged for parties and individuals. Similar schemes operate at Shrewsbury (operated by the town's Tourist and Publicity Centre), at Cambridge and Chester, the last from the City Museum. Elsewhere, as at Norwich, the library assists guide services which are operated by voluntary associations.

Many towns now have strong affiliations with foreign places. These may be based on historical ties, as in Derby's connection with Lowell, Mass., U.S.A., which was founded by a Derby man, Kirk Boott; on sentimental bonds, as in Coventry's close association with Stalingrad, born of war-time destruction; or they may be merely toponymical, as when a British town exchanges visits and information with one bearing the same name in another country. The 'twin town' idea, in which English towns link with a continental counterpart, preferably of a similar size and character, is also growing and any of these will present opportunities for the library to build up a collection of material on the foreign town and to act as a centre for the exchange of information for the people of both places. The 'adoption' by the civic authority of regiments, ships and other bodies presents similar opportunities.

There are many national schemes and enterprises in which the local library can assist, and in which help and advice could be given, not only when requested, but offered in some cases where information in the local library would be of obvious interest or value. Apart from national and regional projects concerned with Victoria County Histories and other county histories such as the volumes published by the Cheshire Community Council there are a number of less obvious undertakings engaged upon recording various aspects of local information. The Council for British Archaeology, through Mr M. W. Barley at Nottingham University, has nearly completed a guide to collections of topographical drawings and similar material in libraries, museums and record offices; the Railway and Canal Historical Society is compiling an index of the research material available on British railway and canal history; a new national society, The Names Society, 7 Aragon Avenue, Thames Ditton, Surrey, was formed in 1967 originally for the study of house names, but has already widened its scope to include place-names, personal names, street names and other names and has embarked upon a national survey of street names that will include a bibliography of street-name literature; and the Paul Mellon Foundation for British Art has a publishing programme that includes a comprehensive *Dictionary of British Painters*. Organisations such as these need to make use of local source material and it is the librarian's function to make this known to such potential users, and to offer the help of the library at least by drawing attention to printed and manuscript sources. Many national and regional surveys of this kind are ultimately dependent upon this help for their success and completeness.

Co-operation with the local press is essential if the department is to make a real impact upon the community, and editors and journalists, for their part, recognise this section of the library as having for them, great news value. The wise librarian will encourage them to make use of the material by reporting unusual or valuable acquisitions, by drawing attention to material on topics which are 'in the news', by supplying full details of the library's activities, exhibitions and displays, and by offering bibliographical help in writing up obituary notices, local centenaries and the like. The goodwill of editors can be fruitful in many ways, since they are often in closer touch with the community than librarians.

In such contacts the librarian should be impartial and news emanating from the library should reach all local newspapers at the same time, unless there are good reasons to the contrary. It must be impartial, too, in its scope and content, and free from any suggestion of bias, its only purpose being to bring the resources of the library to the notice of the public. Some librarians contribute a regular series of articles or booklists to the local press and in these local history matters are prominently featured. Radio and television are media offering avenues of publicity to the live local history collection and the help of local librarians is constantly sought by producers. This help has been more frequently acknowledged in the credits of programmes produced in recent years than was the case formerly, but the enterprising librarian will not always wait for his help to be sought. Producers are always interested in important exhibitions, centenaries of the famous and unusual items of local history. Regional services of the BBC, local radio stations and the independent companies controlled by the ITA are all interested in local matters and good scripts based on original material will always be considered.

Chapter 8

Exhibitions, Publicity and Display

The librarian has long been convinced of the necessity of bringing his stock to the attention of the public through publicity, exhibitions and display. These media enable him to fulfil one of his primary duties, that of making the stock known to the ordinary citizen, and they are particularly applicable to local history material and to local records, which lend themselves to display to a greater extent than other library material and which also need to be publicised because of their comparative inaccessibility to the general public. Library display, as an art, may indeed be said to have had its origins in this department and the great majority of successful exhibitions organised by libraries have had some aspect of local studies as their theme. The catalogues and other publicity attendant upon the staging of an exhibition, if well produced and illustrated, can become important means of reference or students' aids to the material exhibited.

Opportunities for displays are in this field literally inexhaustible and many librarians arrange a constantly changing series of exhibits in their entrance halls, in display windows, corridors or, with less justification, in the local room itself. Much of the material – maps, engravings, photographs, manuscripts and documents, broadsides, playbills, examples of early printing – is little used and may well be given an occasional airing. Mobile exhibition cases which can be moved about the building are useful for these temporary displays. Items from the local history collection are regularly displayed in exhibition cases and display units in the entrance halls of many libraries, and in some towns it has been found that shop windows of banks,

building societies and department stores can often be utilised
for attractive displays of material. Liverpool arranges small
monthly exhibitions of recent acquisitions in the spacious
entrance foyer to its record office and local history department,
but has also organised a permanent display of books, documents,
prints and water colours illustrating the city's development
from 1207, which occupies special accommodation in the
record office.

A display should, if possible, have a theme or a purpose,
something concrete which the viewer can see, appreciate and
remember. For this reason topical displays, built around a centenary or anniversary, a parliamentary election, the demolition
of a well-known building, or the opening of a new one, the
death or anniversary of a local worthy, the publication of a
new book by a local writer, and so on, are the most effective.
Opportunities occasionally arise outside the library. The
annual mayor-making ceremony, a civic reception or an
appropriate conference, provides the occasion for a display of
the borough charters or its regalia, with the librarian on hand
to talk about them.

Local centenaries are an opportune time for exhibitions on a
larger scale than the small display. Burnley's exhibition in
connection with the centenary of the Charter of Incorporation
in 1961 attracted 12,000 visitors and similar exhibitions have
been staged at Northampton in 1964, Southport in 1967 as
well as at Bootle, Huddersfield and St Helens in 1968; whilst the
granting of much earlier charters and events have also been
celebrated with considerable pride at Macclesfield in 1961,
where the charter celebrations covered the period 1261–1961,
and at Stockport where the 750th anniversary of the charter
took place in 1970. At Hastings in 1966 the millennium of the
Norman Conquest was the occasion for an exhibition and a
well-produced booklist. At Kensington in 1961, an exhibition
depicting seven centuries of the parish of Kensington was
mounted in Derry and Toms departmental store by the
library. Tynemouth celebrated the centenary of its library with
an exhibition and Cardiff chose a centenary of Cardiff elections
as a suitable theme for the display of local material. At Bournemouth, the 75th anniversary of the Bournemouth Symphony
Orchestra provided a theme; at Sunderland it was the 250th

anniversary of the River Wear Commissioners; whilst at Salford in 1970, a theme was found in the Golden Jubilee of the Manchester and Salford Council of Social Service.

Many libraries responded to the National Library Week organisers by staging exhibitions of local history material and national events always present an acceptable opportunity for mounting sizeable exhibitions of a library's bibliographical and manuscript treasures. Cardiff responded to the Investiture of the Prince of Wales with an exhibition entitled 'They Came to Wales' and both Southwark and Plymouth made good use of their local material during the 'Mayflower' celebrations in 1970. In 1970 also, the celebration of the centenary of the 1870 Education Act found a ready response in many towns: Burnley's exhibition was simply called 'Our Schools', whilst at Leeds education in Yorkshire was depicted under the heading 'How They Learned'. Similar exhibitions were also held at many other places including Lincoln, Oxford, Wakefield and Warley, but at Macclesfield it was decided to devote an exhibition to the 'History of the Macclesfield High School from 1880–1970'.

It is possible that the proposals to change the face of local government itself has caused many people to take a serious look at the locality in which they live, with the result that in many towns and cities, exhibitions depicting various aspects of town and city life and history have attracted thousands of visitors in recent years. At Burnley in 1967 a 'Down Your Way' exhibition attracted 7,000 visitors. 'Our Town' has been the simplest theme and title of these exhibitions but variations have been produced both in titles and in content. Whilst 'A Prospect of Aldershot' has a pleasing sound and 'Memories of Bath' a more nostalgic flavour, 'The History and Redevelopment of Belfast' sounds severely practical. Brighton decided to limit two exhibitions to 'Brighton in Regency Times' and 'Charles II and Brighton' and Macclesfield also staged an exhibition devoted to 'Georgian Macclesfield'. Leeds concentrated on 'How They Lived 1200–1900' whilst Shrewsbury was concerned with its 'Changing Face' and Southwark looked at 'Southwark through the Centuries'. Several exhibitions were devoted to trade and industry, and in Tower Hamlets the docks and shipping were depicted, as they were in Bootle. A different aspect of transport was featured in Rochdale's exhibition 'From Turnpike to

Motorway' and this title should prove a useful one in many other towns. Enthusiasts enjoyed Warrington's selection of photographs and literature relating to 'Warrington Trams'. Similar enthusiasm was no doubt generated by a 'Canals of Bath' exhibition and for this Bath Municipal Libraries produced a neatly cyclostyled exhibition guide. Providing sufficient exhibition space is available, local maps always attract attention and stimulate interest in the history of any locality, and an exhibition of 'Yorkshire Maps' at Harrogate in 1967 was no exception, nor was the display of 'Local Maps' at Huddersfield in 1969, or a similar exhibition of 'Early Printed Maps of the British Isles and Hampshire' that was mounted at Winchester.

Although maps, prints, sketches, paintings and photographs are always attractive exhibits and were the essential ingredients of such successful exhibitions as Cambridge's exhibition of the 'W. Martin Lane Collection of Fen Flood Photographs' which resulted in BBC television and extensive press publicity; Sunderland's exhibition of 'Durham Cathedral Prints'; and of Oxford's exhibitions of 'Taunt and Minn Photographs Taken between 1870 and 1930', it is also clear that success can be achieved without the aid of such pictorial exhibits. At Bolton in 1969 an exhibition based on an analysis of the frequency of occurrence of Christian names in Bolton during the last three centuries, entitled 'Alice Where Art Thou?' achieved national press publicity and was referred to on radio. The source material for this exhibition was the collection of local parish registers in the library.

Most towns fortunate enough to have strong links with men and women of national importance have little difficulty in finding a theme for an exhibition certain to attract considerable local attention. Not all figures, of course, are likely to attract as much attention as 'Juliana of Norwich', the subject of a scholarly exhibition and exhibition guide in the Norwich Central Library in 1970, or of the exhibition at Shoreditch on the occasion of the Shakespeare quatercentenary in 1964, which was also marked by the publication of a booklet entitled *Shakespeare Came to Shoreditch*. Wordsworth's bicentenary was marked at Carlisle with an exhibition in the cathedral and also by the publication of an extensively printed *Catalogue of the Wordsworth Collection, 1970*. The 150th anniversary of George

Eliot in 1969 and the centenary of John Clare in 1964 were marked by exhibitions in Coventry and Nuneaton, and in Northampton and Peterborough respectively. Northampton also paid respect to Charles Bradlaugh in 1968, whilst Halesowen has devoted exhibitions to both Francis Brett Young and William Shenstone. Several London boroughs, of course, have established connections with many national personalities, and exhibitions in these libraries nearly always manage to achieve publicity in the national press, the London borough of Camden, for example, has arranged exhibitions in recent years devoted to Dickens, Kate Greenaway, Beatrix Potter, Karl Marx, Hogarth, Thomas Coram and Henry Wood. The H. G. Wells centenary exhibition featuring the extensive Wells Collection at Bromley in 1966 was used by the producers of radio and television programmes on Wells. Perhaps a more unusual type of exhibit has been used at Warrington in two exhibitions devoted to the work of local violin makers. Apart from photographs and printed items, both of these exhibitions included violins made by Harry Clare and Harry Roberts.

The enterprising librarian, however, readily recognises that a local history exhibition organised solely or primarily to draw attention to the contents of the local collection is an unfailing method of arousing public interest in it and acts not only in an informative manner but often arouses the interest of those who have useful material to donate. Public co-operation in building a collection is thus often obtained and a number of exhibitions have been mounted for the specific purpose of discovering material available in a locality. Swadlincote organised a 'Do You Remember?' exhibition for which the public was invited to lend photographs, programmes of events and anything which tended to re-create the past. A considerable amount of the material lent was subsequently donated to the local collection.

Far too many small displays and even some larger exhibitions in public libraries, however, tend to be distinctly amateurish in presentation, a tendency that seldom creates respect for the library or the care it bestows upon material that locally is priceless. Extra care or expense is often needed to change the amateur appearance of a display into a presentation bearing a professional look. Care and neatness in labelling and lettering are sometimes all that is required, but a stylish mounting of photographs and the ruthless rejection of hastily or poorly executed lettering and other untidy methods of displaying exhibits is essential to success. Sufficient space and good display media – properly designed cases or other display units – are basic essentials, and where these are lacking it is better to turn to the art gallery or museum, or even to hire a special room for an important exhibition. The director of the former will, if approached in good time, usually place accommodation at the disposal of the organisers, and can offer useful help and advice in the best methods of presentation. For a large exhibition the local surveyors and architects department can be helpful in making suitable display units and advice and assistance can also often be obtained from the local school of art.

A fruitful source of co-operation in local history exhibitions will be with county record offices which are frequently willing to participate by loaning material in their care, so long as it can be properly safeguarded. At Preston in 1952 an exhibition of material on the history of the local gild merchants was organised by the librarian, jointly with the director of the Museum and Art Gallery and the county archivist, its catalogue indicating the location of the material displayed and containing an annotated bibliography. A similar exhibition was held in 1972. At Norwich there is also frequent co-operation in staging exhibitions jointly with the record office, as in 1964 when such a jointly executed exhibition for the Norfolk and Norwich Triennial Festival depicted 'The Festival through 140 Years'. During the Harrow Civic Week in 1965 an exhibition entitled 'Harrow – from Villages to Borough' was organised by the Harrow Local Archives Committee in conjunction with the Middlesex County Record Office and the Harrow Arts Council and was held at the County Library, Wealdstone. A sixty-page catalogue was produced for the occasion.

Occasionally the librarian is invited and is permitted by his authority to arrange 'outside' exhibitions to celebrate special events unconnected with the library or the local authority and not always held on library premises. This may be the centenary of a local church, a firm or a public utility, or perhaps the visit of some special body such as the British Association or the Archaeological Institute. 'Conference' towns have special opportunities here: Norwich City Libraries arranged three exhibitions for the Conference of the Historical Association in 1959. Harrow provided the majority of exhibits for a local archives exhibition organised by the Local Archives Committee on the occasion of the opening of a new parish hall at Weald-stone. Material from the library will occasionally be loaned on these occasions, if safety can be ensured.

Exhibitions of this kind afford an opportunity to enrich the library permanently, either by stimulating the gift or loan of additional material, or by encouraging the copying of material from other sources which may be borrowed for display. Warrington arranged a comprehensive exhibition in honour of the bicentenary of the Warrington Academy, the famous dissenting seminary, and published a limited edition of William Turner's *Historical Account of the Warrington Academy* (1957); the librarian also broadcast a talk on the event. The exhibition which was staged in the Old Academy building, was organised by a joint-committee representing Library, Museum and Warrington Society. The library exhibits attempted to show every important book and manuscript relating to the Academy, its tutors and students, and one result was that many items were purchased, either as originals or photocopies, to add to the local history library. These included the minute books and register of admissions, which were microfilmed from the originals in Manchester College, Oxford.

The librarian will seek to help his local museum and art gallery by freely allowing his own material to be displayed in those institutions for limited periods. Documents, prints and watercolours should not remain on display indefinitely, as both natural and artificial light can be deleterious. It is possible to provide adequate protection from the ill-effects of artificial light by the use of appropriate electric lamps, and of natural light by the use of an appropriate ultraviolet absorbing filter such as Perspex ve, Oroglas uf3, Perspex va and Plexiglas ol. Information on the use of these materials and on the protection of exhibits from light in general is given in a Museums Association Information Sheet, *Conservation and Museum Lighting*, by Garry Thomson (Museums Association, 1970). The subject of lighting was also considered in four articles by N. S. Brommelle and J. B. Harris under the title 'Museum Lighting' (*Museums Journal*, vol. 61, no. 3, December 1961; vol. 61, no. 4,

March 1962; vol. 62, no. 1, June 1962; vol. 62, no. 3, December 1962). The effects of daylight may also be controlled by the use of protective blinds or shutters. At Liverpool some items displayed are equipped with a small blind attached to the framework of the exhibit and in the Warrington local history library the blinds on the outside windows are easily controlled to allow either diffused or direct light to enter the room.

Some libraries with inadequate display space of their own lend some of their best prints, paintings and maps for display in council offices and other public buildings in the town, especially those which are accessible to the public. Annual displays of pictures by local artists or photographers are held in lecture rooms or halls at central or branch libraries. There are also the small travelling displays which are arranged, often by county libraries, for agricultural shows, local conferences and the like, similar to the peg-board display units often circulated to schools. Displays by local bodies interested in local history should also be encouraged and the greatest hospitality extended to them. Many societies wish to celebrate their centenaries or other occasions by recounting their history and the library can help greatly. County libraries and record offices are frequently called upon to assist village exhibitions.

It cannot be insisted too strongly or too often that the modern local collection should be an up-to-date arsenal of facts and figures concerning the area, its local authority and its social services, its cultural amenities and activities of all kinds. The library is, or should be, the first port of call to which the visitor requiring information on the entertainment facilities of the locality, the commercial representative wanting information on firms and businesses, or the newcomer wishing to know what is available in the way of sporting clubs or cultural societies, or the ordinary resident requiring information of various kinds should turn, and they should not be disappointed.

Many libraries do keep a 'Diary of Local Events' in one form or another, some as exhibition boards or visible indexes, others as folders or lists which have to be sought inside the library. It must be admitted that they are *not* easy to maintain properly without good organisation and keen public relations work. The essential ingredient to ensure the success of such a venture is that it should appear to offer worthwhile publicity from the society's point of view. Many diaries which commenced with high hopes and confidence that support would come from the various organisations which it is intended to help, have foundered against the apathy of these amateur bodies. The London borough of Hackney publishes a monthly programme of activities as part of the library magazine *Profile*, and at Dudley a printed leaflet *The Dudley Scene* also gives information about local societies and forthcoming activities. Other libraries display the syllabuses of local societies or use a peg-board for the display of standard-size cards containing information about forthcoming events in their entrance halls or in other prominent positions. Where an attractive diary of this kind is available it frees the librarian from the necessity of accepting posters of these events, which are often poorly produced and can be a source of embarrassment.

Another useful tool is a directory of official information concerning societies and clubs in the town, with names and addresses of secretaries and other officers, rates of subscription and place and time of meetings. It is essential that this information should be kept up-to-date, and here again the co-operation of the societies is necessary. It can be done by keeping a keen watch on the local papers in which annual meetings are recorded, or by sending circulars to the secretaries regularly. This information is useful not only in the library, but as outside publicity and many such lists are printed or cyclostyled for local distribution. Newcomers and visitors to the town, travellers, social workers, school teachers and the press find them of great value. Bath's *Directory of Local Societies* is now published on a subscription basis and a master file is kept in the Reference Library. At Cambridge six sectional lists, covering the majority of the societies included in the Reference Library files, are compiled and distributed from the libraries each year. In addition, separate indexes are maintained of people lecturing on particular local topics and of local historians.

Library publicity, well directed and produced, is recognised as the most effective means of acquainting the public with the contents of the library and its potentialities in various directions. The local collection is no exception and much of the early publicity issued by libraries was an endeavour to secure recognition for the collection and to make its resources more widely known. Serving, as it does, a large number of people outside the immediate area, this department must publicise its resources if these are to become widely known to its potential clientele. This is particularly true of manuscript and archival material.

Again it must be said that publicity, like other forms of extension work, must be based upon adequate resources, and there is little point in publishing a guide to a poor collection. The result will only be disappointed readers, who may not return even when the stock has been built up to a reasonable level. It is better, then, to delay publication until the coverage is fairly complete. In spite of the prohibitive cost of printing a complete catalogue of the local history collection, a printed catalogue is the most valuable and useful method of ensuring that the fullest use is made of the collection and such catalogues have been issued by a number of libraries in the post-war years. Those published by Gillingham, Guildford and Reading have already had supplements issued in 1955, 1958 and 1967 respectively, whilst the Dagenham catalogue achieved a second edition in 1961. Epsom and Ewell also joined those authorities that have published catalogues in 1970 and several county libraries have also produced catalogues of their collections.

Where a complete catalogue is out of the question, either by virtue of the cost or because the collection is not yet sufficiently representative, a select catalogue or bibliography listing the more important works may fulfil a useful purpose at a fraction of the cost. Sheffield's *Basic Books on Sheffield History*, 1966, lists, chronologically and with annotations, the material considered to be most useful to the average student. Gateshead's *Historical Gateshead: A Select Bibliography*, 1967; Southampton's *Southampton's History: A Guide to the Printed Resources*, 1968; Torbay's *The Hundred of Heytor: A Guide to the Printed Sources relating to South Devon*, 1967, with its *1st Supplement*, 1970; and although multilithed, Blackburn's *Sources of Local History*, 2nd ed., 1968, are all good examples of select lists that are well produced and fairly comprehensive in content, but an increasing number of select and short guides, some printed and some multilithed, issued in the past ten years by Bradford, Bromley, Castleford, Dartford, Edinburgh, Hull, Ilkeston, Kensington, Lambeth, Plymouth, Salford, Southport, Stockport, Surrey County, Swinton and Warrington, have all demonstrated the value of this type of publication. These lists, usually confined to printed material, are useful in bringing the general resources of the collection to the attention of the public; they help the student and the amateur rather than the researcher.

Local subject lists are sometimes produced when the quantity of material in the collection is sufficient to justify a separate list and often these lists are of considerable interest to people who do not live in the locality but who are interested in the subject. Derbyshire County Library's bibliography of Derbyshire *Lead and Lead Mining* being a good example of such a list. Shropshire County also has issued a mining catalogue, *The Coalbrookdale Coalfield Catalogue of Mines and Mining Bibliography*, compiled by Ivor J. Brown, 1968, and Sunderland has produced a list of the *Potteries of Sunderland and District*. Bath's *Architecture and Planning*, 1969, demonstrates the architectural wealth of an historic town and other recent subject lists have included such diverse interests as Newcastle's *Blaydon Races*, Manchester's *Peterloo Bibliography* and Chester's *Mystery Plays*. Whenever a library is called upon to prepare a booklist on specific local topics in connection with courses or lectures consideration should be given to the duplication or printing for more general distribution.

Another very useful subject guide to material in a local history collection is to be found in a publication of the Kensington and Chelsea Public Libraries, *Kensington and Chelsea Streetnames: A Guide to their Meanings*, compiled by B. R. Curle and Miss P. Meara, 1968. This admirably produced, although multilithed, booklet not only lists street names and their meanings but also lists the principal sources used as well as giving notes on various estates in the borough. The same libraries have also produced a select list of local maps and it is evident that the desirability of publishing a list of local maps fulfils a separate need since a number of libraries, including Crosby, Edinburgh, Leeds, Manchester and Stockport, have all published catalogues or guides to their maps in various forms.

Perhaps the most valuable form of publicity for the average ratepayer is a general guide, listing the principal sources of material in the various subjects represented in the collection. Such a handbook describes the scope of the collection, the area covered, the classification system and the public catalogues and indexes, with general notes and rules for the use of the material, hours of opening, etc. Any special collections or material of particular importance will be mentioned. Designed to provide an introduction to the collection as a whole it may be given away to potential users and students such as grammar school pupils, school leavers and people attending local history classes.

In place of guides some libraries have issued a small booklet, drawing attention briefly to the collection and incorporating an appeal for further donations or deposits. This may largely ignore printed material and concentrate on the preservation of manuscript records, being directed at the owners of various kinds of record and stressing the advantages of official custody and the value of the records to future historians.

Publicity has sometimes been given in the transactions or proceedings of local historical societies to articles describing briefly the library resources in local history. A typical example is Miss D. M. Norris's article 'Materials for a History of Birmingham in the Reference Library' which appeared in the *Transactions of the Birmingham Archaeological Society for 1945 and 1946*, Birmingham, 1950. These societies invariably welcome an annual list of books and articles on local history and several librarians regularly contribute a list based on additions to the local collection. Leeds prepares a 'Yorkshire Bibliography' annually for publication in the *Yorkshire Archaeological Journal*. Similar lists of manuscript additions are contributed by librarians and archivists. All archive repositories should, as a matter of course, submit annual returns of their documentary accessions to the Historical Manuscripts Commission for publication in the *List of Accessions to Repositories*, and these could usefully be included in local publications for wider publicity. The magazine *Archives*, issued by the British Records Association, has for some years included a series of articles dealing with the history and contents of local repositories under the general title 'Local Archives of Great Britain'. Plymouth Archives Department (1961), Worcester Record Office (1962), Newcastle-upon-Tyne City Archives (1962) and Norfolk and Norwich Record Office (1967) have been included in the series, which offers an excellent medium of publicity for libraries possessing large archive collections.

The needs of students are not wholly met by notice of recent accessions in the Historical Manuscripts Commission bulletins, in the library's annual reports and other local publications, and many libraries ought to emulate the more progressive record offices by issuing a general guide to their archive collections. It should indeed be regarded as a duty both to the records and to the public, for otherwise the material will be little known and less used. 'Every research library with manuscript resources ought to recognise as one of its primary responsibilities the compilation and publication of a guide to those materials.'[1] Students may expect to find county records in a county record office, diocesan records in an ecclesiastical repository and so on, but the library collection, often the result of many years' patient collecting, usually contains a wide variety of records from several sources, and it is only through publicity of this kind that students will be directed to its contents.

The essence of the guide will be a brief general description of each component collection, with covering dates, classified according to the type of record, and an index of subjects. The introduction should briefly describe the arrangement of the collections, with a note on any guides or transcripts previously published to any part of these, and a note of the fuller catalogues or calendars available within the library. Fortunately there are now many excellent guides to county record offices available, which provide the librarian or archivist with invaluable help in the preparation of a similar guide to his own collections. The publications of the Essex Record Office, covering a variety of subjects, are models of their kind and they have proved that, well produced and publicised, they can more than pay for themselves. In libraries, efforts to make more widely known the manuscript resources available have grown in recent years and apart from such well-known guides as those published by the Guildhall Library, Sheffield and Newcastle, more recent publications have been issued by Gateshead (1968), Plymouth (1962) and Wigan (1970). A number of authorities have also issued calendars to special collections. The first printing should not be larger than can be disposed of fairly quickly, for it can then be kept up-to-date by

1. Lester J. Cappon. 'Reference Works and Historical Texts' in *Manuscripts and Archives*, edited by R. W. G. Vail. *Library Trends*, January 1957. p. 373.

subsequent editions. Another useful publication is a slighter handlist confined to a certain limited class of material in the library such as the series issued by the Guildhall Library of the City of London covering vestry minutes, churchwardens' accounts, inhabitants lists, rate assessments and parish registers. Shrewsbury has published a list of its parish register transcripts and an index to wills and marriage settlements amongst its manuscript collections.

Bequests of valuable material do place the recipient libraries under a considerable moral obligation not only to house, catalogue and arrange it in a fitting manner, but also to publicise the existence and contents of the collection as widely as possible.

If the library possesses collections, either of records or printed books, of some considerable or unique importance, it may be thought advisable to print a catalogue or guide thereto but this should not, generally speaking, take the place of a guide to the full collection. Occasionally special considerations supervene, such as the provision of an endowment for publishing a catalogue of a bequest, or a promise given by the local authority on its acceptance that a guide would be published. Belfast has published a catalogue of the Irish Collection presented by F. J. Bigger, and has undertaken to do the same for the John S. Crone bequest in compliance with the conditions of its acceptance.

Catalogues of special collections in libraries are often so complete as to become definitive bibliographies of their subject, and this is particularly true of those devoted to local authors and personalities, such as the Burns Collection at Glasgow and the Edward Carpenter Collection at Sheffield. *A Shakespeare Bibliography: the Catalogue of the Birmingham Shakespeare Library* (Mansell, London, 1971), the recently published catalogue of the Shakespeare Memorial Library at Birmingham, consists of seven volumes containing 100,000 entries and provides an unrivalled index to every aspect of Shakespeare's life and work. The centenaries of such celebrities often provide the occasion for the issue of a bibliography, a select list or a commemorative booklet. Carlisle published a *Catalogue of the Wordsworth Collection* in 1970 in connection with the Wordsworth bicentenary, whilst the centenary of John Clare in 1964 resulted in a catalogue from Northampton and a booklist from

Peterborough. Swindon issued a Richard Jefferies bibliography and Chesterfield a list dealing with George Stephenson in 1949. Others worthy of mention include Edinburgh's *R. L. Stevenson Centenary Catalogue*, the catalogue of Bedford's John Bunyan Library, and Newcastle's *Catalogue of the Bewick Collection*. Miss Lucy Edwards of Nottingham City Library has compiled an extensive finding list of the works of D. H. Lawrence in the city, county and university libraries of Nottingham whilst at Castleford a booklist was produced in 1968 to mark the seventieth birthday of Henry Moore. These publications are no less important, and indeed often more so, when they concern lesser known literary or historical figures. Examples include the centenary booklet commemorating Amelia Opie (1769–1853) and the catalogue of an exhibition illustrating the life and work of Francis Blomefield (1705–52), the historian and topographer, both issued by Norwich City Library. Publication, by bringing the material to public notice, often results in the donation of further items. A guide to the work of Rider Haggard, issued by Norwich, recorded several gaps in the author's printed works, but within a year of publication all had been filled.

An interesting example of collaboration in this field is afforded by the commemorative brochure honouring the centenary of the death of Ebenezer Elliott, the Corn-Law Rhymer, which was issued jointly by the libraries of Rotherham, where Elliott was born in 1781, and Sheffield, where he spent most of his life.

Where it is proposed to publish certain classes of the official records, the decision is usually a matter for the council, but some library committees have assumed or have been delegated responsibility for publication, and not a few of these have been transcribed or edited by members of library staffs. Nottingham published nine volumes of the Corporation records between 1877 and 1956, the later volumes owing much to the enthusiasm and talent of the former City Librarian, Duncan Gray, and the archivist, Miss Violet W. Walker. Transcriptions from the Liverpool Town Books edited by Dr G. Chandler have appeared under the titles: *Liverpool Under James I* and *Liverpool Under Charles I*. The First Ledger Book of High Wycombe, a unique record of the civic life of the town from the fourteenth to the eighteenth centuries, has been published by the Buckinghamshire Record Society with the help of donations from the Buckinghamshire County Council and the High Wycombe Borough Council. The Second Ledger Book, 1684–1770, has been published by the High Wycombe Historic Society, in duplicated form, 1965. General articles based on original records may appear in the journals of local societies, but transcripts of records, accompanied by translations or a summary of texts, usually appear as separate publications or in volumes issued by record societies.

In some places, too, library committees have taken the lead in publishing local histories. A *History of Widnes* by George E. Diggle was sponsored and published in 1961 by the Corporation of Widnes; Middlesbrough Corporation commissioned and published in 1968 a *History of Middlesbrough* by a former borough librarian, W. Lillie; and in 1970 the Burnley Libraries and Arts Committee republished in one volume parts 1 and 2 of *The History of Burnley* by Walter Bennett. At West Bromwich a short history was prepared by the staff of the Reference Library in 1964 and a brief history of Whitehaven published by the Corporation in 1966 was reprinted in 1968. At Wallasey the revision of the second edition of *The Rise and Progress of Wallasey* by E. C. Woods and P. C. Brown was undertaken by the library staff in 1960. *A Brief History of Barking and Dagenham* written by James Howson, Borough Reference Librarian, was published in 1968 and Barrow published, also in 1968, a second edition of the illustrated history of *Barrow and District* by the Borough Librarian, F. Barnes. Often a local authority will generously sanction the publication of an official history on the occasion of a centenary and subsequently fail to provide the means for the publication of a revised edition when this becomes necessary. It would seem, therefore, to be a practicable suggestion that whenever such official histories are published, the selling price should be determined so as to provide a publications fund from which subsequent editions and other publications can be financed. A scheme in accordance with this idea operated at Southend where a 'Museums Publications Fund' gradually developed from publications at Prittlewell Priory Museum. The fund is now self-contained and new publications are financed from the fund and from the sales of publications in print. Six Southend publications dealing with various aspects of Southend history are currently in print and three volumes dealing with South-East Essex in Prehistoric, Roman and Saxon times were published in 1971.

Various aspects of local studies have provided an interesting range of publications, often sponsored by the library, museum or arts committee. Burnley published *The Natural History of the Burnley Area* in 1968, Scarborough published an account of *The Archaeology of Scarborough District* in 1956, and Manchester published in the same year *The Architecture of Manchester: An Index of the Principal Buildings and their Architecture, 1800–1900* by C. Stewart. Dissatisfaction with the existing local histories led the librarian of High Wycombe to collaborate with the head of the history department of Wycombe Royal Grammar School in filling the gap, and three volumes, one of which deals with the local chair trade, have been published by a national publishing firm.

The text of many official guides to many towns emanates from the library. Every two years at Bootle the library department is responsible for editing the *Official Handbook of Bootle*. The Carlisle guide is very pleasingly produced and the text is by Kenneth Smith, the City Librarian. A magnificent handbook of Sheffield, originally compiled and edited by J. P. Lamb, has been substantially revised and reprinted on several occasions since its first appearance, the last edition was produced especially for the 1966 World Cup year. It is also of interest in connection with the financing of local publications that Mary Walton's *Sheffield: Its Story and Its Achievements*, originally published in 1948 by Kemsley Newspapers (later Sheffield Newspapers Ltd.) has been reissued in facsimile with a new preface and appendix by Miss Walton. This has been made possible by the acquisition by the Corporation of the copyright from Sheffield Newspapers Ltd. and the sharing of all costs of publication between the Corporation of Sheffield and S. R. Publishers Ltd. Occasionally a local history written or edited by the librarian is published by a local society and on the occasion of the Scarborough millennium, the Scarborough and District Archaeological Society published *Scarborough 966–1966*, a history edited by the director of the Libraries, Museums and Art Gallery.

There are, too, libraries which are seeking to encourage

local historical studies by publishing a regular series of pamphlets dealing with local history. Coventry's local history pamphlets, prepared by Miss Alice Lynes, formerly librarian in charge of the Coventry and Warwickshire Collection, are excellent examples of recurrent local publicity and include subjects ranging from Lady Godiva to the Coventry miracle plays. Sheffield's local history leaflets are cyclostyled in attractive printed covers and have dealt with a wide variety of topics including a railway chronology of the Sheffield area; the water mills of Abbeydale and the prisons of Mary Queen of Scots in Yorkshire and Derbyshire. Fleetwood has also shown what an enthusiastic small authority can do by issuing a series of Occasional Papers that have described the Fleetwood ferry and early buildings of Fleetwood as well as an outline history of Fleetwood. Other libraries which have issued a series of local history leaflets include Colchester, Hull, Nottingham and Stoke.

The local department deserves greater mention in the general publicity produced by the library than it usually receives. In the guide which is intended for new readers joining the service, the resources of the department should be prominently featured, since it is one which the average reader often overlooks. Few booklists or bulletins seem to include additions of local interest, which need not be confined to book material, and the collection should receive more prominent mention in our annual reports than it often does.

The cost of printing and especially of printing records *in extenso* is so high today that alternative methods have been examined. Calendars, catalogues and handlists and other publicity likely to be of permanent value should always be printed, if possible, but the flow of these publications has slowed down as production costs have risen. Essex Record Office has shown, however, that well-produced printed publicity can cover its cost and even make a modest profit. Worthwhile publications may be brought to the attention of other libraries by means of a prospectus, and if the support of the education department, either in the form of a financial grant or a guarantee of the purchase of a certain number of copies, can be secured, so much the better.

Where printing is not possible, a variety of processes and machines is available for alternative reproduction methods and care should be taken to select the most suitable for the particular purpose. A good guide is H. R. Verry's *Document Copying and Reproduction Processes* (Fountain Press, London, 1958). With photocopies we are not now concerned since their use is principally to produce single or small numbers of copies from existing originals and they are rarely economic for publishing purposes, although the advantages of microcard and fiche will be considered in future for specialist purposes and where wide distribution is not envisaged.

The most generally useful process, where printing is not feasible, is the duplication process, of which there are several variants in use today. Normally the stencil is typed but photographic and electronic methods of preparing stencils can be used, e.g. for illustrations, covers or title-pages. Where duplicating is used for any but very temporary kinds of publicity or for leaflets of a few pages, a printed cover should be provided and the booklet may be stapled and taped with adhesive linen. Improved machines and techniques, as H. R. Verry has shown, have improved the quality, appearance and readability of duplicated work, but where a fairly long run of bulky material is desired duplicating is not economical and the offset litho process might be considered. The resultant quality is often very high, approaching that of type-set print. Illustrations, especially line drawings and sketches, are no more expensive than text, since blocks are not needed. The type consists of thin aluminium sheets and is easily stored, so that reprinting is a simple matter.

Ordinary plan-copying and photocopying processes are cost repetitive and useful only when a small number of copies is required, but the dyeline process produces copies from a translucent master copy which can be typed on a typewriter. Further information about the variety of copying processes available is contained in Donald Mason's *Document Reproduction in Libraries* (Association Assistant Librarians, London, 1968); in Harry T. Chambers' *Copying, Duplication and Microfilm: Systems and Equipment for Use in Business and Administration* (Business Books Ltd., London, 1970); and in *Modern Office Copying* by S. B. Page (Deutsch, London, 1966).

Chapter 9

Photography and the Local Collection

Photography today can play an important part in extending the resources of all research libraries and, properly used, it has a great deal to offer to the local collection. The case for collecting photographic records in libraries is self-evident and is based upon the necessity of linking together all the evidence, printed, manuscript and visual, pertaining to an area, building or natural feature. Photographs do more than merely supplement the written record – in many fields they are vital to the full and proper recording of history.

They may also provide a truer record. It may not be true that the camera cannot lie or distort, but it is true that the photograph has some advantages over the printed or written word. It is unselective; it is incontrovertible and convincing, providing within its limits authentic evidence of the state of affairs at a given time; it is graphic and interesting and its message is easily assimilated.

It is not only in the topographical sphere that the photograph can play a vital part. In the field of architecture and town planning it is essential as providing an authentic picture of the state of the town or village at a given time and its subsequent development. In social history, customs and costume can be accurately recorded; developments in transport history and industrial archaeology are made clearer, while in archaeology a photographic record of excavations and discoveries is essential and preliminary aerial survey necessary in many instances.

Professor Jack Simmons[1] has spoken of the need for strong

1. At a one-day conference on 'Photographic Records for Local History' held at Chaucer House, London on 19 May, 1960. Printed in the *Library Association Record*, vol. 62, October 1960. pp. 328–33.

subject collections of photographs to supplement the topo-graphical collections maintained locally by libraries, and the importance of co-operation between the two. Examples of these are the collection of the British Transport Commission in London and that relating to agriculture at the Museum of Rural Life at Reading University. Paramount, of course, is the National Buildings Record which now has more than half a million photographs and drawings of buildings and architec-tural features in England and Wales, and which contains several special collections covering subjects such as barns, bridges, dovecotes, roof bosses in ecclesiastical buildings, etc.

Long before the modern developments which have had such a salutary effect upon the preservation and distribution of research materials, the photograph was recognised as a vital local record, and many early photographs are treasured as providing data on things long past which are unrecorded in literature. Libraries began to collect photographs to supplement the written and manuscript records, and in some areas systematic surveys were attempted. In the early years of the twentieth century several photographic record societies were flourishing, the products of which were placed in libraries. Others followed as a result of the publication in 1916 of *The Camera as Historian* by H. D. Gower, L. S. Jast and W. W. Topley, in which the organisation of a survey or record society is described in detail, model rules given and notes supplied on the classification, cataloguing and arrangement of the resultant prints.

From the experience of these early schemes it would seem to be difficult to keep them active for long periods. Many start with a fine burst of enthusiasm, due to the initiative of a librarian and the keenness of a group of amateur photographers, do excellent work for some years but gradually decline as interest wanes or as members leave or die. Or a major upheaval deals it a death-blow, as happened to many early surveys during the First World War, and to many which were flourishing in 1939. Some well-known early surveys are now defunct or pro-ducing little. There often comes a time when the initial impetus has slackened, little fresh material comes in and it seems to be advisable to let them die for a while and to re-suscitate them later with a fresh start under new officers, rather than to attempt to keep them alive in a state of torpor.

1. Norwich Local History Library from the Colman Room

2. Norfolk and Norwich Record Office in the Norwich Central Library. The County Archivist Miss J. Kennedy, examining documents in the Bradfer-Lawrence Collection

3. Norfolk and Norwich Record Office in the Norwich Central Library on the occasion of the visit (February 1967) of Mr G. Belov, Director of Archives in the USSR

4. Norfolk and Norwich Record Office in the Norwich Central Library, Archives repair room

5. Mr A. O. Elmhirst, Chairman of the South Yorkshire Committee, N.R.A., examining documents at his home prior to sending them to the Sheffield City Libraries

City of Liverpool Record Office and Local History Library. Exhibition

City of Liverpool Record Office and Local History Library. Exhibition

8. Nuneaton Public Library. Local History Collection showing large atlas stand ar microfilm cabinet

9. Nuneaton Public Library. Local History collection. Bound volumes of press cuttings

10. City of Plymouth. Local History Library showing single study tables

11. City of Plymouth. New Library of Naval History

12. Warrington Municipal Library. Entrance to Local Studies Library and Local Record Office showing microfilm readers and a microfilm reader-printer

Although photographic surveys in various towns and counties have produced a large number of photographic records for local history libraries it is evident that many collections of photographs in libraries have developed without the aid of a systematic survey, and that in spite of the considerable acceleration that has taken place in the growth of photographic collections in the past ten years, it is apparent that no single method of recording the changing face of any locality is practised in a sufficient number of libraries to commend a general acceptance. Some methods are obviously superior to others and are producing useful photographic records; others are clearly failing to produce the records that are necessary in a period when modern planning and redevelopment schemes are causing rapid changes in the appearance of most towns and cities.

Because of rapid redevelopment programmes there has been a substantial increase in the number of photographic records added to local history libraries in recent years. In 1961 a survey of 261 libraries showed that only 21 possessed more than 5,000 prints, whereas in 1970 a similar survey of 253 libraries revealed that 52 possessed more than 10,000 prints. At Sheffield, for example, the picture collection, which includes photographs, numbered 2,300 items in 1960 but in 1970 this total had risen to 25,500. The collection at Manchester now numbers 80,000 items and grows at an annual rate of 5–6,000 prints each year. On the other hand, 25 libraries representing 10 per cent of the total responding to a questionnaire in 1970, were unable to report the possession of any collection of photographs at all, and the overriding impression is that the majority of library collections still develop in a haphazard rather than in an organised manner.

Very few libraries report a separate financial allocation for photographic purposes and many libraries seem to depend upon the good nature of amateur photographers and others for the donation of suitable material. It is plainly apparent that only where a library is prepared to spend a reasonable amount on photography can it be hoped that a full photographic record of the locality will be obtained. At Manchester suitable prints are selected by the local history librarian from photographs submitted by the Manchester Amateur

6

Photographic Society and an expenditure for the year 1970–71 of £1,700 was necessary for the purchase of more than 6,800 prints. In this comprehensive collection the prints generally are 10 in. x 8 in. in size and are suitably mounted on cards. Streets are photographed in their entirety in such a way that each photograph slightly overlaps another and an effort is made to include details useful in dating such as advertisements and other notices frequently posted on walls, and in windows. Care is taken in this and other ways to secure the best photographs possible for record purposes as opposed to artistic views or exhibition photographs.

A comprehensive co-operative photographic survey of Chester has been undertaken by using 35 mm. film giving standard 35 mm. negatives, positives, and slides in black and white only. Between 1964 and 1970 the number of slides added amounted to about 8,000 at a current annual cost of about £50.[2]

Clearly the extent of amateur co-operation through local photographic and other societies, as well as the type of photograph secured, determines the cost of a systematic survey and it is also evident that only comprehensiveness can be regarded as a reasonable aim in recording streets and buildings liable to sudden and dramatic changes.

Some libraries rely upon members of the library staff using their own cameras, or cameras owned by the library, to make the necessary records. At Dudley members of the library staff have used 35 mm. film in a systematic survey of streets and buildings. About 2,000 photographs were added in 1970 to a collection containing 10,000 pictures.[3] Similarly at Nottingham, photography is part of the duties of a member of the local history library staff. The considerable growth in the collection of photographs at Oxford, however, now numbering 12,000 items, has largely arisen as a result of obtaining financial assistance from a Trust to acquire 3,000 photographs taken between 1968 and 1970 by a local photographer, and in the further acquisition of 1,000 photographs taken between 1870

2. This survey was described by Miss Yvonne Fennell in 'Chester Photographic Survey'. *Library Association Record*, May, 1970. pp. 197–9.
3. The Dudley Survey is described by D. F. Radmore in 'Suggestions for a Photographic Survey'. *Local Historian*, vol. 9, no. 5, February 1971. pp. 222–5.

and 1930 of Victorian and Edwardian Oxford. The London Borough of Harrow reports that:

The main area of growth has been the photographic collection; a standing order with the G.L.C. Photo Library for prints by the Photographic Unit of the Department of Architecture and Civic Design placed in 1968 resulted in the addition of 130 photographs, and 220 photographs were added in the year February 1969–February 1970. Surveys of high technical quality were carried out by teams of students from the School of Photography of Harrow College of Technology and Art to our advice in 1969 in two great houses in private hands and impossible for amateurs to photograph (one was the RAF HQ at Bentley Priory). Many aerial photographs have been bought in the last few years from Aerofilms Ltd. and Fairey Surveys Ltd. Many photographs are also obtained from the local newspaper.

The Harrow collection contains 5,000 items. An aerofilm survey of Kensington and Chelsea also forms a part of the large collection (approximately 15,000 items) in the Royal Borough of Kensington and Chelsea where a ground survey (street by street and sometimes house by house) is in progress. The largest collections of photographic records (all in excess of 15,000 items) are at Liverpool, Manchester, Birmingham, Norwich, Westminster, Cardiff, Waltham Forest, Sheffield, Nottingham, Brighton, Edinburgh and in the Bedfordshire County Library and Record Office which holds a collection of about 100,000 photographic plates from the office of the *Bedfordshire Times.*

Whatever method is chosen to obtain a photographic survey it should be planned systematically instead of leaving contributions to individual preference. Experience has shown that photographers prefer to be given definite assignments. This is obviously easier when the area is limited, as for a single town, but with good organisation of workers and equipment and plenty of enthusiasm, valuable results can be obtained over a wider area. Sometimes the survey has limited objectives or a special purpose such as that undertaken by the Sheffield Council for the Conservation of Antiquities of all buildings in the city considered worthy of preservation which is now housed in the Central Library.

Where a survey exists the librarian will, as his contribution to the corporate endeavour, attend to the administrative organisation, including the details of classifying, indexing, mounting and filing the prints. It is usual for the library to provide filing boxes or vertical files and to defray the costs incurred in housing and preserving the prints. An eye should be kept on the quality and permanency of the prints, although first-class pictorial prints are not essential for record purposes. Most surveys find that they have to accept a certain amount of second-rate material in order not to discourage enthusiasm and a poor print is better than none. Newspaper prints, often done in a hurry, may need to be refixed and rewashed. Correct dating is of great importance and the librarian should take pains to ensure this. The librarian who wishes to study these matters in detail is referred to *The Camera as Historian* (Sampson, Low, London, 1916) which, though somewhat out-of-date, is a complete handbook to photographic record work. They are also dealt with less fully in John L. Hobbs's *Libraries and the Materials of Local History* (Grafton, London, 1948).

Many large photographic collections have been achieved without the help of a survey society or survey organisation due to the activities of research and photographic societies and in some cases to the activities of individual photographers. The Preston Scientific Society has a Record and Survey Committee which has a collection of local photographs dating from Victorian times. Members of the sub-committee keep this up-to-date and the collection is housed in the reference library. At Lowestoft the Port of Lowestoft Research Society has presented to the library a collection of photographs of vessels built, registered or repaired at Lowestoft, or using the port. In 1970 this collection contained about 9,000 photographs and receives annual additions. The collection of photographs of ships and shipping at South Shields includes the Ossie Peterson Collection of sailing ships and the photographic collection in the library also contains another three individual collections (the Parry, the Flagg, and the Willits) of local photographs and negatives. At Norwich the collection includes the Thomas Eaton Collection of early Norwich photographs and individual collections are to be found in a number of large local history libraries including Bexley, Eastbourne and Winchester. Both at South Shields and Hackney the large photographic collections include records of war damage in the respective boroughs and at Hackney the collection has been considerably increased in recent years by the inauguration of a systematic survey of the redevelopment sites.

In many authorities it has been found that appropriate arrangements can be made with the borough surveyor's department for duplicate copies of photographs of buildings scheduled for demolition and of redevelopment sites to be made for the library wherever such photography is normally undertaken, and there are other methods of augmenting the collection which the librarian should explore to save needless duplication of effort. A popular one is a record competition sponsored by the library, either with or without the co-operation of the local photographic society. The Worcestershire Photographic Survey organises expeditions for its constituent societies for the purpose of taking photographs for the collection. These have resulted in as many as a thousand prints of an area from a single day's outing. Some librarians have found the press co-operative to a suggestion that they should pass on to the library press photographs when they are disposed of periodically, and others have found local commercial firms similarly helpful. The acquisition of negatives already existing in the hands of antiquarians, local families and former photographers is important. The death of a local photographer or the closing of a business may present an opportunity to obtain a series of local photographs, while chemists' dark rooms sometimes yield old negative plates.

Many librarians have found that an exhibition of old photographs will prompt local residents to produce prints in their possession either as donations or for the purpose of having copies made for preservation in the library. Aerial photographs can also be purchased from commercial firms such as Aerofilms Ltd. and where a complete aerial survey of any locality is obtained in this way it is useful to plot each photograph on a map and index the collection from map references so that a photograph of any place in the locality can be easily found. Various national organisations are also often able to supply local photographs. The National Buildings Record, which records buildings of architectural interest throughout the country, has already been mentioned but there are others such as the Royal Institute of British Architects, and the Royal Commission on Historical Monuments.

Aerial photographs are an important aid to the study of archaeology in the field[4] and should not be neglected in this connection in the development of the photographic collection. This form of archaeological study was developed by the late O. G. S. Crawford and the late Major W. G. Allen. The negatives of photographs taken by Major Allen are kept at the Ashmolean Museum and this pioneer work was further developed by Dr J. K. St Joseph[5] of Selwyn College, Cambridge, and others. The Ministry of Defence has also done much aerial survey work and sets of prints covering selected areas can be ordered from the Ministry.

Some libraries have collections of lantern slides, both of the older $3\frac{1}{2}$ in. square glass variety as well as the more modern 35 mm. coloured transparencies, which are loaned to lecturers. The collecting of about 5,000 such transparencies at Plymouth during the past ten years is indicative of the value of this medium in building up a natural colour record of the life and appearance of the town and county for the future. Since unmounted colour transparencies can be 'read' in most microfilm readers students have found that the transparency can be used for the reproduction of maps, plans and diagrams to attach to theses and periodical articles.

Edinburgh's collection of 7,926 lantern slides at May 1970 included 3,412 colour transparencies, and the library makes transparencies of its local prints and maps for sale. Suitable prints are also reproduced in black and white or colour and sold as postcards or Christmas cards. Other libraries make colour transparencies of local prints, maps and similar material for loaning to schools in connection with lessons and some have arranged series of slides accompanied by lecture notes for the use of lecturers. A growing use of such collections has often been made by TV companies to provide stills for a wide variety of programmes.

One or two libraries have also used 16 mm. film, both in colour and in black and white, in order to record local events

4. See O. G. S. Crawford. *Archaeology in the Field*. Phoenix House, London, 1953.
5. See M. W. Beresford and J. K. S. St Joseph. *Medieval England: An Aerial Survey*. Cambridge University Press, Cambridge, 1958.

as well as for more ambitious excursions into the art of film-making such as Plymouth's *1,000 Years of Plymouth History* and *Plymouth Before and After the Blitz*. Bootle has made film records on a fairly extensive scale since 1961 and possesses full 16 mm. equipment as well as three sets of 16 mm. projector equipment which schools and societies may borrow. An allocation of £425 per annum for this work is provided and the collection of 81 films in the local history library includes 74 on 16 mm. Similar use of 16 mm. film has been made at Hamilton, Scotland, where the collection now contains 124 films on 16 mm. as well as 25,000 feet of 35 mm. film devoted to Sir Harry Lauder.

Although the use of the wide variety of photocopying and microfilm processes in many libraries is too often confined simply to the microfilming of local newspapers, the number of libraries now possessing microfilm readers, photocopying equipment and making use of copying equipment in other local government departments is increasing rapidly. About 60 per cent of the libraries responding to a questionnaire in 1970 possessed microfilm readers and about 50 per cent possessed photocopying equipment, although very few were able to report the possession of the most sophisticated types of equipment such as microfilm reader/copiers, dual-spectrum or xerox copying machines. Nevertheless the variety of machines in use in libraries, both readers and copiers, is very wide and it is evident that the purchase of the more expensive types of equipment is becoming a much more economic proposition as the use of microfilm and photocopies rapidly increases.

A certain resistance to microfilm copies on the part of scholars was evident in the initial stages, but this has gradually been overcome. Indeed, many today express a preference for using film instead of handling documents which may be frail and easily damaged, or newspaper files where several heavy volumes can be accommodated on one film reel. It is essential that the whole page should appear on the screen without manipulation. A major and perhaps supreme advantage of these processes is that of absolute fidelity to the original. A manuscript or typed copy, even a printed copy, can never be guaranteed to be an exact replica, but in this respect at least the camera cannot lie or distort.

The purposes and advantages of microcopies and photocopies generally as applied to local history research material may be summarised briefly as follows:

1. To allow the wider dissemination of research materials and the collection of copies of material in other institutions at reasonable cost. This enables the library to complete essential series, to provide important manuscript material which is otherwise unobtainable, and to make the lot of the scholar and researcher much easier. This aspect is of primary importance and will be discussed more fully below.

2. To preserve the original or delicate material from unnecessary handling, or from the hazards of war, fire and theft, etc. Unique and irreplaceable records are filmed to guard against their accidental destruction or decay. Modern photographic techniques can produce copies of worn or faded matter which is even more legible than the original. Photocopies of material such as maps, paintings and engravings can be produced first for inspection to the reader, who can then decide whether it is necessary for him to consult the original. This is especially important for rare or fragile items, such as old estate maps, which are liable to be extensively damaged by constant examination.

3. To save storage space and, in certain circumstances, to permit discarding of material. Bulky, trivial and ephemeral items which lack of space may make it inadvisable to retain in their original form may be microfilmed and the originals destroyed to clear vital space. An example might be certain of the less important modern archives scheduled for destruction.

4. To improve reference to long sequences or files of bulky material. It is often easier, with modern equipment, to run through a roll of microfilm than several large and heavy bound newspapers, or to examine a series of archives on film than to consult the separate papers.

To the local history department the most vital concern with microrecording and photocopying rests in its power to increase our resources and augment the collections by providing opportunities for the acquisition of photocopies of local records, both printed and manuscript, from other sources, public and private. It is well known that before the establishment of public libraries (and even since) many important local records and collections gravitated to the national institutions. Consequently the British Museum, the Public Record Office, the Royal College of Arms, the university libraries of Oxford (Bodleian) and Cambridge and the national libraries of Scotland, Wales and Ireland contain large quantities of records which are of local rather than of national interest. Most of these are extremely co-operative in allowing photocopies to be made for the appropriate local library, where the material has a potentially greater use and value.

The principal forms of photocopying and microrecording in general use in libraries are neatly summarised and described in Donald Mason's *Document Reproduction in Libraries* (Association of Assistant Librarians, London, 1968) and microrecording is more fully described in *Microcopying Methods* by H. R. Verry, revised by Gordon H. Wright (Focal Press, London, 1967). Progress in techniques has been very rapid so that a bewildering variety of equipment has been evolved much of which was usefully listed in George H. Davison's *1962 Review of Equipment for Microtext* (Council for Microphotography and Document Reproduction, London, 1962) and in more recent detail in the *International Directory of Micrographic Equipment*, edited by J. Rubin (International Micrographic Congress, Saratoga, California, 1967).

Microcopies may consist either of transparencies on film in roll, strip or sheet form; or of opaques on cards, either printed photographically or by offset litho processes. All microcopies require optical equipment to enable them to be read. Photocopies can usually be read without the aid of optical equipment since they are most generally produced in the size of the original document. They may consist of photographic processes involving the use of a camera or merely the use of sensitised paper. Other pseudo-photographic processes such as xerography involve infra-red or electro-magnetism and result in images printed on non-sensitised paper.

Roll microfilm was the first form to be extensively used in libraries and the other microcopying processes have developed from this. It is still the most popular and useful for long runs of material such as complete books, book-length manuscripts, files of newspapers, university theses, parish registers and archive collections. A large number of libraries have acquired microfilm copies of their local newspapers, either to complete gaps in their holdings, or to secure copies of files in other hands, or have their own files filmed to save originals from wear and tear. Many old files of bound papers in libraries have become dilapidated through long usage, and today it is cheaper to film than to bind them. Nevertheless most libraries retain the original files after filming and simply store them in less expensive storage accommodation than is contained in most central libraries. The need to do this will continue until the life of microfilm has been firmly established.

It is unfortunately true that the majority of libraries possessing microfilm equipment are slowly struggling to complete a programme of microfilming the local newspaper files and there are still a number of large towns and counties that possess neither microfilm equipment nor microfilms. Wherever the use of microfilm has been pursued with more than a modest enthusiasm, however, the acquisition programmes have soon led to the purchase and making of films of a wide variety of local material. Castleford, Eccles, Grimsby, Morley, Shrewsbury, Warrington, York and no doubt a few other libraries have secured copies of the Enumerators' Returns for the Censuses of 1841, 1851 and 1861 from the Public Record Office, which form a valuable directory of every inhabitant in the town for these years. Manchester, which possesses a microfilm camera, has microfilmed all unpublished registers for the Manchester diocese to 1837, and where a parish has ceased to exist the whole register has been filmed. Rate books, manorial court rolls and borough records as well as scarce local histories and unpublished theses on local history topics are all suitable material for microfilming and have all been included in the microfilm collections of some libraries. The microfilm holdings of most British libraries in 1970, however, indicate that a much more vigorous acquisition policy would be beneficial to libraries and users alike.

Micro-editions of material in the library can be made available to researchers who would find it impossible to consult the original material. Many American scholars now regard this as a normal means of gaining access to unique material, and many librarians have supplied microfilms in response to requests. Warrington has sent films of its Joseph Priestley correspondence to the United States, and few libraries with large collections have not had similar requests. Individual items are often made into slides for exhibition purposes: there is no obstacle to the reproduction of colour material.

Microfiche is used in a relatively small number of local history libraries but has been used extensively on the Continent as a publishing media. As a micro-transparency it has an advantage over the micro-opaque in that the optics required for viewing and copying are simpler, and as the sheets of film can be stored in protective transparent envelopes which need not be removed when the film is placed in a viewer the film is protected at all times – unlike the roll form of microfilm which is subject to heavy damage in some microfilm readers. Birkenhead has put 3,000 of its early documents relating to Cheshire on microfiche. The library retains the negatives and frequently lends the positives to other libraries, including university libraries, for students to work on them. One 5 in. x 3½ in. microfiche card contains 10 foolscap sheets and 3,000 deeds occupy one 12 in. drawer.

Micro-opaques are principally used by the publishers of micro-texts for books and periodicals, generally in sets of material which is out-of-print and not obtainable through normal publishing channels. The Microcard Foundation uses 3 in. x 5 in. microcards and since 1961 Microcard Editions Inc., of Washington, D.C., has produced an annual *Guide to Microforms in Print*. The Readex Microprint Corporation uses 6 in. x 9 in. microprint and the Lawyer's Co-operative Publishing Co. uses 6½ in. x 8½ in. microlex.

The material so far published is not such as is needed in the normal local collection, since the process is economic only in reasonable editions,[6] rather than single copies, but some material available on microcards would be valuable reference stock to supplement local records, such as the Annual Register, the Rolls Series of early chronicles and histories and the publications of the Early English Text Society. Their chief use is in the technical field, but there is little doubt that small reference libraries will ultimately find this a useful method of stock building, as several county libraries are doing.

A wide variety of photocopying processes are in use by about

6. The Microcard Foundation requires a minimum of five orders and copyright clearance before it will consider microcarding a title.

half of the libraries responding to a questionnaire in 1970 and it is also evident that increasing use is being made of the equipment possessed by these libraries. More and more users are able to save time by having non-copyright items copied from local history libraries. A better indication can be given to correspondents by sending them photocopies of material in a collection than by sending a written description thus enabling these correspondents to decide whether a visit to the library is worthwhile. Items in private possession can be copied and thus the photocopies fill gaps in the library collection. Most photocopying machines are used in fact to copy single sheet items, extracts from books and periodicals, and on occasion to reproduce a copy of a complete thesis, all in the size of the original which means that many machines are restricted to the reproduction of items less than 18 in. × 14 in. although some machines are able to produce reproductions up to 60 in. × 40 in. in size.

The increase in the need for photocopies both by the library as a collector of local history material and by users of the library has meant that machines producing dry copies with rapidity are essential in order to save operational time and reduce the cost of copies. Unfortunately the speediest and most sophisticated equipment is the costliest and requires heavy use to prove economically viable. The dry copies produced on ordinary paper by the Rank Xerox 3600 machine, for example, are completed by the machine before the next original can be placed in position, whilst the 3M Company Ltd. has produced a dual spectrum machine with an automatic feed. If these machines are used to a reasonable capacity the copies can be produced at a fraction of the cost of any modern reflex copying machine. Copies produced by xerography and other electrostatic processes on ordinary paper are not subject to the subsequent staining and fading that sometimes occurs with the sensitised papers used on reflex and other photographic machines, but illustrations, except line drawings, do not reproduce well in the pseudo-photographic processes employed in xerography. The active local history library really requires a fast electrostatic copier as well as a good reflex copier to handle the variety and volume of photocopies necessary for the library and its users, and where any variety of items is contained in the holdings of microfilm material a microfilm reader/copier is also a most useful and necessary piece of copying equipment. So far very few libraries possess such a range of modern equipment. No more than fifty of the public and county libraries responding to a questionnaire in 1970 possessed xerox or electrostatic copying machines although many other libraries have reasonable access to such equipment in other local government offices, whilst less than a dozen libraries appear to possess microfilm reader/copiers.

Approximately fifty different types of photocopying machines and twenty-five different microfilm readers were listed by the libraries possessing photocopying and microfilm equipment and as all equipment is subject to rapid change and development it would be invidious to name particular products. Except perhaps to mention that a microfilm camera such as one manufactured by the 3M Co. Ltd. (2000 AO) will take a photograph of any item up to the standard AO size (841 mm. × 1189 mm.) and, in the incredibly short space of forty-five seconds, will produce an aperture card in standard column size for data processing containing a single frame of 35 mm. microfilm set in the aperture ready for enlargement or filing. Clearly this creates tremendous possibilities for the duplication of collections of illustrations and press cuttings as well as providing a ready instrument for information retrieval. Microfilm reader/printers such as the Kodak Magnaprint and the 3M 400M are also machines capable of usefully extending the service provided by all libraries possessing microfilm. The cost of equipment varies from less than £100 to several thousand pounds and obviously it cannot be hoped to provide the best in optics or film transport, speed of operation, perfection of the final image (whether a photocopy or projected image) in any one or two very low-priced machines. The abundant literature available from the various manufacturers must be carefully studied and a selection made of the machine most likely to meet the needs of each library.

Making photocopies of copyright material has increasingly been a cause for concern on the part of authors and publishers as photocopying practices have increased in libraries, schools and other institutions so that a new Copyright Act, 1956, together with Copyright (Libraries) Regulations, 1957, became necessary and in 1965 the Society of Authors and the Publishers Association published a helpful pamphlet entitled: *Photocopying and the Law: A Guide for Librarians and Teachers and Other Suppliers of Photocopies of Copyright Works*. This pamphlet was reprinted in the *Library Association Record*, vol. 67, no. 11, November 1965, and should be carefully studied by all who are concerned with the supply of photocopies of copyright material.

Chapter 10

Local History in County Libraries

Unlike municipal authorities where the majority of local history collections consist of archival and printed material, most county authorities have developed separate collections of archives in the county record offices and printed material in the county libraries. There is often close co-operation between the two services, especially where both the county headquarters and record offices are situated in the same building or, as at Hereford, where the county librarian is director of both services, and it is also evident that the leading role in the promotion of local history studies in most counties has been taken by the county archivists, many of whom have also encouraged and assisted librarians in charge of municipal collections.

The comparatively recent establishment of the County Library Service in the early 1920s has meant that much early printed local material has been difficult to collect and it is only in recent years, as attractive branch buildings and new county headquarters have been erected, that donors of useful collections have been sufficiently persuaded that their donations could be housed, maintained and displayed in suitable conditions.

The earliest county record office preceded the earliest county library service and it was founded in 1913 by Dr Herbert Fowler in Bedfordshire. Because of the pioneering efforts of Dr Fowler, who became the first chairman of the Library Sub-Committee after the inauguration of the County Library Service in Bedfordshire in 1925, this county now affords one of the best examples of a well-developed and sensibly integrated collection of county local history material. In July 1969 the Bedfordshire County Record Office and County Central

Library came together in a new purpose-built four-storey building on the County Hall site and an impressive new centre for local studies was thus created. The main collection in Bedfordshire is a central one for reference with duplicate copies (including sixteen sets of the Victoria County Histories as well as 200 bound volumes of the various parts) available for loan. All the branch libraries have a collection of the basic books on the county and on their own locality whilst the area libraries have much larger collections. Area and branch librarians are urged to participate in local history society activities, to search for, buy and acquire material for their collections, to contribute to local guides, and to get to know those working individually in local history studies. The county council published Joyce Godber's *History of Bedfordshire* in 1969 which was based on published and manuscript records of the record office, the Fowler Library and the county local history collection. Close co-operation is also maintained with the Bedfordshire Historical Record Society, which published a Bedfordshire Bibliography compiled by L. R. Conisbee in 1962 and issued a 1st supplement in 1967.

In other counties the development of local history collections and the exploitation of material varies considerably and has depended upon individual enthusiasm as well as on the extent of urban areas under county control within each county authority. Since county libraries were established to serve the predominantly rural areas originally controlled by county councils, it is scarcely surprising to find that the majority of those county libraries that have developed local history collections have established central collections, and that three separate policies have been pursued concerning these central collections. Of 53 county libraries responding to a questionnaire in 1970, 51 had established centralised collections and 9 of these were stated to be for reference only; 7 were mainly for lending and 35 were for reference only with duplicate copies of books, obtained wherever possible, for lending. In 27 counties there were reasonably strong collections in branch or area libraries, but 22 counties did not provide such branch or area collections and 27 counties had no considered overall plan for developing the collection of local history material within the county.

The decision to confine central collections to a reference only policy must be a difficult one to take. There exists a very real conflict between on the one hand, the duty of any librarian to conserve scarce, often valuable and sometimes unique printed material for the use of future generations as well as for the varying needs of the present generation, and on the other, the desirability in a county where access to a centralised collection is not always a simple practicability, to lend as much material as possible in order that the needs of the majority of users may be met with the least inconvenience. The compromise of combining reference only and lending functions by means of duplicate copies has prevailed in a majority of counties and many emphasise that modern copying techniques have enabled rare items to be made available for lending purposes.

Whatever the original policy concerning the central collection, however, a gradual change has occurred in some counties as urban areas have been added to county control, and these changes are of special interest at the present moment since the allocation of main functions contained in the 1972 Local Government Act place many additional urban areas under the control of county councils. In those counties that have already become responsible for the library services of urban areas that formerly possessed independent library services, it would appear that the tendency has been to leave well-established collections of local history material in their original locality, and in some instances, to strengthen these collections with additional material. Derbyshire County, for example, reports that the main collection of unique first copies is largely centralised and kept for reference, but there are some unique copies at branch libraries, especially at those, in particular at Buxton, which were formerly independent libraries. Of great significance, however, has been the reorganisation of local history material that has taken place in Shropshire since local government changes took place in 1966.

The Shropshire County Library has pursued a policy, since several small boroughs and Telford New Town came under county control, of establishing strong local collections in a number of key market towns, thus demonstrating what would appear to be an eminently sensible approach to the disposition of local history material for the greatest convenience of all those likely to be concerned with the use of the material in the county. In pursuing this policy the County Library's main collection was first moved from Shrewsbury but as the level of demand was not sufficient to justify the continuation of the service in the new location the collection was regarded as 'development' and used to strengthen and form collections in new branches. At the new Madeley Branch Library, part of Telford New Town, and opened in 1969, a sizeable local history reference collection was made up from this development stock. It is proposed to transfer the remainder of this stock (7,000 vols.) to a new central library, now being planned, for Telford New Town and also to move to Telford the local history catalogue at present housed at the Shropshire Headquarters. This re-allocation of the main collection has been made possible partly because a sensible consideration of the collection in the Shrewsbury Public Library led to an agreement being reached concerning the respective sphere of influence of both libraries. In a new library at Whitchurch, named the Caldecott Library in honour of Randolph E. Caldecott, the Shropshire County Library has placed 1,000 volumes on local history from the Lloyd estate purchase. The local history collection of the former Oswestry Borough Library remains in a separate room at Oswestry with fifteen tables and thirty chairs. A bibliography of Oswestry history is being prepared there by a Birmingham University extra-mural class. The County Library is equipped with a microfilm reader/copier, telex communication and a plan to produce a computer catalogue. Quite clearly the needs of readers have been placed before any administrative convenience in this county authority and the administration has been made first to serve readers.

Shropshire can also claim a prominent position amongst local authorities that have produced and sponsored works of scholarship in the field of local studies. In 1968 the County Library published the *Coalbrookdale Coalfield Catalogue of Mines and Mining Bibliography*, compiled by Ivor J. Brown. It has also gathered together some 10,000 volumes from nine parochial libraries and a *Catalogue of Books from Parochial Libraries in Shropshire*, compiled and edited at Shropshire County Library under the direction of Miss O. S. Newman has been published by Mansell, 1971.

In those counties that have decided to maintain a centralised collection of local history material, either for reference or lending, it is essential to provide catalogues of the collection for use in all branches. Placing such a catalogue on a computer in order to obtain frequent print-offs is perhaps the speediest way of providing branches with up-to-date information concerning the collection. This has been done at Flintshire County Library where the collection has been housed separately in a local history room of the new County Headquarters at Mold since October 1969 and is chiefly for reference only. A copy of the computerised local history catalogue is deposited at each county branch library.

A somewhat different approach to the disposition of local history material throughout a county area has been undertaken in Surrey, where the central collection at Surrey County Library Headquarters in Esher includes a substantial loan collection in order to provide copies for home reading of the more important books on local history normally held for reference use only in district libraries. Substantial collections are held in many district libraries and contain non-book material well organised and indexed. An excellent *Short Guide to the Local History Resources of Surrey County Library* (preliminary edition) was produced at County Headquarters in 1969, which in addition to giving adequate information concerning the collection in the libraries controlled by the Surrey County Library, also mentions for the convenience of local history students, other libraries possessing Surrey local history material such as Chertsey, Croydon, Epsom, Guildford, the Minet Library and the library of the Surrey Archaeological Society at Castle Arch, Guildford. The Surrey County Library also published in 1965 *Surrey People: A Union List of Directories and Allied Material Held in the Libraries of Surrey.*

Although suitable catalogues or guides to the material in the county collections of local history material would appear to be a necessity in view of the large proportion of counties having centralised collections, comparatively few counties have so far issued such essential guides. An early lead was taken by Denbighshire with a three-part bibliography published in 1935–37. Similarly, Huntingdon's *Catalogue of the Local History Collection*, originally published in 1950, reached a second edition in 1958, and Nottingham's catalogue, first published in 1953, achieved a third edition in 1966. A bibliography of Cardiganshire *Llyfryddiaeth Ceredigion 1600–1964,* compiled by G. L. Jones, Deputy County Librarian, as a Library Association fellowship thesis was published by the County Library (3 vols., Aberystwyth, 1967). Other catalogues and guides to county collections which have been issued by county libraries in the past decade have included those from Cambridgeshire and Kent as well as from three Irish counties: Cavan, Galway and Limerick. A printed catalogue of the Derbyshire collection is in production. County bibliographies, however, are in active preparation and in various states of publication through a number of co-operative efforts in several counties and regions including Cheshire, East Anglia, Hertfordshire, Lancashire, Lincolnshire and the East Midlands (formerly the North Midlands Bibliography). Good, duplicated and printed selective lists of local history material have been produced by Merioneth (1969), West Riding (1968), and Wiltshire (1967).

As many new county headquarters, new county branch libraries and new regional libraries have been erected during the past ten years so has the provision for local studies and the housing of local history material in county libraries developed. Not only has separate housing of centralised collections been provided, but provision has been made for meetings of local societies in new branch libraries and the spate of new county building has led to an extension of the material collected in many instances, as well as to an increase in the number of librarians employed specifically to develop and administer local studies and local study material. The percentage of county authorities now employing separate staff for local history purposes (23 per cent) is nearly equal to the percentage of municipal libraries employing local history librarians (26 per cent) although both of course are still pitifully small. Similarly, the growth in the number of county authorities collecting non-book materials such as microfilm, photographs and illustrations, tapes, films, maps, lantern slides, newspaper cuttings and posters has increased considerably. Most county libraries have good map collections and 38 per cent possess microfilms, 51 per cent possess small collections of up to 1,000 photographs and illustrations, 17 per cent have collections ranging to 10,000 items and 2 per cent have large collections in excess of 10,000 items. As in municipal authorities the microfilm and photocopying equipment tends largely to be of the less sophisticated types and there is clearly a need for the purchase of such machines as the microfilm camera, manufactured by the 3M Co. Ltd., which is capable of producing a single 35 mm. frame film set in a standard 80 column data processing aperture card in 45 seconds and which can be used to duplicate quickly and easily collections of illustrations and press cutting material as well as to provide a ready means of information retrieval. The purchase of this type of machine could be one of the benefits to arise from the new local authorities to be set up as a result of the Local Government Act, 1972.

County library local history services, therefore, in many instances are beginning to emerge from the early formative stages. The reason for their slow development seems to have resulted from the almost simultaneous growth of the county record offices. In many counties librarians have found that other aspects of the county library service have required prior attention and these have been developed with the knowledge that local history studies were being given considerable attention in the record office. As county library services have developed and building programmes have been completed, however, the growth of local history collections outlined above has also meant that the county collections of printed and non-book materials have attracted bequests from private collectors and have also grown by purchase of private collections. Such special collections in county libraries are not as yet particularly numerous, but some of them are sufficiently substantial and comprehensive to attract wide attention. In Dorset, for example, the Thomas Hardy Collection consists of 1,522 books, manuscripts and other items and there is a Lock Collection of Hardiana on deposit containing 520 books and MSS. cuttings. Dorset also is one of the few counties with a special fund for the purchase of local books and manuscripts. Collections of books, manuscripts and other items associated with local authors and personalities exist in a number of county library collections including Aberdeenshire where there is a collection of the novelist George Macdonald; Cumberland (part of Hugh Walpole's collection of Lakeland literature as well as material on Lake District writers); Dumfries (the Frank Miller Collection of literary and ballad material and the Burns Club Collection); Notts. County (D. H. Lawrence); Flintshire (Fr Rolfe, W. E. Gladstone, as well as an Arthurian legend collection); Herefordshire (John Masefield); Lindsey and Holland (the Banks Collection of MSS. and original material collected by Sir Joseph Banks who sailed with Captain Cook as a botanist); Norfolk (a Thomas Paine Collection); Shropshire (a collection of a nineteenth-century inventor, Thomas Parker, consisting of papers, drawings and models); and West Riding (Mrs Ewing). Other special collections have been acquired by Bedfordshire where the files of the *Bedfordshire Times* and 100,000 photographic negatives have been acquired; Cornwall (the Ashley Rowe Library of books and manuscripts on Cornish history); Derbyshire (Barmaster's Library of local lead mining interest and the Handford Collection of engravings and maps of Derbyshire); Lindsey and Holland (the Goulding Collection of local history material which under the terms of a bequest has to remain at the Louth branch); Orkney (Dr Marwick's collection on the Norse language and R. Rendall's collection on conchology); Radnorshire (a collection of school board minute books and school log books); and at Westmorland (a collection on the geology of the Lake District and a large map collection).

Many new local history societies have been encouraged to meet in county branch libraries as well as in the new county headquarters erected in recent years and it would seem that the future development of county local history services will rest to a greater extent than ever at a more local level. The successful accomplishment of such an aim can only be achieved if local branch librarians are encouraged, as they are at present in Bedfordshire and one or two other counties, to participate in local history society activities, to search for, buy and acquire material for their collections, to contribute to local guides, and to get to know those working individually in local history studies. The future tasks of those at county headquarters having special responsibility for local history material could very well be to a greater extent devoted to the production of bibliographical material and the reproduction of material by the photographic and other copying processes now available.

Chapter 11

The Use of Local Research Materials

The bibliography of any subject is part of the technical equipment of a librarian, and this is equally true of local history, where the term 'bibliography' should be understood as including manuscript as well as printed source material. In each of the various fields comprising local studies today he should be aware of the important sources, their virtues and limitations, the methods on which they were compiled and their adequacy or otherwise for particular lines of enquiry.

The discovery of source material is a sphere in which the student and the amateur may legitimately look to the library staff for advice and help. It is the library's primary function in fact to provide these, but we have indicated that no library can hope to secure more than a fraction of the available material on local studies. It is surely a logical extension of this to know of similar or related materials to be found elsewhere. This does not mean that the student is to be denied, or is to be carefully shielded from, the delights of searching for his sources on his own account. On the contrary, it is salutary that he should undergo this essential preliminary training and the amount now available is so great that no library can have or even know about *all* that is needed for any specific line of research, however limited it may be.

The writer is not attempting here to give advice on *methods* of historical enquiry or on training in such. Mr C. G. Crump offered excellent advice on these lines some years ago in his admirable essay *History and Historical Research* (Routledge, London, 1928). To try to make this section an exhaustive guide to primary sources of historical information would obviously be impracticable and it will not be attempted. Nor is it aimed at the amateur historian, still less the accomplished scholar, but at the librarian or assistant who has charge of, or who hopes one day to have charge of, a local history collection. That it may also be helpful to the beginner in historical studies is the hope of the author, but this is incidental to its true purpose. Certainly it cannot include the wealth of detail that will be found in Philip Hepworth's *How To Find Out in History* (Pergamon Press, Oxford, 1967), which is an excellent guide to 'sources of information on history and its allied subject biography, and methods of approach to them'.

Attention has already been drawn to the extensive series of original sources for local studies existing in the national and university libraries, and to the fact that these are, for the most part, unprinted and accessible only by enquiry in these libraries. The guides, lists, indexes and calendars of certain classes of these records which have been printed will facilitate reference to them and they should be available to the historical student, and familiar to the local librarian. The need for a guide to these publications has now been met by the appearance of the Royal Historical Society's *Texts and Calendars: An Analytical Guide to Serial Publications*, compiled by E. L. C. Mullins (Royal Historical Society, London, 1958), which covers the output of such official bodies as the Record Commissioners, the Historical Manuscripts Commission, the Public Record Office[1] and the Royal Commission on Historical Monuments, as well as of national and local societies. Many of these are of great local significance with which the librarian needs to be acquainted. In particular the Index Library series, issued by the British Record Society, has published calendars and indexes to wills and administrations in various provincial courts, abstracts of 'inquisitions post mortem' and marriage licences for several counties and similar records; the Harleian Society has published an extensive series of county visitations, pedigrees, allegations for marriage licences and other material of heraldic and genealogical interest; the Pipe Roll Society has published the great rolls of the Exchequer from 1158 to 1212, some feet of fines and similar records; and the Selden Society has issued

1. A more detailed guide to the public records is the Public Record Office's *Guide to the Contents of the Public Record Office*. 2 vols. HMSO, London, 1963.

transcripts and calendars of several series of legal records from the Public Record Office and other sources.

The contents of the local record office should be known intimately and its guides, handlists and calendars should be available. An excellent practical guide for all who wish to use local records which includes useful information on record repositories is F. G. Emmison's *Archives and Local History* (Methuen, London, 1966). There are a large number of secondary sources, too, which may be helpful and access to a good reference collection of historical literature is of inestimable value to a local history department. Basic reference works such as the *Dictionary of National Biography*, and other biographical dictionaries by Harvey, Colvin, Gunnis, Bénézit and others, the *Complete Peerage* and similar publications, clergy and army lists, the Rolls series and the State Papers, the Journals of the House of Commons and the House of Lords, files of historical periodicals and the publications of historical and antiquarian societies will be in frequent demand in the local room. The librarian should be aware, too, of general aids to local history and historical research of the nature of the bibliographies and other publications of the Royal Historical Society and the 'Helps for Students of History' series issued by the Historical Association. Especially useful is *English Local History Handlist, A Select Bibliography and List of Sources for the Study of Local History and Antiquities*, edited by F. W. Kuhlicke and F. G. Emmison (Historical Association, London, 4th ed. 1969. 'Helps for Students of History', no. 69). The bulletins of the Institute of Historical Research have included a series of useful articles dealing with 'Bibliographical Aids to Research', while the files of the *Amateur Historian* (now the *Local Historian*) contain a number of interesting and valuable contributions on many topics allied to local history and its study aimed, in the main, at the untrained researcher.

One other point should be mentioned here. The library is naturally primarily interested in documentary evidence of the past, but there is much material evidence still existing, though rapidly being lost, which should not be neglected. It has been shown by Professor L. Dudley Stamp, Professor W. G. Hoskins and others, that every village has peculiarities of soil, climate and physical features which have, to a large extent, affected its history and conditioned its growth. Professor Tawney's advice to the historian to 'put on his walking boots' has been echoed by Professor Hoskins, who stresses the value of fieldstudy in his book *Local History in England*. 'The English landscape itself', he tells us, 'to those who know how to read it aright is the richest historical record we possess.' Such pursuits are specially important in the study of archaeology, deserted medieval villages and medieval history generally, architecture, agricultural history, industrial archaeology and the history of local topography. Indeed archaeology as a science deals with a period for which documentary evidence is spare, if not non-existent, and only secondary materials will be available.

The earliest written evidences of our history are the pre-conquest chronicles and the comparatively few surviving Anglo-Saxon charters. Such charters, giving the boundaries of the lands or estates granted, do exist for many areas. Some have been transcribed in W. de Gray Birch's *Cartularium Saxonicum* (3 vols., London, 1885–99), and J. M. Kemble's *Codex Diplomaticus Aevi Saxonici* (6 vols., London, 1839–48), while others may still be found in national collections. Mrs Margaret Gelling[2] has indicated the value of these charters in an interesting article, and Dr Grundy, Professor Hoskins, Dr Finberg and others have illustrated how the boundaries delineated can often still be recognised by careful fieldwork allied to later documentary evidence.

The written history of many areas commences with the Domesday entry and innumerable local histories take this as their starting-point. The Victoria County histories invariably contain an introduction and textual transcription, and for other counties there are usually scholarly translations available, although some of the older of these, compiled in the nineteenth century, may need to be reconsidered in the light of modern scholarship. Professor H. C. Darby's studies of the *Domesday Geography of Eastern, Midland and Northern England* (3 vols., Cambridge University Press, London, 1952, 1954 and 1967) are valuable as supplying the general geographical background for the Domesday entry for a particular place. A facsimile edition of Domesday, edited by Professor V. H. Galbraith, is to be published by Gregg International Publishers.

2. Margaret Gelling. 'Pre-Conquest Local History: Evidence from Anglo-Saxon Charters'. *Amateur Historian*, vol. 1, 1953. pp. 241–5.

The sources for the early medieval history of our towns and villages must be largely sought amongst the charters and records in the Public Record Office, and in other national repositories. The Chancery Records, which include the close, charter, fine and patent rolls, are significant for several aspects of the local history of this period. In particular, letters patent, transcribed in the patent rolls, cover grants of rights or liberties to boroughs, schools, guilds, religious houses, etc., for taxes, markets and fairs and other privileges. The Hundred rolls are invaluable for tracing details of manorial history and the descent of medieval manors and they throw much incidental light upon matters of topography, depopulation of villages and early inclosures. Inquisitions post mortem deal with landed families and the hereditary descent of lands and analogous matters like assignments of dower, proofs of age and the property of lunatics. The plea rolls are records of common law actions and the assize rolls record local proceedings, supplementing the rolls of the quarter sessions. Many of the most useful of these from the local historian's point of view have been printed in the Calendars of State Papers published by HMSO whose List Q is a very valuable index to these sources. In some counties the early history has been studied in detail and published, as in R. W. Eyton's *Antiquities of Shropshire* (12 vols., London, 1854–60).

The religious history of the period centres round the monasteries and other religious houses, an essential source book for which is Sir William Dugdale's *Monasticon Anglicanum* (best edition, 8 vols., London, 1817–30). This details the charters of foundation and other deeds, with a historical survey of each. Although the work bears Dugdale's name much of the research was done by Roger Dodsworth. The surviving monastic cartularies are unique sources for this period. Many are still to be found in national and local libraries and G. R. C. Davis's *Medieval Cartularies of Great Britain: A Short Catalogue* (Longmans Green, London, 1958) lists both the monastic and secular cartularies which have been traced in public or private ownership. This describes only three ecclesiastical, as opposed to family or secular cartularies, in public libraries – those of Marham Abbey (Cistercian), Norfolk, in the Norfolk and Norwich Record Office, of Newstead Priory (Augustinian) in Nottingham

City Library, and of Haughmond Abbey, Salop (Augustinian) at Shrewsbury, but Sheffield has since acquired that of Beauchief Abbey in Derbyshire. The Newstead Cartulary was translated by Miss V. W. Walker, formerly of the Nottingham City Library, and published in 1940.

There has been considerable research since the war into the causes of depopulation in medieval England, through the Deserted Medieval Village Research Group. The work of the group owes much to the practical researches of Maurice W. Beresford of Leeds University and J. G. Hurst of the Department of the Environment, and from it has grown the Society for Medieval Archaeology. Its published work is so far small in quantity but it will eventually provide a corpus of research material for the medieval historian and archaeologist. The sources for this study are too detailed to be discussed here, but will be found in W. G. Hoskins's *Local History in England*, the same author's *Fieldwork in Local History* (Faber, London, 1967), and in Maurice Beresford's works, *The Lost Villages of England* (Lutterworth Press, London, 1954) and *Medieval England: An Aerial Survey* (Cambridge University Press, London, 1958).

The best guides to the writing of village history are those of R. B. Pugh, *How To Write a Parish History* (Allen and Unwin, London, 1954) and Miss Joan Wake, *How To Compile a History and Present-day Record of Village Life* (Federation of Women's Institutes, Northampton, 1935), while an older work by the Rev. J. C. Cox, *How To Write the History of a Parish* (4th ed., London, 1895) is still useful. W. E. Tate's *The Parish Chest* Cambridge University Press, London, (3rd ed. 1969) describes the various parish records which the researcher needs to study at first hand.

Sources for the medieval history of towns will be chiefly local and will centre around the borough archives, where they exist, and especially where the major series have been printed, but a good deal of supplementary information can be found in the State Records. F. J. C. Hearnshaw's pamphlet on *Municipal Records* in the S.P.C.K. 'Helps for Students of History' series (no. 2, London, 1918) is still a useful general introduction for the learner. As many parish histories are predominantly manorial and ecclesiastical in scope, so many town histories are primarily constitutional, concentrating on the administrative development and not the town as an organic human community. Professor Hoskins, referring to the fact that few towns have been studied from the viewpoint of their topographical development, has dealt brilliantly and exhaustively with the general sources for the topographic, social and economic history of towns in his *Local History in England*, pp. 71–105, with far greater knowledge than the writer possesses and it is unnecessary to cover the ground again. A reprint of Charles Gross's *A Bibliography of British Municipal History*, which first appeared in 1897, was published as a 2nd edition by Leicester University Press, 1966, and a continuation to include literature published since 1897 is being prepared by G. H. Martin. Real histories of our medieval towns of the calibre of Sir Francis Hill's *Medieval Lincoln* (Cambridge University Press, London, 1948), and *Tudor and Stuart Lincoln* (Cambridge University Press, London, 1956), and Angelo Raine's *Medieval York* are few and of counties even fewer, but several excellent parish histories have appeared during the last thirty years.

One of the best sources for modern history of all kinds is files of local newspapers and periodicals. Every library should try to complete the file of its local newspapers, on microfilm if it does not have the originals. Many are available in the British Museum Newspaper Library at Colindale, which has made remarkable progress in replacing the files destroyed during the last war, while the Bodleian Library also has extensive files of many early provincial newspapers, of which a catalogue down to the year 1800 has been published.[3] Local papers can be traced in *The Times Tercentenary Handlist of English and Welsh Newspapers, 1620–1920* (*The Times*, London, 1920) although this does not give locations.

The *Gentleman's Magazine* (1731–1883) contains much local information of an antiquarian and social nature, while the *Annual Register* (1758 to date) is similarly useful for political matters, and *Notes and Queries* (1849 to date) for literary, biographical and bibliographical data. The *Journal of the House of Commons* (1547–1900, 155 vols.) is the longest continuous parliamentary record in existence. It relates in narrative form the proceedings in the House; most of the petitions presented in

3. R. T. Milford and D. M. Sutherland. *A Catalogue of English Newspapers and Periodicals in the Bodleian Library, 1622–1800*. Oxford, 1936.

the House; records all motions, members appointed to select committees and papers ordered to be printed by the House. It is now available on microprint. The *House of Lords Journal* is of slighter value from the local viewpoint, but the *London Gazette*, which commenced in 1665, includes royal and official pro-clamations, announcements of titles and accolades, orders in council, promotions and appointments to commissions in H.M. Forces and notices of bankruptcy, dissolutions of partnerships and other matters.

Place-name study has made immense strides in recent years, mainly under the influence of Professor Eilert Ekwall and other Swedish scholars, with the result that many early studies, especially at local level, may largely be discounted. 'Few subjects', says Professor Hoskins, 'contain so many pitfalls as the study of place-names.' Professor Ekwall's *Concise Oxford Dictionary of English Place-Names*, the fourth edition of which appeared in 1960, is definitive, as are the county volumes pre-pared by the English Place-Name Society which now covers twenty-four counties. Early original records, Anglo-Saxon charters, Domesday, medieval charters, conveyances and other records, with their contemporary references to forms and spelling, are the basic sources of study.

Field and minor names are similarly recorded in title deeds and conveyances from medieval times onwards; later there are surveys, terriers, enclosure awards, tithe maps and apportion-ments, sale catalogues, etc., but the collection and interpreta-tion of the field and other minor names of our countryside will always depend largely upon local investigations, study and observation on the spot and by enquiry from local inhabitants, especially the farming community. A surprisingly large number of modern field names have their origin in the 'open' fields and monastic lands of the medieval village, and in many places a great deal of enclosure of commons, waste and woodland took place in late medieval and Tudor times. Nevertheless the era of parliamentary enclosure, 1750–1850, when the common lands were parcelled up into fields and given to local pro-prietors, did substantially settle the pattern of our present-day landscape and many field names date from this time. The enclosure maps, and even more so the tithe maps, where they are available, are the best sources for these.

Street names are to the town what field names are to the rural area, and many towns are rich in sources for their study. These range from the official records, especially town rentals, subsidies, etc., to the monastic cartularies and to medieval and later deeds of conveyance of land and property in the town. From these can be built up lists of references to the streets and other features, which can be used by the expert philologist to elucidate the original meaning of the street name. They also point to the date when streets ceased to exist or changed their names. The county volumes issued by the Place-Name Society now contain fairly exhaustive studies of street names for the major towns, while Professor Ekwall's work on London street names (*Street Names of the City of London,* Clarendon Press, Oxford, 1954) shows the student how the available evidence may be collected, collated and interpreted in a most interesting manner. A new national society, the Names Society, 7 Aragon Avenue, Thames Ditton, Surrey, formed originally in 1967 for the study of house names, has widened its scope to include place-names, personal names, and street names and has embarked upon a national survey of street names that will include a bibliography of street-name literature.

Educational Records

Although many of the principal public and grammar schools have their written histories, the general history of local education has rarely been systematically tackled and emphasis has gathered round the development of educational theory to the neglect of the study of the institutions.[4] This is probably because the available records are not as plentiful or as accessible for the smaller schools. The Institute of Education at Leeds University has a good general library on the history of education and a museum of educational history. The writing of comprehensive studies of education in this country, as of many other subjects, has been hindered by the loss of significant records, but these are now increasingly being deposited in county record offices.

4. The late Arthur F. Leach surveyed the educational records in several areas, e.g. in *Early Yorkshire Schools* (2 vols., Huddersfield, 1899–1903) and *Documents Illustrating Early Education in Worcester, 685 to 1700* (Worcestershire Historical Society, Worcester, 1913).

The British Records Association has issued a memorandum on the *Preservation of School Records* (no. 12), giving guiding principles to be observed in the preservation or destruction of this class of archive.

All records of early systems of elementary education on the Bell or Lancasterian model must be preserved intact, as should all records from the eighteenth century or earlier. In fact few records antedating the passing of the Forster Act of 1870 can safely be discarded, and this should be done only at the discretion of a trained archivist. An important point likely to be overlooked is the necessity to preserve even the most trivial record which concerns scholars who have later achieved fame or distinction.

Endowed schools are described in N. Carlisle's *Endowed Grammar Schools* (2 vols., London, 1818), which gives separate accounts of each, and pre-Reformation foundations in A. F. Leach's *English Schools at the Reformation, 1546–8* (Westminster, 1896). Where the school archives, including the charter of foundation, registers of admission, grants of land and property, etc., have survived the task of the historian is much easier, and the records of several schools have been published in record series.[5] Original charters which are missing may be traced in the Public Record Office. Other national sources include those concerning educational charities and the reports of several nineteenth-century government enquiries into educational matters, such as the Taunton Commission of 1868.

Other primary sources include certain kinds of ecclesiastical record, particularly the bishops' registers, subscription lists and records of archdeacons' visitations, usually to be found in the diocesan registry office, and the local vestry minutes. Almost the whole range of our earlier educational history can in fact be studied in the episcopal records, since the Church had a vital concern in schools ranging from the town grammar school to the village 'dame' school. No one was allowed to exercise the office of schoolmaster without licence from the diocesan authority and his licence had to be exhibited at visitations. Canon J. S. Purvis's *Educational Records*, published by the Borthwick Insti-

5. E.g. *The Records of King Edward's School, Birmingham* (4 vols. Dugdale Society, Stratford upon Avon, 1924–48), and *The Records of Blackburn Grammar School*, edited by G. A. Stocks (3 vols. Chetham Society, Manchester, 1909).

tute of Historical Research in 1959, contains many illustrations of documents relative to education from the diocesan records at York, and indicates the extent and wide variety of these records. For later periods much material is available in civil as well as ecclesiastical archives, and for the last two hundred years or so parliamentary records and papers are a rich mine of information.

The registers of Oxford and Cambridge colleges which may have had official connections with the school should also be consulted. The wills of masters, benefactors, clergy and others connected with the school will throw light on its history, and details of their lives discovered through the usual biographical sources may also be helpful. As most of these will have attended a university the registers of alumni by Emden, Foster and the Venns are invaluable.

Religious Affairs

For the history of local churches and the general spiritual life of the locality source materials are numerous and a well-arranged, clearly written survey of *The Records of the Established Church in England Excluding Parochial Records* by Dorothy M. Owen was the first of a new series of publications entitled 'Archives and the User' published by the British Records Association in 1970. Many churches are recorded in Domesday, while the taxation of 1291, published by the Record Commission as *Taxatio Ecclesiastica* in 1802 lists the churches existing at that date. The *Valor Ecclesiasticus* also published by the Record Commission in six volumes (London, 1810–34) is a Reformation survey of all ecclesiastical property. Professor Hoskins draws attention in *Local History in England* (already cited, pp. 48–9) to several sources in the public records, such as ministers' accounts and particulars of grants, covering the fate of monastic property after the Dissolution, when many church benefices changed hands.

Much information relative to churches and to their incumbents may be found in the bishops' registers and visitation books in the diocesan registry. This office will indeed contain many records which throw light on the churches and parish life throughout the diocese and, together with the parochial records

7

of each parish, if these have survived, they form the principal primary sources to be consulted. By far the most useful for this purpose are the churchwardens' accounts, although in later times the wardens had a variety of civil duties thrust upon them which tended to overshadow the care of the church fabric and fittings, the services and the general spiritual care of the parish which had been their chief function in pre-Reformation days.

The types of record to be found in diocesan record offices are dealt with exhaustively in *An Introduction to Ecclesiastical Records* by Canon J. S. Purvis (St Anthony's Press, London, 1953). They include the archbishops' registers, visitation records and records of ecclesiastical courts, and copious examples of the actual documents encountered are given. Calendars and transcripts of bishops' registers and similar episcopal records have been published by societies such as the Canterbury and York Society, the Cantilupe Society and the Alcuin Club.

As has already been mentioned, many counties have prepared lists of surviving parochial records, which invariably include extant churchwardens' accounts. A general list, although it is not complete, is provided by J. Blain's *A List of Churchwardens' Accounts* (Ann Arbor, Michigan, 1933) while John Charles Cox's book on these records in the 'Antiquaries' series is still useful. National inventories of church goods were made in 1552 and are in the Public Record Office, and several county and local lists have been issued by the Alcuin Club and by local societies.

The Nonconformist history of an area is usually more difficult to trace in detail since surviving records are fewer, more difficult of access and harder to trace. Several general sources are indicated in R. B. Pugh's *How To Write a Parish History* (Allen and Unwin, London, 1954, pp. 86–9) and Professor Hoskins' *Local History in England* (already cited, pp. 67–8) and need not be repeated here, while the British Records Association has issued a guide to *Archives of Religious and Ecclesiastical Bodies and Organisations other than the Church of England* (Reports from Committees, no. 3, London, 1936) which gives the location of the principal surviving records. Section 22 ('Archives of non-established churches') of Redstone and Steer's *Local Records* (already cited) gives lists of the types of archives which might be in the custody of local churches and composite collections which may contain material of local interest, and a useful article by W. R. Powell, 'The Sources for the History of Protestant Nonconformist Churches in England', has also appeared in the *Bulletin of the Institute of Historical Research* (vol. 25, no. 72, 1952, pp. 213–27). The publications of the various denominational historical societies should also be consulted.

Dr Williams's Library[6] in London contains many original records of Nonconformist history, especially of Presbyterianism, including the minutes and papers of many early dissenting congregations. Locally, the county records will usually throw much incidental light on early Nonconformity. Surviving Nonconformist registers have been printed for some counties, e.g. Shropshire, and many are available for consultation at the Public Record Office. Registers of several French Nonconformist churches in the British Isles have been printed by the Huguenot Society (Proceedings, 1887–1958, 46 vols.).

Before the founding of the Congregational Union in May 1832, many chapels were independent and local, and this very independence of the early dissenting congregations militated against the careful compilation and preservation of records. Not being required for submission to a central authority, as were those of the established church, they were rarely compiled, or if compiled seldom kept for very long. Those which have survived, chiefly consisting of trust deeds, minutes of church meetings, rolls of members and registers, often remain in the hands of the churches, although some are housed and preserved in the Congregational Library, established in 1831. There may also exist material relating to the dissenting academies which provided training for ministers, such as the Warrington Academy, mentioned above. Some of the modern Congregational theological colleges, especially Hackney College, London, N.W.3, are rich in manuscript material on these academies, whose successors they are.

Methodists were originally a group within the framework of the Church of England and their early records are inseparable from Anglican parochial records. They are included, for example, in parish registers, as Nonconformists seldom are, but several Methodist chapels did keep their own registers

6. See Kenneth Twinn. 'Sources for Church History. 2. Dr. Williams's Library.' *Local Historian*, vol. 9, no. 3, August 1970. pp. 115–20.

which, under the Non-parochial Registers Acts of 1840 and 1858 were deposited in Somerset House, but which will, by the Public Records Act, 1958, be transferred to the Public Record Office. Methodist churches are grouped into circuits under a superintendent minister who has charge of the archives of the churches and who inspects them annually. The Methodist Conference, the annual assembly of the church, has established an Archives Commission to preserve Methodist records and make them available to students, perhaps through local repositories.[7] Many of the administrative records are now kept at the Methodist Book Room, where there is an excellent reference library, while the archives of the Methodist Missionary Society are in the offices of that body.

Quaker records are generally better kept than those of other faiths. There is a large collection of records of the Society of Friends in their library at Friends House in London, including manuscripts of local interest and much biographical information concerning Quaker families. Records of monthly meetings have, however, been deposited in about thirty local record offices. Of sixty monthly meetings in England and Wales, excluding London, thirty-five have deposited some or all of their records. Most of the remainder are in the care of the local meetings. London monthly meeting records and a few others are at Friends House where a record is kept of the whereabouts of all the records of the Society. The records of Leicestershire meetings are in Leicester Museum; those of Worcester and Salop are in the Worcestershire County Record Office. Quaker registers are deposited at Somerset House, but copies of many have been retained by the Society. Many of the older records have been transcribed and printed in the *Journal of the Friends Historical Society*, which commenced in 1903. An excellent article dealing with the archives of the Society of Friends by R. S. Mortimer appeared in the *Amateur Historian*, vol. 3, no. 2, 1956–57, pp. 55–61, and a detailed catalogue of surviving Quaker records is kept at Friends House.

For details of other churches, the general works quoted above should be consulted, especially the British Records Association Report no. 3. This report also contains a section dealing with

7. See Frank Baker. 'Methodist Archives'. *Amateur Historian*, vol. 3, summer 1957. pp. 143–9.

the records of the Roman Catholic Church in England. R. B. Pugh's *How To Write a Parish History* (already cited) also has a useful section dealing with Roman Catholic records. The Catholic Record Society is the principal repository of secondary material on Roman Catholicism and its published volumes supply information on the national organisation and history of the Church, while locally the publications of branches of the Newman Association, formed to study Catholic history and particularly post-Reformation recusancy, are important. The Record Society series includes several Catholic registers. The Jewish Historical Society holds records of many Jewish congregations, but its published work is small and of no local significance.

Medicine

The medical history of most localities in Britain still awaits detailed study and very few hospitals and infirmaries have anything like complete series of their records. Where they do exist their minutes and other records are vital and some do go back three or four centuries. Their administrative archives are valuable material for social and economic, as well as medical historians.

Parish, vestry and diocesan records contain materials of interest to the medical historian. Gaol records are also valuable; parish registers, census returns and similar sources provide evidence for the study of epidemics and vital statistics, while newspaper files are essential for their history over the last two hundred years.

Modern hospital records in the custody of regional boards are now classed as public records under the Public Records Act of 1958, and the Minister of Health has issued a circular to assist the preservation of archives of actual or potential historical interest.

Science and Technology

Science and technology is a wide field and the library's local resources are not, as a rule, very extensive, although some of the larger collections such as the Boulton and Watt Collection in Birmingham are of national rather than of local value, and should be consulted by the historian of other areas. The *Transactions of the Newcomen Society* (1920 to date), *Business History*, first published in December 1958, and the publications of the Iron and Steel Institute and the Institution of Civil Engineers contain much valuable historical material. The *History of Science and Technology*, published in five volumes by the Clarendon Press, Oxford, 1954–58, provides factual data for most industrial developments, and is useful bibliographically as a guide to sources. For primary records the Business Archives Council should be consulted and also the subject index to archive collections maintained at the National Register of Archives. A survey of the papers of scientists and technologists is now being prepared (1972) by a joint committee of the Royal Society and the Historical Manuscripts Commission.

Many libraries probably possess records of some importance in these fields. Shrewsbury, in its not too substantial collection, has the records of the Coalbrookdale Company from 1709 which relate to the discovery by Abraham Darby of the process of smelting iron with coke, a discovery which, say the experts, did more than any other single invention to pave the way for the Industrial Revolution later in the eighteenth century. It also has the records of the Ironbridge Trust which erected the first iron bridge in the world and led to the tremendous development of the use of iron in architecture and other fields. There is also a series of letters from William Strutt, the inventor, to Charles Bage of Shrewsbury which relate to the use of iron beams in buildings, especially cotton mills. This correspondence led to the building of the Flax Mill (now the Maltings) in Shrewsbury in 1796, in which Bage was a partner, and this building, the first in the world to use iron beams as a structural element to ensure fire-proof construction, led directly to the modern multi-storied building and the American skyscraper.

It would obviously be impracticable to detail the respective sources for all major industries and commercial enterprises, for which original sources have been considered in a general way in the section on business records. Most industries have their general histories which give the student the necessary factual background, and which most libraries should try to purchase to start the beginner on his way. A useful list of such general

histories will be found in section ten of F. W. Kuhlicke and
F. G. Emmison's *English Local History Handlist* ('Helps for
Students of History', no. 69, Historical Association, London,
4th ed. 1969).

Social and Economic History

The sources available to the student of social and economic
history are detailed in the works by Professor Hoskins and
R. B. Pugh which have been previously cited. Local economic
studies include population growth and development, the
economic make-up of the population as illustrated in the
occupations of its inhabitants; the distribution of the wealth of
the community; taxation and currency; wages and prices of
commodities of all kinds. Social studies cover poor law administration, charities, care of sick and infirm, rural depopulation and its causes, agrarian organisation and land ownership
and many other aspects of communal life.

The borough records for towns and parochial records for
rural areas are the most fruitful documentary sources for the
economic and the social historian. The former will be interested
primarily in the accounts and fiscal records, in subsidy and
hearth tax rolls from the Public Record Office and in inventories attached to wills; the latter in the legal and poor-law
records, the records of quarter sessions, manorial rolls, churchwardens' accounts and the like.

Episcopal visitation records and those of ecclesiastical courts,
usually in the diocesan registry, throw much light on the social
life of olden days and, for the Industrial Revolution and later
periods, newspaper files, directories and sets of local government reports are useful.

The *Economic History Review* which commenced publication in
1927 under the joint editorship of E. Lipson and R. H. Tawney,
is the principal forum for the economic historian. Its articles are
usually written from the national and not the local viewpoint,
but they are authoritative and contain much factual basic
material of great value on prices, wages and kindred topics.

The economic and social history of the last two centuries is
bound up with the rise and progress of the trade union movement, but its records, largely inaccessible, have generally been

neglected by historians. The great work on trade union history is still that of Sidney and Beatrice Webb, entitled *Industrial Democracy* (Longmans, London, 1897). The large amount of material which they collected and upon which this study was based is available to students in the library of the London School of Economics. There are also the large collections of George Howell in the Bishopsgate Institution in London. An article by Sidney Pollard ('Sources of Trade Union History' in the *Amateur Historian*, vol. 4, no. 5, 1959, pp. 177–81) and Dr Hobsbawm's paper at the British Records Association Conference in 1959 ('Records of the Trade Union Movement' in *Archives*, vol. 4, no. 23, 1960, pp. 129–37) will guide the student to likely sources.

Agricultural History

The history of local agriculture and farming methods has not yet been adequately dealt with in many areas, but these aspects of local history are engaging a great deal of attention at present, due principally to the formation of the British Agricultural History Society in 1953. It will shortly receive further impetus from the publication of the *Agrarian History of England* which is now in the process of compilation.[8] The Museum of English Rural Life at Reading University contains materials on all aspects of country life and crafts, including drawings, photographs and farm accounts, manuscripts and diaries from the late eighteenth century onwards. On the cognate study of folklore the Central Register of Folklore Research is a card-index, classified under subjects and counties, which is held at the headquarters of the Folklore Society at University College, London. It is described by H. A. Lake Barnett in *Folklore*, vol. 70, March 1959.

The library should aim to provide not only the early printed sources such as the original reports made to the Board of Agriculture and Internal Improvement towards the close of the eighteenth century and the county histories, largely based on these, which were published in the early years of the nineteenth century, the 'tours' of Arthur Young and others (many of which

8. See H. P. R. Finberg. 'An Agrarian History of England'. *Agricultural History Review*, vol. 4, 1956. Vol. 4 of *Agrarian History of England*, edited by H. P. R. Finberg, was published by Cambridge University Press, 1967.

are embedded in the *Annals of Agriculture*), but also basic works such as H. L. Gray's *English Field Systems* (Harvard Press, 1915, but reprinted by photography by the Merlin Press, London, 1959) and C. S. Orwin's *The Open Fields* Oxford University Press, London, 3rd ed. 1967). The works of G. E. Fussell give valuable references to books dealing with the history of agriculture and reference should also be made to the Aslib Directory, volume 1: *Information Sources in Science Technology and Commerce* (Aslib, London, 1968), which lists those libraries, research and other organisations specialising in agriculture and allied interests. The resources of four important agricultural libraries in or near London are described in *Agricultural Libraries* (Library Resources in the Greater London Area, no. 5) prepared by the South-East Group of the Reference and Special Libraries Section of the Library Association.

The real history of farming and land utilisation in any area, however, will be traceable only by detailed study of original sources. Chief of these are the tithe maps and awards, enclosure acts and awards and the minutes of enclosure commissioners; early surveys, rentals and accounts of manorial and other estates; old ordnance survey maps, especially the first six-inch edition, *c.* 1850; the probate inventories of farmers and landowners and, to a lesser extent, the manorial records themselves. Lay subsidy rolls are useful for the descent of manors and distribution of wealth, while they also enable deserted villages and settlements to be traced, as Maurice Beresford has shown.[9] The subsidy rolls are in the Public Record Office, but many can also be found in borough archives, and they provide a directory of the principal landowners of the time. Census returns from 1801 onwards and agricultural returns from 1866 provide factual data, and while the files of the *Agricultural History Review* are an increasingly valuable source of general information, the earlier transactions of agricultural societies still have historical value.

Transport History

The history of the various forms of transport is another aspect

9. See 'The Lay Subsidies', two articles in the *Amateur Historian*, vol. 3, no. 8, pp. 325–8 and vol. 4, no. 3, pp. 101–6.

of local and regional studies which has resulted in the publication of two scholarly journals. The *Journal of Transport History* has been published by Leicester University Press since 1953 and was originally the only journal devoted to the history of transport as a whole. Much the same ground is now also covered by *Transport History* which has been published by David and Charles since 1968.

Turnpike roads, canals and railways are of comparatively recent growth and the records pertaining to them are being given increasing attention. An impressive *Bibliography of British Railway History*, compiled by G. Ottley and others, was published in 1965 by Allen and Unwin and a Railway and Canal Historical Society was formed in 1954 which publishes a journal.

Large quantities of records relating to railways and canals have been acquired by the historical records section of the British Transport Commission, and are now (1972) in the care of the British Railways Board, Historical Records Department, which has made great efforts to catalogue them and make them available to students.[10] In addition to its library and record office in London, it has opened branch offices in York and Edinburgh, but the Scottish records were transferred to the Keeper of Scottish Records following the passing of the 1968 Transport Act. A collection of material on transport history is also being built up at Leicester University.

Many transport and public works undertakings were promoted by means of private bills in the Houses of Parliament and the deposited plans and associated books of reference are amongst the parliamentary records.[11] The Acts and Bills, Blue Books and Minutes of Evidence before parliamentary enquiries record the initial stages of many undertakings.

Local sources in this field are not extensive, though occasionally papers relating to local turnpike roads and canals have found their way into libraries and record offices, while local Acts, deposited plans and books of reference relating to railways, canals and bridges can be found amongst the county records,

10. See L. C. Johnson. 'British Transport Historical Records Department: the First Decade'. *Archives*, vol. 6, no. 31, 1964. pp. 163–71.
11. See Maurice Bond. 'Records of Parliament: 2. Private Bill Records'. *Amateur Historian*, vol. 4, no. 7, 1960. pp. 267–74, and 'Material for Transport History amongst the Records of Parliament'. *Journal of Transport History*, vol. 4, no. 1, 1959. pp. 37–52.

and, with quarter sessions records and local newspaper files, will provide valuable evidence of the inception, making and maintenance of these undertakings. Baron F. Duckham has written two helpful articles on transport – 'Short Guide to Records. 18. Turnpike Records' (*History*, vol. 53, June, 1968, pp. 217–20) and also 'Transport and the Local Historian: Some Suggestions for Further Work' (*Amateur Historian*, vol. 7, 1966, pp. 84–7).

Family History and Genealogy

Sir Anthony R. Wagner expresses the belief that 'an interest in family origins is widespread and tending to increase among the peoples of British descent throughout the world, especially perhaps outside the mother country' and many librarians would echo his opinion that 'the volume of enquiry and the variety and geographical dispersion of those from whom it comes grow year by year'.[12] A large number of the enquiries made of library local collections concern these personal aspects of history and although such pursuits are in many instances little more than pastimes for an idle hour, genealogy, family history and heraldry must have their place in a representative collection. They are apt to be denigrated or ridiculed by the serious historian, yet many of their devotees are earnest and well-meaning seekers after knowledge, and something must be said of the subject here, if only because so many genealogical researchers have only the vaguest ideas, not only of the bibliographical basis of the study, but of how to set to work.

Americans, in particular, apart from the Mormon sect, to whom the tracing of their ancestors is a pious duty, take a great deal of interest in genealogy. There are in the United States many 'family' associations which exist for the purpose of promoting and sharing researches, many of which have too blithe an assumption of a common ancestry and little realisation that many 'trade' names, such as Hayward, Walker, and any name deriving from a personal name, can have their origins in widely separated parts of the country. Modern historians are scornful of the activities of the nineteenth-century nobility-conscious

12. Sir Anthony R. Wagner. *English Genealogy*. Oxford University Press, London, 1960. p. 1.

genealogists, yet the more painstaking of them produced masses of well-documented material, which saves the modern student much time and labour, though not necessarily verification of sources. The science of genealogical technique and enquiry has in the present century been placed on a sound footing largely under the aegis of the College of Arms and the Society of Genealogists.

As far as bibliography is concerned, Manchester City Library's catalogue of *Genealogy and Family History* published in three unbound parts, is so comprehensive as to form a general bibliography of the subject. Part 1 deals with pedigrees and family history (and includes manuscript material on these subjects); Part 2 covers parish registers and wills; and Part 3 personal and place-names, heraldry and associated topics. Sir Anthony R. Wagner's book, referred to above, provides a comprehensive picture of genealogy in relation to English history and discusses fully the many primary and secondary sources for its study. Sir Anthony R. Wagner also writes a foreword in Marion J. Kaminkow's *A New Bibliography of British Genealogy with Notes* (already cited) and the same author has also written a descriptive guide to *Genealogical Manuscripts in British Libraries* (already cited). Genealogical research is also dealt with in Derek Harland's *A Basic Course in Genealogy*, 2 vols., 1958 and D. E. Gardner and F. Smith's *Genealogical Research in England and Wales*, 2 vols., 1956, both published by Bookcraft Inc., Salt Lake City, which cover in an extremely detailed manner the chief genealogical sources in England and Wales. Works such as these are helping to place the science of genealogy and the construction of pedigrees on a scientific footing, and are removing some of the stigma which became attached to it as a result of the unscientific work often done in the nineteenth century. This was acquired by the enthusiastic, but frequently inaccurate, pedigrees drawn up by family historians and antiquarians who lacked both a critical sense and training and experience in documentary research. They were also inclined to quote manuscript sources, such as the Egerton and Harleian manuscripts in the British Museum, without assessing their accuracy and thus often perpetuated errors.

Some of the most valuable sources for starting genealogical research are national, such as the General Registers of Births,

Deaths and Marriages at Somerset House, and the census returns at the Public Record Office. The general register includes these vital statistics from 1 July 1837, prior to which date they remain at the churches or in local record offices, with the exception of certain Nonconformist registers. The procedure for using the Register and its indexes is fully described in an article by Lawrence Maidbury ('The General Register of Births, Deaths and Marriages', *Amateur Historian*, vol. 3, no. 3, Spring 1951, pp. 108–12). A following article (ibid., pp. 112–14) by Kenneth D. Baird describes the procedure for Scottish registers at H. M. Register House in Edinburgh.

The registers of dissenting congregations deposited at the Public Record Office are indicated in *Lists of Non-parochial Registers*, published by HMSO in 1841. The value of registers before 1837 has been mentioned earlier. They are vitally important for other purposes besides family history, and the librarian should know the location of any transcripts of local registers, as well as of the originals which are included in the surveys of parish records made for many areas. The Society of Genealogists has published two lists of parish register transcripts, the *Catalogue of the Parish Registers in the Possession of the Society of Genealogists* (rev. ed., 1963) and the *National Index of Parish Register Copies* (to be published in 12 vols.: vol. 1, 1968; vol. 5, 1966; vol. 12, 1970 already published). Older works still of value are A. M. Burke's *Key to the Ancient Parish Registers of England and Wales* (London, 1908), an alphabetical list with the date of the commencement of the register and the *Parish Register Abstract, 1831* (HMSO, London, 1833), which was compiled from the replies to a government enquiry sent to each incumbent in 1831. This lists the dates covered by 10,984 ancient parishes. Where parish registers are not available information may still be found in the bishops' transcripts, usually in the diocesan registry office or the county record office. These transcripts are specially useful for the Commonwealth period when the parochial registers were often neglected. The bonds and allegations made in connection with marriages by licence, which are usually amongst the diocesan records, are particularly useful for genealogical purposes. *Boyd's Marriage Index*, which covers marriages in most of the registers which have been printed or transcribed and which was the life-work of the late Percival

Boyd,[13] can be consulted at the Society of Genealogists in London, which also has a wide collection of printed and transcribed registers. Other collections are in the British Museum and in the College of Arms.

The census returns for 1841, 1851, 1861 and 1871 are available for consultation in the search room of the Public Record Office in Chancery Lane, London. The later censuses are in the custody of the Registrar General at Somerset House and are not yet open to public inspection. From the genealogist's point of view the 1851 return is the most valuable, since it adds the relationship of each person to the head of the family, gives the condition (i.e. married, unmarried, widow, etc.), occupations and ages of each occupant, and for those born in England and Wales the county and parish of birth are given. The census provides a useful starting point for most genealogical enquiries and with the added assistance of parish registers a skeleton of most families can be compiled. This can be supplemented from wills, administrations and other probate records, poor law records, local directories, poll books, school registers, etc. The British Record Society has published many indexes to wills in the various probate registries, while B. C. Bouwens' *Wills and their Whereabouts*, has been revised by Anthony J. Camp and published for the Society of Genealogists, 1963, and is a valuable guide to the location of wills from the various ancient courts of probate.

For earlier periods, in which for practical purposes genealogical study is almost confined to the landed classes, inquisitions post mortem, plea rolls and other public records, medieval cartularies and deeds, gild rolls, subsidies and tax assessments, burgess and apprenticeship rolls, etc. are all useful as are the printed and manuscript visitations. Professor W. G. Hoskins, assisted by the staff of the City Library, has transcribed five seventeenth-century assessment lists for the City of Exeter in *Exeter in the Seventeenth Century: Tax and Rate Assessments, 1602–1699* (Devon and Cornwall Record Society, new series, vol. 2, 1957). This gives a clear indication of the value and scope of this type of record, many of which are duplicated at the Public Record Office. Manorial records are also helpful as early

---

13. The Marriage Index has been microfilmed. Boyd also compiled an index of apprenticeships (1710–1774), a copy of which is at the Society of Genealogists.

genealogy is closely linked with the system of land tenures. They are, as Walter Rye indicated in his *Records and Record Searching* (London, 1888), the only means of tracing non-armigerous families before the parish registers. Fairly accurate genealogies of the aristocratic and land-owning families may be found in the various peerages and the standard works of Burke, Lodge, Debrett and others, and there are several indexes to published family histories and pedigrees, ranging from the early works of Richard Sims, Charles Bridger and James Coleman to T. R. Thomson's *A Catalogue of British Family Histories* (Oxford University Press, London, 2nd ed. 1935), G. W. Marshall's *The Genealogist's Guide* (1903, reprinted Genealogical Publishing Co., New York, 1967) and *A Genealogical Guide* by J. B. Whitmore (published in four parts by the Harleian Society, 1947–53). For Scotland, Miss Joan P. S. Ferguson of the Scottish Central Library, has compiled a list of *Scottish Family Histories Held in Scottish Libraries* (Scottish Central Library, Edinburgh, 1960) which gives locations.

Sources for biographical data are so ubiquitous as to defy analysis. Family papers and letters, if they are available, are the best and obvious source, and the files of local newspapers, periodicals such as the *Gentleman's Magazine*, the *Annual Register*, the *London Gazette* and *Notes and Queries* provide much local biographical information. Sir William Musgrave's *Obituaries*, published in six volumes by the Harleian Society are useful for people who died prior to 1800 and the nineteenth-century biographical dictionaries occasionally supplement the *Dictionary of National Biography*. *British Diaries* compiled by W. Matthews (Cambridge University Press, London, 1950) is an annotated bibliography of printed and manuscript diaries written between 1442 and 1942, giving locations for those in manuscript form. The same author's *British Autobiographies* (University of California Press, Berkeley, 1955) records 6,654 entries relating to persons born in the British Isles. The Personal Index to the National Register of Archives contains references to biographical material in hundreds of collections throughout the country, but it is limited to people who appear in the *Dictionary of National Biography* or the Complete Peerage. Reference should also be made to the Standing Conference of National and University libraries (SCONUL) index at London University library which covers primarily manuscript material relating to literary figures, and to the Library Association's Biographical Register Index which has now been incorporated in the indexes to the National Register of Archives and this was published in 1971 by the Library Association as a research project: *Select Biographical Sources: the Library Association Manuscripts Survey*, edited by Philip Hepworth.

Local sources are rarely of great importance for biographies of military and naval personnel, since the persons concerned spent much of their time away from home and even overseas. Local regimental and volunteer records are, of course, vital where they exist. Admiralty and War Office records are not normally available until they are a hundred years old, when they are transferred to the Public Record Office. The muster rolls for the eighteenth and nineteenth centuries are particularly helpful, and regimental registers, available at Somerset House, record births, marriages and deaths of service personnel from 1790 to 1924. A brief guide to the sources suitable for studying the lives and careers of members of the former Indian Army will be found in the *Amateur Historian*, vol. 1, 1953, pp. 117–22. Nearly a hundred volumes of naval records of various kinds have been published by the Navy Records Society. A naval history library was opened in the Plymouth Central Library in 1962 in a room adjacent to the Plymouth local history library and this new library houses a large collection of naval material.

For politicians there are a number of specialist sources such as the State Papers, the Journals of the Houses of Commons and Lords. Of the State Papers, the calendars of patent rolls, State Letters and Papers, State Papers Domestic, the feet of fines, inquisitions post mortem and the Acts of the Privy Council are all likely to throw light upon figures prominent in political or parliamentary life. If the person served in the foreign diplomatic service the various calendars of Foreign Papers should be consulted.

Much material relating to political personalities may be found amongst the records of the great landed families. We may instance the Newcastle mss. from Clumber in the Dukeries, now in the Nottingham University Library, which includes a mass of political correspondence, and the Wentworth Woodhouse Collection at the Sheffield City Library, which includes 3,000 letters of Edmund Burke, as well as the papers of the 2nd Marquess of Rockingham, the Whig Prime Minister. The reports of the Deputy Keeper of the Records and some of the Historical Manuscripts Commission reports, such as the Hatfield and Cecil MSS. should be examined, while the *Transactions of the Royal Historical Society* and the publications of the Camden Society also contain much useful information.

Clergymen usually had the benefit of a university education so that the works of Foster, Emden and the Venns are a useful starting-point, while many of the older clerics are included in Fuller's *Worthies of England* (London, 1662), Foster's *Index Ecclesiasticus* (Oxford, 1890) and other general biographical dictionaries, including Crockford's *Clerical Directory* which commenced publication in 1858.

References to the consecration and ordination of early clerics are to be found in the bishops' registers, which in several dioceses commence in the thirteenth century. Many volumes of these registers have been published by the Canterbury and York Society and the Cantilupe Society. Many classes of episcopal archives naturally assist this study and certain national records such as the certificates of institutions to benefices and the list of institutions at the Public Record Office offer material dealing with the local clergy and ecclesiastical affairs.

Chapter 12

Problems of Organisation and Administration

The physical boundaries of the area to be covered by any local history collection have to be considered initially and they may have to be varied at a later stage for a number of reasons. A major cause of subsequent change arises when local government reorganisation occurs in the area covered. Such changes have taken place in recent years in the county of Shropshire, in the boroughs of the Greater London Council, in the Midlands and elsewhere. Less occasionally, the creation of new libraries, such as university or college libraries in any locality, may also cause fresh thought to be given to the coverage of an established collection. Finally, a change in the pattern of usage has brought about a need in some libraries to intensify the 'depth' of the contents of the local history collection by decreasing the extent of the area covered.

Considerable thought will have to be given to the problems arising from the physical boundaries covered by local history collections in many localities as further local government reorganisation takes place as a result of the 1972 Local Government Act and various other proposals at present under consideration.

Just as the recent local government changes have reduced the number of controlling authorities, so will the proposed changes cause further reductions. The problem of the areas covered by many more local history collections, therefore, may become much less a matter for the independent judgement of a large number of separately controlled libraries, all making individual decisions on what to acquire, and become a matter for a smaller number of large authorities who will have to decide where to house to the best advantage the collections of material in the areas they control.

No doubt there are advantages to be obtained from the centralisation or regionalisation of the materials of local history collections, perhaps because economies may be effected, and possibly because such centralisation could result in a more efficient administrative machine. It should be emphasised, therefore, that in any proposals to change the disposition of local history material, the first consideration should be the advantage and convenience of the users of the material.

It is abundantly clear that, because all the existing library authorities of the country did not come into being at the same time, and because their respective local history collections were not initiated simultaneously, that there exists in many areas a duplication of coverage and use of resources that may appear to some to be unnecessary. When two or three adjacent or neighbouring library authorities compete for the same scarce material the problem is highlighted, and the objectives of each competing authority are likely to be called into question. Often, however, a matter that is overlooked on such occasions is that although a duplication of effort and resources may exist, there may also be sufficient demand to justify both the duplication of effort and the competition.

It must be admitted, however, that as the number of library authorities – municipal, county and university – has increased during the past century in particular, the coverage by separate authorities in some areas has not always been a question of duplicating of demand. There have been some continuations of established practices that might have been reviewed in the light of the services developed by new authorities, and also some services have been brought into being by new authorities without a full appraisal being made of existing services.

A reduction in the number of controlling local government authorities is going to provide no simple solution to these problems. It has already been emphasised throughout this book that local history studies are essentially concerned with local areas – they are, in fact, basically parochial. Obviously every parish cannot hope to have an adequate collection of local material on the spot, but any fresh consideration of the disposition of local history material must ensure that the strongest collections are maintained in the most convenient centres of population and are not simply centralised or regionalised for the sake of administrative convenience, or as a sacrifice to appeals for economy.

Because a rapid increase in interest in local studies has been accompanied by a more intense approach to them, often described as a greater approach 'in depth', some reappraisal of the area covered by a few local history collections had already occurred before any question arose of local government reorganisation. Current user demands require the strongest possible collections in each locality dealing with all aspects of the locality in depth. This need has prompted a number of authorities to cover a smaller area with their collections than was originally envisaged in order to strengthen and intensify the depth of the material available for the benefit of users.

Towns and cities which, in addition to collecting material relating to the town and its immediate environs, had also collected material for a wide county area, have in some cases decided to restrict their efforts to their own boundaries. Gateshead, for example, states that 'prior to 1961 this library was the officially recognised repository for records relating to Northern Durham. Since the opening of the Durham County Record Office, we have restricted ourselves to the area of the County Borough only.' Birkenhead reports that it now places less emphasis on Cheshire material and more on Wirral and Merseyside. Perhaps the most significant reappraisal of an area covered, because of a need to acquire a greater 'in depth' coverage of more local material, has taken place in Belfast where the collection began as an Irish collection, and where for many years an attempt was made to collect material on the whole of Ireland. The Librarian now reports that 'Consequent upon a recent Organisation and Methods Study of our service we are in the process of reorganising the collection as a true Local History Library which in our case means all material relating to Northern Ireland and in particular the City of Belfast.'

Many librarians consider the appropriate locality of their collection to be the catchment area of their town from the viewpoint of shopping and other services, and many urban local history collections seem to be based on a radius of between five and twelve miles surrounding the individual town. The area served is more often likely to coincide with the area served by the local newspaper, or perhaps the local postal district, rather than an area prescribed by a local government boundary. Local government boundaries generally are modern and bear little relationship to older parish boundaries on which so much local history is based. Overlapping of areas served by different local history collections, therefore, certainly exists and it would seem that it should continue if the convenience of users is to be fully considered.

It is also clear that no hard and fast rule can be adopted for all the wide variety of local authorities at present in existence, or likely to be created as a result of future reorganisation. Conditions vary tremendously between the new local authorities of the metropolis and the more rural types of counties; between the proposed metropolitan districts and the proposed county councils; and between an industrial type of county, liberally sprinkled with populous county boroughs, boroughs and urban areas, and an agricultural county with perhaps only one dominating city or town at the centre. Any attempt, therefore, to propound a universal solution to the problem of providing the best local history service for every area of the country is most unlikely to meet with universal acceptance – or success.

Without a really intimate working knowledge of all the circumstances appertaining at the time that various authorities in widely different parts of the country were amalgamated as a result of recent local government changes, it is not possible to be sure whether all the actions that were taken concerning the disposition of local history material were good. Two or three or more local authorities which are to amalgamate are unlikely to have the same standards of service. The amalgamation should, therefore, result in attempts to improve the level in all parts of the new authority. Such attempts could be frustrated by the need for new or additional buildings, shortage of suitable staff, or by lack of suitable material. Compromise would then become inevitable and could result in the production of a better service in one part of the new authority, perhaps at the cost of some convenience to users in terms of distances to be travelled or in other ways. This means, of course, that geographic compactness of an area, transport facilities, the physical condition of existing buildings, and the availability of staff have all to be considered in reaching decisions concerning the location and development of collections of specialised material.

That consideration of all these matters took place following the reorganisation of library services in the new London boroughs is clear, and it is also evident that many different solutions were found as a result of the varying circumstances appertaining at the time of change. Some of the new London boroughs indeed state quite clearly that the original solution to their problems is not likely to be the permanent answer as they would like to organise things differently as soon as new buildings become available, or when staff are able to reorganise collections effectively.

From returns submitted in 1970 by twenty-four of the new London boroughs, it appears that two-thirds decided to leave collections of local history material where they were before amalgamation took place, although one or two state that changes may occur in the future as new buildings are erected. Movement of local history material in the remaining third has not always been in the nature of a complete centralisation of resources. Some have moved parts of a collection, or perhaps joined two collections out of three according to the availability of suitable premises or staff, or after consideration of the geography of the area.

Perhaps the two extreme courses of action likely to occur following amalgamation, namely the almost complete centralisation of resources on the one hand, or the decision to leave collections in their former locations on the other, are exemplified in the cases of the new London boroughs of Bexley and Hounslow respectively. Bexley states that the various parts of the local history collection have been 'mainly brought together in the Reference Library' which means that 'people must travel more, but find more supporting material in one place'; whilst Hounslow reports that the various parts of the collection are 'still housed separately because of the shape of the borough and the lack of public transport', so that the reorganisation has not affected users. Tower Hamlets has also decided to move collections to the local history library in the central library and claims that this reorganisation has had very little (presumably adverse) effect on users. Bromley, on the other hand, states that substantial local collections are held at the main branches – Orpington, Beckenham and Penge – with nucleus collections at smaller branches covering their immediate areas. Thus whilst the various collections of this new London borough still remain largely in their original homes, the central collection is being expanded to cover the whole area by duplication (or transferring second copies) where possible so that eventually the very rare books and in general all manuscript material should be at the central library. As in other London boroughs, the amalgamation at Bromley resulted in the acquisition of municipal archives from the former authorities and the result, it is stated, is that 'Gradually more readers are using the Central Library. It is anticipated that this tendency will be more marked when the new Central Library is completed.'

Partial centralisation of resources seems to have taken place at Richmond upon Thames where it is stated that 'The Local Collection for Richmond upon Thames is divided into two. The material on the former Borough of Twickenham remains at the Twickenham Library. Material on the former Boroughs of Richmond and Barnes has been brought together in one collection at the Central Reference Library, Richmond.' The result of this is that 'Material on Barnes and Mortlake is now housed outside the area to which it refers. Although this necessitates local residents having further to travel, the enlarged collection, by the amalgamation of the two collections, has improved the service.'

Rather more complex, however, has been the reorganisation in the City of Westminster comprising the library systems of Westminster, Paddington and St Marylebone, which all maintained local history libraries prior to 1965, and have since been amalgamated. The first effect of amalgamation was that the City Librarian was given responsibility for all the City Council's archives up to the period of amalgamation, whereas responsibility for the historic records in the former boroughs of St Marylebone and Paddington had not previously been deputed to the former librarians who had responsibility for the donated and deposited records only. Nevertheless library staff in these two former boroughs had access to the Council's historical records for purposes of research; and a catalogue of the records had been produced in Paddington and a microfilm project covering the local rate books had been introduced in St Marylebone. The Paddington archives were moved to St Marylebone after amalgamation into improved strongrooms in what had been the Marylebone Town Hall, and thus the records of these two boroughs were brought together under one roof. The archives of the present City of Westminster, therefore, that are under the control of the City Librarian are maintained in three repositories: at the former Marylebone Town Hall (now Westminster Council House); at Buckingham Palace Road where the senior archivist and her staff operate; and at Cavell House, Charing Cross Road (the former Westminster City Hall). The former Paddington local history library was also moved to join forces with the Marylebone local history collection and in 1969 the whole of the Reference Library at Marylebone was re-structured[1] and the opportunity taken to provide better accommodation and greater space for the local history library which contains books on London and collections on Paddington and St Marylebone. There are thus now two local history libraries in the City of Westminster, one at the Buckingham Palace Road library and a smaller library at the Marylebone Road library. More staff devoted exclusively to local history are now employed than formerly, the total local history library staff now amounting to 3 professional librarians, 3 archivists, 3 library assistants and 1 archives' repairer.

It is stated that in consequence of these changes the transfer of the Paddington archives has given them greater accessibility and that the use of local history material in the city is ever on the increase as is the number of enquiries handled by the staff.

Changes in the disposition of local history material in Shropshire County following recent local government changes have been described in Chapter 10 and so it is not necessary to repeat them. It is evident that the changes already described that have occurred as a result of recent local government changes in London and Shropshire illustrate the point that there can be no one simple solution, capable of universal application, to any further changes in the local government structure of the country. Each new area must give careful

1. R. F. Vollans. 'Westminster's Modernised District Reference Library'. *Library World*, vol. 71, March 1970. pp. 275–8.

consideration to its needs and resources regarding as the first priority the essentially local nature of local history services and their users. Then providing that changes are not made simply for administrative convenience or, because a change in control may seem to demand some drastic alteration to justify the new administration, it would seem that some readjustments could be made in many areas that would result in improvements beneficial to the community of users.

Another administrative decision which should be decided before the collection takes shape concerns the degree of independence to be allowed to the local librarian. The degree of autonomy permitted in specialised subject departments within the large library systems varies according to the size and resources of the authority, but no librarian in charge of such a department can be expected to create the highest standard of service if his freedom of action is too severely restricted. The general encouragement given to branch and area librarians in Bedfordshire concerning local history collections should perhaps be considered as appropriate to any librarian responsible for a collection of local history material if engaged for that purpose on a whole time basis. Bedfordshire states that 'Area and Branch librarians are urged to participate in local history society activities, to search for, buy and acquire material for their collections, to contribute to local guides and to get to know those working individually in local history studies.' We have already stated, in Chapter 6 that qualified archivists working in libraries should have a great deal of freedom to treat their material according to their own concepts and training, and should be independent, as far as possible, of normal library duties. While matters of policy and negotiations for deposit of material must obviously be dealt with by the chief librarian, the archivist may be encouraged to initiate action, and to take a full part in all extramural activities. Where librarians and archivists work in concert in local history departments, there must be mutual understanding of one another's problems and the chief librarian must often employ delicacy and tact in resolving the problems and jealousies which may occasionally arise. If they prove intractable or happen with recurring monotony then there is clearly something wrong with the administrative set-up and this should be re-examined. The official policy of the

Library Association states that 'where special departments may appropriately be staffed either by archivists or by librarians their chances of advancement within the department should be equal.'

The content of the collection can be a difficult matter in large libraries with a number of subject departments, for whilst everything local is usually placed in the local history collections of the small and medium-sized libraries, the largest systems find that perhaps local music is claimed by the music library, local authors by a literature and arts department, and so on. Decisions about the location of local items in a large system, therefore, can be complicated by the claims of other subject departments, and also because the name of 'local history library' tends to cause a somewhat restricted view to be taken of the scope and purpose of the local collection.

Although the terms 'local history studies' and 'local history collections' have been used throughout this book these terms clearly apply to collections of material and the associated studies that are nowadays gradually becoming known by what is perhaps the more appropriate term of 'environmental studies'. Under the heading of environmental studies, therefore, the widest concept of local history studies is embraced and a subject department devoted to such studies in the largest library systems could contain all the local material available both for lending as well as reference. Bradford's local history library is situated within the social sciences library and the disposition of material in the Bradford Central Library is described by Michael A. Overington in his book *The Subject Departmentalized Public Library* (Library Association, London, 1969). In libraries that do not operate complete subject departmentalisation, as many of the books in the local history library as possible should be duplicated and made available in the lending library.

Much local history material consists of books and pamphlets that are unique and clearly a considerable responsibility rests with librarians having charge of these collections to ensure that such unique material is preserved as far as possible from the ravages of the wear and tear of heavy use, as well as other risks often associated with unrestricted lending. Unique single copies should always be for reference only and fortunately modern copying techniques have made this a much easier decision to apply. It is also necessary to duplicate material for lending wherever possible, either when local books are first published or by the acquisition of second-hand copies as they become available. Whilst those engaged in research are expected to visit the library in order to use collections of research material, and they in turn expect to find all the material available when they come, it must also be recognised that to visit a library is not always convenient and that the duplication of material wherever possible can often assist those who may be unable to spend more than a very limited time in the library.

Standard works, such as Victoria County Histories *can* be duplicated and made available for lending as well as reference and so can many of the volumes of record societies. Newly published local histories often appear in small editions only and quickly go out of print. In buying sufficient working copies for all departments and branches upon publication, therefore, the needs of the future should also be borne in mind and a sufficient number of reserve copies should be purchased for future replacement purposes.

Works that are out of print and unduplicated are occasionally lent on condition that they are consulted in another library conveniently situated to the home of the user, but unhappy experiences of damage to books in the post and whilst on loan in this manner create a nice exercise in probabilities for the librarian asked to lend rare material. Manuscript and archival material will only be loaned in the most unusual circumstances. 'Archives may be lent only under conditions that will preserve them physically and preserve their record character.'[2] Archives depend for a great deal of their value and authenticity upon continuous public or official ownership and we are not justified in risking the loss of this unique archival quality. The only exceptions which may be made are when the material can be safely deposited temporarily in another library or archive centre, in which case official custody is deemed to be un- broken, or when records have to leave the library to enable them to be photocopied, when adequate steps for their safety should be assured. They may also occasionally be returned for reference or official purposes to the agency which produced

2. T. R. Schellenberg. *Modern Archives: Principles and Techniques*. F. W. Cheshire, Melbourne, 1956. p. 233.

them. In the same category comes the temporary loan of items for exhibitions and lectures, or their production in courts of law. They should always be lent *only* to institutions, never to private individuals.

The loan of archive material even between repositories is not generally encouraged, but there seems to be no good reason why occasional loans should not be made under due safeguards. This might be particularly useful between repositories in the same area, where the convenience of readers might be served, for example, by the temporary transfer of a series of documents from the borough records or from an estate or solicitor's office, to the library, where the student could use them in greater comfort and for longer periods. In cases where important local manuscripts are located in county record offices it may be possible to arrange for temporary deposit in the library for the convenience of particular students. The Essex Record Office, enlightened in so many respects, frequently loans material to libraries in the county for the use of local students, and Southend has recognised the record office's helpful attitude in lending to the extent that the Corporation now pays £1,500 a year to assist its work with the ultimate intention that the Southend archive repository will become the Southend branch of the Essex Record Office.

Open access to the printed material should, as a rule, be permitted, not perhaps as a matter of right for the beginner but certainly as a privilege for the person who knows how to use books. Unfettered examination of the shelves is a genuine boon to the scholar and even to the keen student and it should not be withheld without good reason. They may indeed be trusted to browse at leisure amongst the shelves. This is not, of course, possible in the muniment rooms but here too the trained worker may be allowed to look through series of records with a minimum of supervision. It is obviously impracticable to expect him to detail each item he wishes to consult on an application form and the necessity to skim through a whole archive group in a search for possibly relevant items arises not infrequently in a serious piece of research.

The recording of issues has become almost a fetish in the library profession and the local history department is not exempt from this general tendency in spite of the fact that, in this section of the library more than any other, an 'issue' is an intangible and indefinable thing, due firstly to the great disparity in the material in the collection, which ranges from newscuttings to archive series, and secondly to the wide variation in the purposes for which it is used. Since standardisation in collecting, tabulating, presenting and evaluating statistics has not yet been achieved in the comparatively simple and serene atmosphere of the lending library, it is scarcely to be hoped that uniformity can be introduced into the collection of local statistics. Nonetheless 'issues' are zealously recorded, each being a separate item whether it be the largest local history or the flimsiest pamphlet, a manuscript cartulary or a single letter. Indeed, often photographs, drawings and maps will all feature as single issues and are not differentiated in any way.

Many record offices have a more practical approach to this question which libraries might well emulate. Fortunate in being untrammelled by the need to justify their existence and funds for their support by producing high issue figures to impress their committees, a process which has bedevilled public libraries throughout their history, they merely record the number of visitors as a suitable guide to the use of the material. These are usually totalled from the visitors book or the issue slips which students are required to sign on each occasion. In libraries, however, the tradition of counting and recording issues dies hard and so long as local authorities expect numerical evidence of the popularity of their services, issues will continue to be recorded, more or less religiously. If kept, local statistics should be based on clear definitions and should, if possible, be related to the value of the material used. To equate a fleeting reference to the local directory with prolonged study of a medieval cartulary or of an archive group is patently absurd. Common sense dictates that there should be a distinction between the use of printed and of manuscript material, even where these are produced at the same desk or counter, and consultations of visual material might well form a third category.

If these points are borne in mind it is immaterial whether the collection of statistics is based upon the material used, the nature of the query or the persons using it. A mere record of queries or visitors does not necessarily give *more* information unless these are analysed, i.e. as quick-reference queries, local history queries, study of original source material, loans for home reading and inter-library loans. Issues are useful as being indicative of general trends in the use of material, and libraries with expanding collections have noted in the post-war years a tendency towards original research and the greater use of documentary sources as well as a substantial increase in the use of local history material generally.

The procedure for dealing with donations should be standard and simple. Elaborate forms are not necessary, and the ornate, lavishly worded and eulogistic circulars formerly sent out in response to gifts by many libraries have given way to the more personal and sincere informal letter. A suitable official form of acknowledgement can be used, and this should mention the special collections maintained by the library, including the local collection, and thus serve as useful publicity. My own practice is to send a short personal letter immediately on receipt of the material and, unless it is of very slight importance, to follow with the official letter of thanks when the gift has been reported to the library committee or, perhaps, to the council.

All donations should be entered in the donations book, with the fullest details. These are usually reported to the committee *in toto*, but sometimes the librarian makes a selection for this purpose. Important gifts should be brought to the notice of the council and appear in its printed agenda, a method which attracts publicity. Most donors are not unmindful of, and usually welcome, dignified publicity while, from the librarian's point of view it is invariably a good thing *pour encourager les autres*. There are occasions, however, when publicity may not be desired and the librarian has to use tact and a fine judgement in this matter.

When several items have been presented at the same time, and particularly in the case of a collection of documents, a brief schedule should be prepared and a copy should accompany acknowledgement of the gift to the donor, and a duplicate should be entered in the donations book. This is even more important with deposited material, where a receipt has been given for the loan. In some cases a more detailed calendar of the records will have been promised and this will be attended to as soon as possible. Where some delay in supplying this seems likely, either from pressure of work or other causes, this should be explained at the time.

Libraries with archive collections will have to be prepared to accept collections on deposit or 'permanent loan'. For larger collections this is often the usual method of acquisition today and such collections, once deposited, are rarely moved. The details of the transaction may vary considerably in different depositories or with different collections. Some record offices have drawn up a standard agreement, authorised by the clerk of the council or town clerk, which is entered into with the owner. Some find more virtue in an informal agreement, rather than a formal one setting out the precise extent to which the records may be available to students and other points, feeling that these matters are better left to the discretion of the librarian or archivist. The library authority should at least give the undertaking to keep the records in safe custody, accept the owner's right to inspection or the recall of particular items, and should secure the right to make records available for public inspection. It must be remembered that deposited collections do restrict the library's rights in several ways, and the attention of students must be drawn to these in appropriate cases, especially where the possibility of publication arises. The owner would have the right to know and even to place a veto on unauthorised publication of his records.

Regulations for use of material

The presence of valuable and even unique material makes it imperative to have regulations which must be observed by readers. The library whose local collection is confined to the possession of printed materials may find the rules for its general reference library adequate, but manuscript material should be subject to special safeguards.

We have previously stated that, ideally, documentary material should not be consulted in the reference library, where it is difficult to achieve the desired standard of supervision. If, in a small library, this has to be done, a table near to the reference librarian's desk should be set aside for the use of records, which should be taken away as soon as they are finished with. Where there is a local history or manuscripts room they should be consulted in this, provided that the necessary continuous supervision is available. In a small archive repository a reader's desk may be provided in the archivist's work-room.

Most archive repositories require the visitor to sign an admission register or visitors book, stating briefly, in addition to personal details, the purpose of his research and the collection he wishes to consult, and this is an idea which could be adopted with advantage in the local room. Alternatively, the reader is required to complete an application form on each and every visit, which is signed by the assistant who receives the material after use. The reverse of the form should contain the rules for the consultation and handling of documents, or extracts from these.

Deliberate theft or damage to records is much less to be feared than unthinking neglect or damage due to carelessness or unskilled handling. Archives in particular, being unique and irreplaceable, must be produced only under safeguards which will avoid any possibility of loss or damage. Printed books and visual material attract the thief far more than documentary material, although there is always the occasional unscrupulous collector. An overcrowded table or desk is one of the chief sources of danger to records and readers should not be allowed to have too many documents in use at a time, though hard and fast rules are difficult to enforce on this point. Some students working with manuscripts appear to think it impressive to be surrounded by a large number of manuscripts, but this should be discouraged and it should be insisted that material used should be handed in before a fresh collection is produced. Some repositories limit the number of independent records which the reader can have at one time, three being regarded as a suitable number, but this rule should be waived at the archivist's discretion.

Copious stamping of records, while unsightly, is a deterrent to theft, and careful and clear numbering also helps to minimise misplacement and to simplify the restoration of the misplaced document to its proper place. Adequate oversight, careful checking and the observance of regulations are usually effective in preventing theft, or at least in limiting the opportunities for it.

The librarian must reserve the right to withhold from use documents or books in a frail or damaged condition. Where possible a photocopy should be made for public use. Similarly where donors or depositors of material have imposed regulations or restrictions on its use, these must be scrupulously observed.

We have mentioned that some archive repositories seek to limit the use of documents to 'accredited' students which means that the would-be researcher must produce an introduction from his tutor or other responsible authority. A more acceptable alternative is for the repository to reserve the right to ask for independent evidence of the applicant's capacity to work on documentary materials. It is also usual to request that, wherever practicable, notice in writing should be given to the librarian or archivist of the intention to consult archive material, stating the object of the enquiry or search. This need not be insisted upon, but it is a courtesy appreciated by the staff, and will also save the reader's time since the documents can be looked out in advance.

Smoking is invariably prohibited and tracing or photographing records should require specific permission from the archivist. The use of pens should also be at the archivist's discretion.

Sheffield has no special regulations for students wishing to consult manuscripts and archives (apart from the general regulations of the library) but it requires the completion of a special form of application before allowing access to certain of the major deposit collections. This is to meet the individual requirements which are often laid down by the depositors and is conditioned by the legal agreement signed between the owner and the Corporation. In the case of the Arundel Castle manuscripts lent by the Duke of Norfolk, the agreement stipulates that only 'accredited students' shall have access to them and that no publication of any document shall be allowed without permission. Students doing long-term research with a view to publication may be asked to submit an application in writing which may be referred to the Duke, and the form embodies an undertaking not to publish without such consent. The application form respecting the use of the Wentworth Woodhouse Muniments deposited by Earl Fitzwilliam is reproduced herewith (Figure 1).

8

SHEFFIELD CITY LIBRARIES

Application to use the Wentworth Woodhouse Muniments

The agreement between the Corporation of Sheffield and Earl Fitzwilliam and his Trustees of the Wentworth Woodhouse Estate concerning the deposit of the Wentworth Woodhouse Muniments in the City Library, stipulates that only accredited students shall be allowed access to them (Clause 2(f)). You will, therefore, understand that it is necessary for me to ask you to provide the particulars indicated on the form below. I shall be glad if you will complete the form and return it before your visit.

City Librarian and Information Officer.

NAME:
ADDRESS:
DEGREE(S) AND UNIVERSITY (if any):
*PRESENT ACADEMIC OR OTHER STATUS:
RESEARCH FOR WHICH DOCUMENTS ARE REQUIRED:
For research workers not attached to any University or similar Institution:
PARTICULARS OF ANY SCHOLARLY PUBLICATION(S):
or
NAME OF PERSON TO WHOM REFERENCE CAN IF NECESSARY BE MADE:

---

*Any postgraduate student studying for a higher degree should here name director of studies under whom he is working. An overseas student who is attached to any such person at an English University is asked to name him.

I undertake, before publishing any extracts from documents in the Wentworth Woodhouse Muniments, to obtain the permission of the City Librarian, and to make acknowledgement in the publication to Earl Fitzwilliam and his Trustees.

(Signed) ....

Date...

Figure 1. Application form respecting the use of the Wentworth Woodhouse Muniments

Leeds has a rule to the effect that the archivist may not give legal advice to students and that any attempt to use the department for legal purposes shall exclude the applicant from further access, unless application has been made to the respective owners concerned and written permission obtained and produced. Such a rule might tend to allay possible misgivings of depositors of smaller collections. Any records subject to fees or statutory charges should be clearly designated in the rules or on the application form.

The British Records Association has issued a Memorandum (no. 15) on 'The Smaller Muniment Room and Its Use by Searchers', which includes a series of draft rules, but this is intended primarily for owners of private muniment rooms. The Association has also issued another Memorandum (no. 20) giving 'Advice to Private Owners and Small Repositories on How To Exhibit Their Documents'.

In repositories where the archive staff is small there will inevitably be occasions when the qualified archivist or archivists are not on duty. This happens frequently in those libraries which seek to help students by allowing access to records during the longer opening hours of the reference library, a laudable purpose but one not without its dangers. In such cases the staff, whether librarians or trainee archivists, should have procedures clearly explained to them and should receive written instructions covering the basic points. Important deposited collections should be specifically exempted from this practice, and be produced only by qualified staff, but there is no reason why collections belonging to the library which have been catalogued should not be produced in the local history or reference library, especially if the student is known to have made an appointment.

Chapter 13

Accommodation

The accommodation devoted to local history collections in libraries varies in extent to the same degree as that of the libraries themselves. In large city libraries the provision for local records is often very substantial, consisting of a suite of rooms, including study rooms, muniment rooms, strong rooms, photographic laboratory, students' carrels, etc. In small libraries the collection occupies a shelf or two of books in the reference library and between these two extremes all levels of size and efficiency exist.

As new libraries have been erected during the past decade the inclusion of special accommodation for local history collections seems to have been accepted as an essential part of most new major library buildings. Including the accommodation in new buildings, local history collections have been given separate housing with public access in some fifty libraries in the past ten years. Many of these local rooms have been developed or greatly extended to meet the growth of local studies and the plans of a number of projected new buildings are also stated to include separate accommodation for local history collections. In several large cities the local history library is a subject department fulfilling both lending and reference functions. Manchester's department of local history is of this nature as are those of Bradford, Edinburgh and Liverpool. At Bradford the local history library occupies a balcony floor within the social sciences library and includes eighteen tables with twenty-six seats. Sheffield on the other hand states that 'The Department of Local History here has never really been a true subject department. Any lending which has been done has never been done on a systematic basis but within the discretion of the

Local History Librarian. We are building up a duplicate collection as rapidly as possible with a view to having systematic lending at some time in the future.' The department consists of a large room fifty-nine feet long divided by a low partition with room for ten and eighteen readers respectively in the two sections of the department, the smaller number being for students of manuscripts. The Liverpool record office and local history department occupies parts of floors five and six of the Brown Library. This comprises reading, exhibition and lecture room, an open-access book stack, secure room accommodation for manuscripts and rare books, and accommodation for watercolours, prints and maps. The repair department responsible for the repair of books, manuscripts and prints occupies premises on the same floor.

When the first department of this kind, the Edinburgh Room, was opened in 1932 by Dr Savage, it was anticipated that the accommodation would suffice for many years. In the first full year of working, 9,349 items were issued from a gross stock of 9,945 but the separation of local material from the general reference collection resulted in a rapid increase in interest and in use, so much so that by 1960 the stock had grown to 46,435 items and the annual issue to 34,529. This remarkable growth led to considerable congestion and an urgent need for further expansion which was met by building an entirely new department in close proximity to the new Scottish Collection. This was opened in 1961.

Complete subject departmentalisation necessitates planning the entire library in such a way as to permit access to each subject library for lending and reference purposes so that heavy traffic for lending purposes does not disturb those engaged in reference work. As many local history libraries are situated as departments with access from the reference library only, a majority of separately housed local history collections can only function with convenience as reference collections.

In a number of new buildings in medium-sized towns, however, the planning does permit complete subject departmentalisation and the new central libraries of Eastbourne and Nuneaton are described by Michael A. Overington[1] as libraries

1. Michael A. Overington. *The Subject Departmentalized Public Library*. Library Association, London, 1969.

of this kind. The accommodation for local history material at Nuneaton was described by S. H. Barlow as follows:

The Study Room (30′ × 30′) contains 12 individual study desks and the Local History and George Eliot collections. The card dictionary catalogue of both collections incorporates an index to a dozen large newscuttings books; such scrap books have been used for newscuttings, photographs and other fugitive material instead of vertical files, since the books are easier to consult and are in themselves an interesting feature. There is a map cabinet here for the collection of historical maps, a microfilm cabinet and a microfilm reader.[2]

At Swinton and Pendlebury also, the new Central Library and Lancastrian Hall, opened in 1970, the planning permits complete subject departmentalisation. On the lower library floor staff are dispersed in two control areas. The reception desk, immediately inside the main library entrance, deals with issue and return of books, and an enquiry desk in the centre of the library houses the readers' adviser, reference and local studies librarian and the record and print library. A local studies library is located near the enquiry desk and facilities are provided for map tracing and reading microfilm. Allied to this library is the small lecture theatre, designed to take classes or small meetings. Although most of the items in this local studies library are for use on the premises only, lending copies of books are provided wherever possible, and some items are available in sufficient numbers for class use in schools. This local history library provides seating facilities for eleven readers, but as most local history collections contain far more material for reference purposes than for lending, there must be far more space devoted to shelving and storage proportionately than can be devoted to the seating of readers. Some extremely large local history libraries have very few seats available in the local history room itself, and the number of seats available in a variety of large libraries ranges from four to fifty-nine.

The new Birmingham Central Library which will house a collection of 90,000 books and pamphlets, 170,700 manuscripts, 35,000 photographs and illustrations, 6,000 maps, 3,000 microfilms and other items on two floors and in two strong rooms will

2. S. H. Barlow. 'Nuneaton's New Library'. *Library World*, vol. 65, July 1963. pp. 3–8.

provide fifty-nine seats. The Norwich Central Library, opened in 1963, houses a collection of some 50,000 books, 50,000 prints and photographs and many other items on two floors and provides twenty-two seats. Exeter's new Central Library, opened in 1965, has only two tables in the West Country room but twelve seats are immediately adjacent in the reference library. Both Norwich and Exeter have separate accommodation for record offices in the same building as the library. In the county of Bedfordshire also, the county record office and the county local history library jointly occupy a new (1969) purpose-built County Central Library. Here on three floors are housed 12,000 books and pamphlets and 58 tons of archive material. On the floor housing the local history library, thirty tables and chairs and five study carrels are provided.

In other new buildings of the past ten years in the separate accommodation provided for local history libraries the ratio of seats to books offers some interesting comparisons: 10 seats for 20,000 books are allocated at Doncaster (1969); 10 seats for 1,500 books at Greenock (1970); 5 seats for 5,000 books at Grimsby (1968); 12 seats for 3,200 books at Guildford (1962); 10 seats for 15,000 books at Newcastle-upon-Tyne (1968); 12 seats for 14,000 books at Plymouth (1956) and 4 seats for 10,000 books at Warrington (1965). In most of these libraries, of course, there are many items other than books in the collection, often in substantial quantity, and additional seating arrangements can often be provided in adjacent reference departments.

As many readers use local history collections for long periods it is essential that considerable thought should be given to their working comfort by providing the most suitable tables and chairs and by ensuring that the general surroundings and atmosphere of the library is attractive and conducive to study.

Tables in the local history library at Warrington were supplied in 1965 at what is often regarded as a standard height of 30 in. These were used with cushioned chairs having a seat height of 18 in. from the floor and were observed to be causing discomfort to a majority of readers. When the table height was reduced to $29\frac{1}{4}$ in. and the chairs raised $\frac{1}{2}$ in. by means of a rubber pad on each leg the comfort of readers was increased considerably, and in the subsequent refurnishing of the reference library these new dimensions were used for all study tables and chairs. The tables used have a central division and give each reader a working space of 30 in. × 24 in. The chairs have both cushioned seats and backs and were selected to provide comfort for those working for lengthy periods.

One or more tables with a larger surface area should also be provided for the consultation of maps and large books. At Swinton and Pendlebury, in addition to a long desk surface measuring 80 in. × 36 in. for the consultation of large maps and books, there is an extension 41 in. in width having a glass panel inset 36 in. × 30 in. with electric lighting beneath as an aid to the tracing of maps. Provision is also made for the vertical and horizontal filing of maps in standard metal map cabinets, as well as in locally constructed cupboards for roll maps.

A considerable amount of information concerning the dimensions of tables, together with details of other components of the library is to be found in Michael Brawne's *Libraries: Architecture and Equipment* (Praeger, New York, 1970).

Often a research worker needs a large number of separate items for regular use extending over a period of several days or weeks, and the time of both staff and student can be saved considerably if the majority of these items can be kept together throughout the period during which they are required. To this end some libraries have provided study carrels in their local history libraries or in situations in close proximity. Such carrels may take the form of separate small rooms as in the Manchester central library, or may be partitioned desks situated within the local history library giving greater privacy and better study facilities than the normal reading desk by allowing, for example, a limited amount of shelving in addition to table space. Partitioned carrels have the advantage of permitting the staff to have the oversight necessary when manuscripts are being consulted, and are also often pleasanter places in which to work than carrels that are no more than large cupboards lacking natural light.

If possible tables should be situated adjacent to, or at right angles to, windows but it should also be possible to control the light from such windows easily by means of modern blinds, such as the 'Louverdrape', so that readers are never discomforted by the glare of sunlight on the white pages of a book. Control of ventilation and temperature should be equally easy to operate so that unobtrusive alterations can be made as conditions change.

Although the display of a limited number of maps, prints or pictures of local significance can be used effectively as a means of decoration within a local history library in order to create a pleasing atmosphere, the temptation to use the library as a miniature local history museum or art gallery should be resisted, as such a display could prove distracting to readers. A separate exhibition room or exhibition facilities should be provided where the movement of people attracted to such exhibitions would not disturb those engaged in reference work.

Some microfilm readers are noisy in operation and the intermittent clicking or whirring of these essential appliances is often annoying to those who are working nearby. If possible, therefore, these machines should be placed as far from study tables as possible. The storage of microfilm also needs some care. Various suitable metal cabinets are available, some containing humidifying devices. Generally, however, it is sufficient to avoid wide ranges of storage temperatures and not to exceed a temperature of 70°F., or a relative humidity of 40 per cent.[3]

A classroom or small lecture room in close proximity to the local history library is also very useful, not only for assembling visiting classes for preliminary talks before they proceed to inspect the library, but it can be used for other purposes such as committee meetings or by members of the public who wish to use a typewriter or tape recorder. Such a classroom should be provided with the necessary aids to lecturing – projection equipment and facilities for displaying books and documents as well as an easy and effective method of blacking out natural light during the daytime.

In libraries containing large quantities of appropriate material an archive repository may be planned in addition to or in conjunction with the local history library. In two large central libraries of the past decade (Norwich and Exeter), both of which house large collections of archives, the archives repositories have separate accommodation in the same building. In the Norwich Central Library the repository is the Norfolk and Norwich Record Office and the strongroom provision for the storage of archival material appears to be the largest in any central public library building, having an area of

3. See 'Cause and Prevention of Microfilm Blemishes'. *British Journal of Photography*, vol. 117, no. 5745, August 1970. p. 827.

12,000 square feet and a cubic capacity of 96,000 cubic feet. The City Record Office at Exeter, situated within the same building as the Central Library, has a strongroom area of 8,550 square feet whilst the new Birmingham Central Library will contain two strongrooms with a cubic capacity of 48,340 cubic feet.

An archives department should be planned as a compact unit to include strongrooms, repair and workroom, as well as facilities for studying the records. For the latter purpose the local room *may* be considered in small libraries, although ideally archive material should be used in a room of its own. Where documents *are* produced for public inspection in the reference library or local room they must be carefully stored away in the strongroom each evening. If the local room is of the study type previously referred to it is preferable to using a busy reference library for consulting manuscripts, but where this is so, casual readers (i.e. of magazines) should not be encouraged and there should be no displays to attract the visitor. Otherwise a small room should be placed exclusively at the disposal of manuscript users. Large archival repositories and many libraries have properly equipped photographic studios in the charge of expert photographers.

Although Dr G. H. Fowler described the essential attributes of a muniment room many years ago in his book *The Care of County Muniments* (County Council Association, London, 2nd ed. 1928, p. 39), and the British Records Association has published a pamphlet on the ideal lay-out of a record office, architects have not as yet given much attention to the planning of archive repositories. Ideally the entire office should be on one floor, preferably at ground level and contained within fireproof walls, but this is practicable only where a new building is being erected, and existing premises show a variety of adapted and makeshift expedients. Archive accumulations occupy considerable space and future libraries will need to devote much more room than hitherto to the housing of records. Collections tend ever to increase, shortage of storage space becomes almost a congenital condition and the remedies sought are often unusual and varied.

High standards are required to give maximum protection to records in the strongrooms, and the muniment room, even more than other departments, must plan for future needs which can only be guessed, but which may be based upon the rate of growth in former years. At Leeds the quantity of archives has increased nearly threefold during the past ten years and the archives department is now housed in a separate building (a branch library) with a further repository in another branch library. The capacity of the total storage accommodation is 27,450 cubic feet and this accommodation is stated to be completely full. Sheffield now has six strongrooms with a total capacity of 13,600 cubic feet. In addition, a small amount of material is at various branch libraries. Although an attempt is made to avoid local material being placed anywhere but in the central library and the strongrooms, not all of the local records at Sheffield can be housed in the latter.

Adequate and ideal protection of records is difficult to achieve in a building which has been occupied for many years, or which is shared with other services. Every library needs a strongroom for its records, and in these days it is often possible to add one to the basement of buildings. The drawbacks to a basement location are the additional transport of records involved, the possibility of damp and the lack of good ventilation, but these can be overcome by modern building methods. Danger from floods is another matter entirely and records should never be stored below ground level in a building exposed by nature or location to this hazard. In case of fire, too, the basement becomes the repository for most of the water poured into the building.

Library strongrooms need to be fire, rather than burglar, proof, and for further security the walls and roof may be reinforced with fire-resisting alloy or asbestos-lining. Sprinkler systems are inadvisable, water usually doing much more damage than fire, but carbon dioxide extinguishers should be plentifully supplied. The best protection is the installation of a smoke-detector fire-alarm system with direct access to the fire service headquarters. Modern systems using electronic or nucleonic detector devices are in use in several record offices and libraries, including Berkshire and Devon county archives, Reading borough and Leicester museum muniment room. There should be no heating in the strongrooms and all electric switches, points and fuses should be sited outside. The door should be completely fire-proof and made by a reputable firm of safemakers. Small metal grilles fitted in the walls will assist the natural ventilation.

The normal library strongroom will not need the extensive shelving required in a county record office with its immensely long runs of official records. The shelves and presses should be of steel, not wood, and they should be deeper than normal book-shelves, at least 14 in. is suggested by Sir Hilary Jenkinson. They should also be as light and open as possible to permit free circulation of air, and adjustable in height to suit the size of box used for storing documents, since vertical storing means easier removal. Special equipment may be needed for bound volumes, large packages, rolled maps and perhaps microfilms. Great height is not essential in the room, for records should not be stored out of reach from the ground. Leicester Museum recently almost doubled its storage space by building a mez-zanine floor and installing Acrow rolling racking storage in its repository. This system has proved so successful in practice that other libraries and archive departments are using it. Apart from reducing space, the close packing which results induces a considerable stabilisation of atmospheric humidity and prevents the growth of mildew. The Library of Congress is using shelving which does not rest on the floor, but which is suspended from overhead beams which, it is claimed, permits better circulation of air and assists floor cleaning.

Records should be stored in boxes with well-fitting lids which give protection from sunlight, damp and dust. They are better filed vertically than flat, but maps and large deeds which cannot be folded should be stored flat in portfolios or special cabinets. If it can be avoided, records should not be shelved against the outside walls of the building, which are particularly susceptible to damp and damage due to faulty drainage.

Large repositories will need to consider installing an air-conditioning system, whereby forced and heated air is drawn through the rooms by suction. It is virtually a necessity in a window-less basement room, improving the quality of the air, making it pleasanter for work and improving storage con-ditions for the records. For one or two rooms, the plant need not be elaborate, nor need it be within the room itself. Air can be drawn from outside the building by a distant window, filtered to prevent the entry of dust and circulated through the muniment room. Tests have proved that air-conditioning eliminates the harmful effects of varying or excessive heat and humidity, and by preventing the formation of mildew, which can cause rapid deterioration in paper records, it increases the life of books and manuscripts. The humidity should be tested periodically. Simple and inexpensive portable dehumidifier units which dry the air without the use of heat are on the market. They are easily installed in strongrooms and a series can be placed in different rooms. They are fitted with humidistats and switch off automatically once the humidity has been brought below the prescribed level at which they are set, which should be about 50 per cent.[4] In industrial areas protection may be needed against the high sulphur dioxide content in the air.

The provision of chutes for the rapid evacuation of material in an emergency may be considered, but the general view amongst archivists is that the removal of large quantities of records is not really practicable. Most fires take place at night and to open strongrooms to try to remove records might be more disastrous than leaving them to take their chance in the fire. A strongroom must, of course, be locked carefully each night, but the outer door should be opened during the working day to allow air to pass through the inner grille door.

The staff workroom where documents are received, unpacked, cleaned, fumigated and, where necessary, repaired, needs careful planning if these tasks are to be carried out effectively. Storage accommodation should never be used for working and a small room for repair work is a necessity in any library with many manuscript records. Dr Fowler considers the equipment of such a room in *The Care of County Muniments* (already cited, pp. 39–45). A fairly heavy press, since most repairs depend on pressure for their effectiveness, paper weights and a guillotine for trimming are desirable. All records will be cleaned and fumigated before being placed on the shelves of the repository. A simple, but satisfactory, fumigating cabinet may be made quite easily by a handyman and will help to prevent and cure mildew on records. A receptacle with thymol crystals, suspended over an electric bulb and below the documents to be treated, is built into a wooden cabinet.

4. The British Standards Institute is finalising recommendations on record storage which should be issued in 1973.

Chapter 14

Staffing

Approximately one quarter of the municipal authorities having local history collections employ separate staff to administer them. Returns from 200 municipal authorities in 1970 showed that 51 authorities employed between them 64 professional librarians, 38 archivists and 55 library assistants on full-time local history duties. The number of local history staff employed by each authority varied from 1 to 21 and the salaries of the professionally qualified librarians and archivists engaged ranged from the 'librarian scale' to the 'senior officer' and 'principal officer' level. Archivists employed in separately established county and other record offices are not included in these figures which relate to municipal local history collections only. It is also necessary to observe that in many authorities there are professional librarians engaged upon local history activities who are not designated as local history librarians, but who undertake their local history library work as part of their duty in a general reference library or department having a wider subject coverage.

In some instances, professional posts in reference libraries where the occupant is engaged mainly on local history duties, have not been designated as local history librarian simply to secure the better career prospects offered in general reference library work. As the number of separately housed local history libraries has increased during recent years, however, the number of those designated as local history librarians has also increased, although not at the same rate. It is now considered that the creation of new local government authorities will result in the establishment of new specialist posts at a high level, so that there should be a considerable improvement in the career prospects in local history work.

The slow but steady growth in the number of specialist posts combined with an assessment of the career prospects in a reorganised local government structure has led various bodies responsible for professional education to include local history and libraries as a field of study in their examination syllabuses. The revised syllabus of the Library Association became effective in 1971 and included for the first time a paper (List B, Paper 36) devoted to 'The Library and Local History'. Similarly a paper (Section B, Paper G 18) has been included in the Library Association's post-graduate professional examination entitled the 'Literature and Librarianship of Local History'. Combined with existing papers on 'Archive Administration and Records Management' and 'Palaeography and Diplomatic' as well as suitable bibliographical studies offered as List C papers, provision has now been made in the Library Association's syllabus of professional examinations for those who wish to specialise as local history librarians. Teaching provision for these new options has still to be fully organised, but some schools of librarianship have already made such provision, and the new local history studies will surely eventually be included in most syllabuses for library degree and diploma courses as well as in the courses organised for the Library Association's own examinations. It is, however, to be noted that as Council for National Academic Awards degree courses are introduced by the library schools, the ability to provide courses for the Library Association syllabus will diminish and therefore the provision of a suitable qualification in local history studies may ultimately depend upon the inclusion of these studies in the new library degree courses alone.

An early lead for the future teaching of local history studies has already been taken by the Polytechnic of North London where an optional paper (A2 : 4 'English Local History') lasting five terms within the course entitled 'The Universe of Knowledge', has been included in the CNAA degree course, following the Polytechnic's syllabus approved by the CNAA. The first intake to this course was in January 1971 and some of these students reached the local history option in their sixth term during the late summer of 1972.

The local history studies associated with the new options now included in professional examination syllabuses will prove of great value to those wishing to specialise in the work of the local history library in the future. There can be little doubt, however, that the first requisite of all successful and competent local history librarians so far is that they have been primarily librarians, able to organise and administer a collection of specialised material for the convenience and benefit of users. Knowledge of the specialised requirements of a local history library and knowledge of local literature and the history of the locality itself has been acquired slowly as experience with the collection has extended over a considerable period of time. Such knowledge can only be attained gradually and is only likely to be acquired and used to best advantage by those who have a real feeling for history as well as the ability to understand the requirements of those who are concerned, often deeply, with the history of a particular locality. Work in local history libraries has produced many dedicated librarians whose names have become widely known because of their devotion to their work. Improved career prospects and improved methods of training in local history work will not mean that dedication to this work will become considerably less vital than it has been in the past, although it is possible to visualise a situation where the progress of the good local history librarian may become somewhat less arduous and promotion be much speedier in attainment than has been possible hitherto.

The size, nature and use of any local history library will determine both the number and the desirable qualifications of those employed therein. Since public library collections vary from those without archives to those containing a considerable number, it is necessary to decide whether the employment of archivists as well as librarians is necessary. The qualifications, qualities and functions of the two professions, though related, are quite distinct and, where the size of the archive collection does not seem to be large enough to justify the employment of a separate archivist, a librarian possessing passes in the Library Association's professional examinations in archive administration and palaeography is often considered as suitably qualified to administer a combined local history library and small to medium collection of archival material. The Library Association's statement of policy on *The Place of Archives and Manuscripts in the Field of Librarianship* (Appendix I) dictates that: 'Just as library authorities should not be in charge of archives without employing qualified archivists, so records committees or similar employing bodies should not be in charge of considerable libraries without engaging qualified librarians.' Libraries with considerable archive collections already employ qualified archivists and endeavour to secure adequate career prospects for those so employed. Some librarians have discovered to their surprise and satisfaction that the employment of an archivist has not only secured the expected services of one capable of applying appropriate administrative methods to an existing collection, but has also provided unexpected talent in securing new accessions for the repository.

The diploma in archive administration of either London or Liverpool universities has long been considered as a suitable qualification for an archivist, although both diplomas have critics. Some have thought that there has been undue emphasis on medieval records to the detriment of the study of modern archives, and concern has also been expressed about the suitability of the London qualification for those intending to work in local repositories. The diploma course in archive studies of London University has recently been re-structured and from October, 1970, lecture courses commenced leading to examinations under the new syllabus. The effect of the new syllabus 'is to increase the number of options and to create three "streams" designed to meet the needs of (1) British archivists who need instruction in handling older material, (2) British archivists who are concerned with post-medieval, in fact, mainly modern documents, (3) archivists from overseas whose needs will be partly the same as those of British modern archivists but who will also need instruction relevant to their own countries.' Liverpool University has also now proposed a three-week pre-entry practical course at a record office selected by the university.

Other universities (Bangor and Aberystwyth) also offer diploma courses in archive administration, and suitable qualifications, both for the professional archivist and the professional librarian intending to work in a record office or local history library, or a combination of the two, now seem to be provided by universities and library schools.

The dedication of two librarians employed in the Nottingham City Libraries will perhaps serve to indicate some of the problems to be resolved in the staffing of a modern local history library. In an earlier chapter of this book it was mentioned that W. E. Doubleday compiled at intervals throughout his working life a vast index-bibliography of Nottingham on cards, which nowadays is a tool of immense value in the Nottingham City Library to whom he presented it, and where with regular updating it now contains about half a million cards. The present local history librarian of Nottingham, Miss Lucy I. Edwards, has also compiled, over a period of two years, a finding list, which extends to 125 pages and was published in 1968, of the D. H. Lawrence holdings in the city, county and university libraries of Nottingham. It is this kind of detailed indexing of the contents of a local history library and this type of bibliographical work – which every local history librarian knows to be necessary if the fullest use is to be made of the collection – that is so time-consuming. Because local history librarians realise the essential nature of this slow work a problem of some magnitude has to be solved, therefore, as the increasing number of more exacting research enquiries from the public requires a growing degree of attention from professional staff, thus reducing the time available for indexing and other work.

Time has to be found for the other duties indicated in earlier chapters of this book such as the acquisition of material, the organisation of exhibitions, work with school classes, copying and duplicating material in the collection, suitably mounting photographic and press-cutting material, lecturing and various activities with local societies. No doubt in the largest libraries some of these tasks, such as repair work, mounting photographs and press-cuttings, photography and photocopying, will be undertaken in separate repair and photographic departments, but in the medium-sized and small libraries the widest variety of duties is likely to be the responsibility of a single department with only one or two full-time staff. It is evident, therefore, that the demands made on staff time by the requirements of the department should be subjected to frequent scrutiny and that a standard policy should be adopted concerning the extent of the assistance that can be given by the staff to those engaged upon research, and also to the quantity of indexing and biblio-graphical work that can be reasonably undertaken by the staff employed. An indication has been given earlier that one solution to the detailed indexing of local newspapers has been found in some libraries by the use of volunteer indexers. This method of compiling a useful index nevertheless requires a little organisation and certainly necessitates some time to be spent by full-time staff for editing.

Reminders sent to local societies and other organisations to obtain their programmes, reports or other published literature can only be really effective if an up-to-date list of the secretaries and other officers of these organisations is maintained. An index of local organisations is but one small aspect of the detailed indexing of information in the local history library, and serves to illustrate the value of such indexing since, on this tiny aspect of a comprehensive index, depends the flow of a considerable quantity of material into the collection.

The arrangement, listing and indexing of archive collections is much more exacting than the cataloguing and indexing of printed material so that the archivist to a much greater extent than the librarian must be free to engage upon technical duties. This can lead to a feeling of frustration when an archivist is working in a library, often in isolation, where he may miss the friendly day-to-day contact with colleagues of his own pro-fession. The chief librarian must be sympathetic and show understanding of these problems and difficulties. He should allow the archivist all possible freedom and should not interfere in technical matters and, if he is wise, he will also discuss matters of policy affecting records.

He should be encouraged to meet his fellow archivists by joining the Society of Archivists and attending meetings and conferences of the British Records Association and other bodies. Visits to nearby record offices and to libraries with a good repu-tation in archive work are another means of improving one's knowledge and technique.

The local librarian and the archivist have a far more intimate contact with their readers than those in charge of other depart-ments, for the reader often looks for help beyond the mere provision of catalogues and indexes. An archive collection, in particular, consists of largely virgin soil not previously worked upon, and there are many interesting finds to be made, some of which will come to light as the archivist lists and calendars the collection. In these circumstances he will, by the very nature of his work, acquire a deep and detailed knowledge of his stock and he must occasionally make discoveries which are important in local history, or which perhaps tend to disprove tenets and opinions previously held. In other words he will, perhaps without conscious effort on his part, become accepted as an 'authority' on the history and records of his own locality, and will receive many requests for advice and help.

The archivist cannot calendar extensive collections of documents or the local librarian index, say, the files of the local newspaper without gaining a wide knowledge of the history of the area and its families, genealogy, heraldry, customs and the like. This is one of his more tangible assets and one which may make him almost indispensable to the library, for no indexing system, however efficient, is a substitute for intimate personal knowledge of the collections and a wider acquaintance with the local background. It may also militate against his promotion within the service or his chances of a change of post, but that is another story. There may, therefore, be a tendency for him to develop a keenness for research and to use his knowledge to write on local affairs. He should not spend his time as a 'paid' researcher, nor even write papers for local societies in working hours, although such activity, time-consuming as it is, is often looked for as a normal spare-time occupation by the local community. An exception to the statement above may be the searching of wills, parish registers, and similar records, especially for foreign students. In some areas, unless the local archivist can be persuaded to undertake such paid work, which could not reasonably be regarded as part of the normal service of a record office or library, there would be nobody to do it. As a public servant, however, the librarian or archivist must recognise that he has no right to use material in his care for private ends, or to deprive others of the opportunities for original research: he should secure general official approval for private genealogical searching, broadcasting or television appearances.

Like all general rules, however, there are occasions when this needs to be modified in practice and Miss Walton puts forward the original view that the assistant in charge of manuscripts *should* occupy himself with gathering together scattered information on the sort of subject for which readers are always asking, and she quotes 'local worked-out mines, activities locally during the Civil War, the history of demolished mansions, important developments in industries and trade, lists of mayors and masters of guilds, place-names and dialect words, the sites of vanished land-marks and the like.'[1] She advocates placing these in manuscript form on the shelves of the local room, suitably catalogued, thereby easing the task of students. In her opinion, 'the archivist can become what corresponds to a bibliographer in the library world, without hurt to his professional impartiality and to the very great advantage of the library in general and the ordinary reader in the Local Room in particular.'[2]

It is perhaps unfortunate, but true, that the public librarian is often the obvious choice as author or compiler on those occasions when the local authority decides to publish a centenary volume on the history of the town, or to edit a series of its official records. Such confidence is rarely misplaced, and in such circumstances, the librarian would find it difficult, if not churlish, to refuse the request. The works of Dr Chandler, John O'Leary, Duncan Gray, L. J. Mayes and many others show what an excellent job can be made of these assignments, and doubtless they will continue to be produced by active and retired librarians, who often feel in undertaking such a task that they are in some measure recompensing the city or town which has given them a pleasant livelihood for many years.

1. Mary Walton. 'Local Records and the Public Library'. A thesis submitted for the honours Diploma of the Library Association, 1938. Unpublished. Copy in L. A. Library. p. 279.
2. op. cit. p. 3.

Chapter 15

Cataloguing, Indexing and Local Bibliography

The cataloguing and indexing of local material is not a topic on which much that is new has been written in recent years, and it may be considered that little more needs to be said, especially since the local catalogue is often the only one in a library where entries are given in any degree of fullness and where the general rules of bibliographical cataloguing are strictly applied. The facts are, however, that most local catalogues are not detailed enough to serve as authoritative guides to the stock, that many are extremely imperfect, and that there are very few local collections in which the material is so closely indexed that all the available material on a subject can be produced readily and rapidly. This material is so diverse in its nature and content that only by the most minute indexing can the fugitive items be brought to the notice of readers. This is especially true of the non-bibliothecal material which can be such an important part of a 'live' local history department. The tendency is to rely upon the knowledge gained by the local librarian in familiarity with the books and records in his charge, rather than on detailed catalogues and indexes, with the result that when he or she leaves or is absent for any reason, the efficiency of the department drops alarmingly.

This is a subject capable of study and development in the light of advances being made in the scientific and industrial information fields. Documentation principles and systems, as adapted to the problems of making recorded knowledge more freely available, are as apposite to this sphere of librarianship as to any other, and the local librarian can learn much from the modern techniques of information retrieval, particularly in the field of indexing. For it is in the local collection, and perhaps here alone, that the public library may claim to be considered as a 'special' library, and where techniques are automatically raised to the documentation level, with all the detailed synthesis of classification, cataloguing, indexing and abstracting which this necessitates. The type of analytical abstracting and phase designation advocated in the scientific field could help considerably to bring to light and to the attention of readers the fugitive information concealed in local books, and much more could be done in the way of evaluating and abstracting periodical articles and contributions to newspapers in the various avenues of local study.

Centralised cataloguing, successfully initiated through the British National Bibliography, gives the librarian of today very few opportunities to exercise the craft of compiling a catalogue, but in a local collection, to which the major proportion of the material added does not appear on printed cards, the catalogue must still be largely constructed by the staff.

Cataloguing and indexing procedure should be well established and familiar to the staff so that new material, as it comes into the library, can be readily assimilated, falls into its proper place and is available to the reader with the minimum of delay. It is better, in most libraries, to allow the staff of the department to do their own cataloguing, rather than to delegate this to the cataloguing section. Not only are the special problems involved more readily appreciated by the staff, but the experience in dealing with the material is a vital factor in gaining familiarity with it.

The choice of the most appropriate form of the catalogue: classified, dictionary, or alphabetico-classed is a personal one and the repetition of the arguments in favour of one form of catalogue or another is not necessary here. Much more important than the form of catalogue selected is the determination necessary to make the catalogue fulfil every possible requirement as a key to a specialised collection of material, and to repeat that apart from cataloguing the items in the collection, the detailed indexing of many parts of every local history library is the most certain way of ensuring that the contents of the library can be used to full advantage.

To those confronted with a choice concerning the most

appropriate form of catalogue it may be helpful to note that existing local history catalogues in 1970 were divided into two principal groups, of which 58 per cent were classified catalogues and 36 per cent were dictionary. The remaining 6 per cent represented a small variety of mixed forms. No matter what form of catalogue is selected, considerable flexibility in the duplication of entries under appropriate subject headings is desirable in order to overcome the deficiency of all classification schemes which only permit any item to be placed in a single location. In the local history collection the conflict arising from the choice between district and subject is especially acute and appropriate added entries both in the classified and dictionary catalogues can overcome this difficulty.

No classified catalogue can be considered to be an efficient instrument unless it is equipped with an alphabetical subject index and an author catalogue. The subject index should be more analytical than either the classification tables or the general body of the catalogue, since it includes specific terms, as well as individual places and also synonymous, alternative and related terms. It should be based upon the principles of synthesis and phase analysis, and the classifier should compile his index as he classifies the books. J. Mills has detailed an effective way of doing this, using Ranganathan's chain procedure, in 'Chain Indexing and the Classified Catalogue' in the *Library Association Record* (vol. 57, April 1955, pp. 141–8).

With the exception of the subject index to the classified catalogue, unit cards may be used for the construction of either classified or dictionary catalogues, and if BNB printed cards are used for any recently published works added to the collection the practice advocated in the *Anglo-American Cataloguing Rules* (Library Association, London, 1967) should be followed. In order to distinguish between different authors bearing the same names, a circumstance that is quite common in local history collections, dates should be added after the name of each author in the catalogue. This information, though sometimes troublesome to obtain often proves very useful when enquiries concerning local authors are made.

The essential information to be included for each item on the unit card for local collection purposes is:

1. Author's name in full, with dates on the first card in the file at least.
2. Title and description.
3. Place of publication (London can be assumed, but where a book published in London also has a local imprint, this should be given).
4. Publisher and/or printer (the name of the printer should never be omitted from a local work).
5. Date of publication (undated books can often be dated approximately from internal evidence or from local knowledge).
6. Imprint, consisting of the number of pages, type and number of illustrations, maps, plans, etc, and size.
7. Notes or annotations (these may cover such points as the physical condition of the book; evidence of former ownership; the connection of the work with the district, where this is not obvious, etc.).
8. Tracings (an indication of the subject and other headings under which additional entries have been made) and number of copies. These details may go on the reverse of the card.

The problem facing the cataloguer when choosing the appropriate subject heading for a dictionary catalogue is often similar to that confronting the classifier, and apart from a decision concerning the location of entries or items when there is a choice between place or subject, another conflict frequently arising in local history collections concerns Acts of Parliament. Should all local acts be grouped in one place or, should those having specific reference to a single topic, such as a school, a railway, or a canal, be placed with the topic? In a classified collection any item can only be allocated to a single shelf location, but in both the dictionary and the classified catalogue subject entries for any item can be made in more than one place and the catalogue becomes much more useful when such additional entries are made. It means, for example, that in a town collection covering neighbouring parishes, a book or pamphlet concerning a village school and classified with other material relating to the village, would receive entries in a classified catalogue under the location of the village as well as under the location for schools, and two similar headings would also appear in a dictionary catalogue. The duplication of these entries would satisfy the needs of those looking for all the information concerning the village, and would also satisfy the needs of those interested in the schools of the locality.

In many dictionary catalogues there are often comprehensive sub-headings which bring related topics together and thereby provide some of the advantages of a classified arrangement, at the same time reducing the necessity of a large number of cross-references. The *A.L.A. List of Subject Headings for Use in Dictionary Catalogs* (American Library Association, Chicago, 3rd ed. 1911) contains a list of sub-headings to be used under cities which is useful in this connection. A similar list, adapted to the needs of English libraries, will be found in J. L. Hobbs's *Libraries and the Materials of Local History* (Grafton, London, 1948, Appendix 1), whilst the general practice to be followed in the choice of subject headings is considered in E. J. Coates's *Subject Catalogues: Headings and Structure* (Library Association, London, 1960).

Since an entry for each work by every local author included in a collection will be made under the name of the author, and these local authors will represent a major proportion of the material in the collection, it is not justifiable to represent these works with a series of unit cards under the place heading in a dictionary catalogue, nor under a subject location for local authors in the classified catalogue. In both types of catalogue it may be considered useful to list the names of local authors under the place or subject location such as:

SHREWSBURY – Authors

For works by Shrewsbury authors *See*

    COKE, DESMOND

    GALLETLY, LEONARD, etc.

or in a classified catalogue to have a similar reference under a location for local authors. In the Warrington classified catalogue this has not been considered necessary as, in the author index, all local authors are distinguished by the addition of the words '*of Warrington*' or '*Warrington*' to the author's name and dates in the heading. '*Of Warrington*' means that the author was born in Warrington, and '*Warrington*' means that the author was resident in the town for a substantial period of time. For the arrangement of cards under an author the *A.L.A. Rules for*

Filing Catalog Cards (American Library Association, Chicago, 1942) should be followed.

Subject entries in the local catalogue may, of course, be limited by including only those which are of intrinsic 'local' interest. This practice is invariably followed in printed catalogues of local collections, chiefly for reasons of economy. Analytical entries for contributions in local periodicals will be made only for those articles which relate to the area. Selective cataloguing of this nature can be indulged in to a considerable extent, the treatment being confined to covering the reasons for which the book or item is included in the collection, but it must be done with care and moderation. Author entries can never be dispensed with safely, but title and series entries can be reduced to a minimum. Books by a local author, but not otherwise pertaining to the district, would thus receive no subject entry, but this ignores the needs of the person who may use the collection in pursuance of the study of the *history* of a subject.

It is permissible to adopt collective cataloguing for many of the minor items, such as trade cards, church magazines, election material, theatre bills, clippings and miscellaneous notes, which may be brought together at one number under an omnibus catalogue entry. Here again discretion is advised – it would be wrong to mix material dealing with different elections or for different constituencies, or playbills relating to several theatres on one card.

Analytical entries must be extensively used since their neglect leads to the value of many books being largely lost. It goes without saying that the transactions and proceedings of all local societies, magazines and newspapers should be fully analysed for both author and subject entries. For cataloguing purposes each article or contribution is treated as a separate work, except that the source or reference will be noted within brackets. Many of the standard local histories need such treatment. R. W. Eyton's *Antiquities of Shropshire* contains a scholarly summary of the early history of almost every village in the county, and although it is familiar to most historical students, catalogue entries under the villages will direct the attention of lesser qualified readers to its important articles. No rigid rules can be laid down for making such entries: the cataloguer should be guided by the value of the material, but their judicious use means that the catalogue will consist of miniature bibliographies under place, subject and author. The catalogue of the library of the Society of Friends in Euston Road, London, contains under the names of prominent Quakers such as Abraham Darby and Elizabeth Fry, a detailed, and fairly exhaustive list of material both by and about them, including not only the separate publications but numerous references to articles, letters and parts of books. Our local worthies and our villages should be similarly treated in library catalogues, since the greater the number of analytical entries and the greater the detail in general entries, the more time is saved the student in assembling his source material.

Most libraries make full bibliographical entries for early or rare books in the collection, and sometimes a special date is selected for this purpose. Edinburgh makes full entries for all books issued prior to 1700. The form and style of entry may be based on the published bibliographies of Pollard and Redgrave and Wing with, of course, a reference to the appropriate catalogue number, and a full collation of the particular copy. If it is a first edition this should be stated, otherwise the date of the first edition will be given, if known.

Books printed or published locally should receive distinctive treatment only if it is considered that they are significant in the history or development of the local printing, publishing or bookselling trades. Here again, only examples earlier than, say, 1800, 1820 or 1850, according to local circumstances, should be included. Otherwise in large provincial centres the catalogue would be swamped by this material. The arrangement of this part of the catalogue should be first by places, then by firms and finally chronologically.

A chronological sub-arrangement of entries is also to be preferred to alphabetical arrangement by author's name in one or two other sections of the catalogue. Several librarians, indeed, adopt this order throughout their classified catalogues, as may be seen in the printed catalogues of Gloucester and Margate, but the necessity of keeping the various editions of the same work together leads to breaks in the strict chronological sequence. In the dictionary catalogue filing in date order would be more logical in many form classes, such as poll-books, directories, maps and subjects such as elections. Entries for various classes of parochial records such as parish registers, church-wardens' accounts, land enclosures and Local Acts, are best arranged alphabetically by place. In most of these, in any event, the author is either corporate or non-existent.

It is desirable to include as much of the printed material as possible in the catalogue, so long as there is no risk of confusing the reader as to its nature. Additional sources such as pamphlets, broadsides, civil war tracts, election 'squibs', theatre bills, may all be treated like books, substituting a title card for the author entry in the case of anonymous material. A collection of cartoons relating to a particular election, or theatre bills from one theatre need receive a collective entry only.

Substantial articles from periodicals and newspapers should be placed in manila covers and then treated like pamphlets and fully catalogued. Those in local newspapers and magazines which are permanently filed will receive analytical entries. Many librarians have acquired miscellaneous volumes of clippings and other matter which defy close classification and cataloguing, although a main entry may be made under the collector, as author or compiler, where this is known. Apart from this, the subject matter should be indexed and consulted when the catalogue fails to answer a query. Volumes of local 'Notes and Queries' from the local papers can be similarly treated.

The treatment of manuscripts and archives has been dealt with in Chapter 6 and it would be superfluous to mention it here, except to say that there is no reason why important manuscript material should not receive subject entries in the general catalogue which will normally be the first source to be inspected by the general enquirer. When they form part of archive groups they will, of course, remain physically in the group to which they belong. Where the library has a large collection of manuscript material with a separate printed or card catalogue, or special handlists and calendars, this is a different matter.

Special problems may arise in a library which commenced with a card catalogue for a mixed collection of printed material and non-archival manuscripts and proceeded at a later date to collect archives. The library whose manuscript resources are limited to non-archival material, mainly in book form, will probably decide to treat these as an integral part of its local

254 Local History and the Library

collection and to catalogue them accordingly, and for these the rules for cataloguing manuscripts in the accepted codes will be found satisfactory.

Examples of manuscript material which it is desirable to include in the main catalogue include the literary manuscripts of local authors, diaries, letter-books, manuscript copies of poll-books, business accounts and certain kinds of local record such as terriers, rentals, surveys and tax-assessments, account books of churchwardens and parish overseers. In fact, a good general rule would allow such entries for any manuscripts in paged and bound form. The description and collation should be detailed and accurate, with notes of any imperfections, so that individual manuscripts can be identified and that there may be no possibility of confusion with other copies. It is often necessary to give fuller details than the standard catalogue card can conveniently accommodate. Entries for similar manuscripts in the publications of important repositories such as the *Handlist of Manuscripts Added to the National Library of Wales*, the *Bulletin of the John Rylands Library* and the *Bodleian Library Quarterly* will indicate the style and fullness of entry required.

Most libraries keep separate indexes of maps and prints, although in small libraries the entries may be included in the main catalogue. For printed maps essential details include the name of the cartographer, the title, if any (this is often to be found within a cartouche in a corner of the map), the edition, and the name of the engraver, publisher or printer, and the date, size and scale. These will appear on each card and added entries should be made for subject, place and engraver.

For prints the name of the original artist, if it can be found, appears as author for the main entry. Otherwise use the engraver's name, or, in the absence of both, the publisher. Many engravings lack all three of these and must be treated as anonymous. Added entries will in any case be made for engravers and the student is helped if cards of different colours are used for artists and engravers. A process often neglected is that of making entries for prints in books, which is specially important for biographical illustrations. The dating of engravings is often difficult and a clear distinction must be made between the date of the engraving and the date of its appearance in a book or magazine, since the difference may be one of many years. The precise process used (etching, line engraving, mezzotint) should be mentioned, as should the size and shape (oval, vignette, etc.) of the illustration. Special subject indexes are necessary for print collections, especially for biographical and topographical engravings.

The library catalogue, although the main key to the collection, can never, of itself, answer all the questions asked of it, and it should not be expected to. It requires to be supplemented by many special indexes and bibliographies. Only knowledge of the particular collection will indicate those likely to be needed in any library, but the preparation of guides and indexes is the best way of ensuring that the widest possible use is made of the collections, for it ensures that students are not faced with the necessity of unearthing their sources from a conglomerate mass. The ability to abstract, to index and to calendar is perhaps the most important single asset of the local librarian, whose collection should be indexed so minutely that any item can be traced and produced with a minimum of delay and by other members of the staff in his absence.

Most libraries find the need to make special indexes for some of the special non-bibliothecal material in the collection. Maps, broadsides, and other printed material – and, in certain circumstances, as indicated, manuscripts – may be catalogued along with the printed books and pamphlets, but it will not generally be wise to add visual materials. Photographs, prints, drawings and paintings should have a separate catalogue or catalogues on cards or sheaf-slips. Local films, filmstrips, lantern slides and tape recordings should also be indexed separately. Cards for microfilm may be included in the general catalogue if the card is clearly marked to show the nature of the material, but it would also be wise to have an independent index which could take the form of, or be incorporated with, an accessions register. The number of film reels, size of the film, whether perforate or not, date and other details will replace the normal book collation.

Several libraries have supplemented the catalogue by compiling a detailed analytical index to the material, covering personal names, place-names and subjects. Often information and references are gathered from many sources, current newspapers and periodicals, books, letters and personal information.

Canterbury has such an index containing 100,000 entries, the librarian noting that it has been made possible by the use of printed cards for general cataloguing, which has freed the qualified staff to compile the index. Leeds states that most of the information added to its index is in anticipation of demand, but that many entries *are* made after the facts have been found in response to a query. Methodical research workers often compile indexes of their own and fortunate is the library which acquires a card-index such as the one Arthur L. Humphreys, the historian, presented to Reading Public Library. This is not, however, a means of reference to the contents of the library collections, but records a vast number of references to Berkshire from materials in the British Museum, the Public Record Office and other sources. Similar is the vast index relating to Nottinghamshire, presented to Nottingham Public Library by W. E. Doubleday, himself a librarian. It often takes the form of a detailed topographical index, as at Malvern, with entries arranged under villages, wards, etc. Newcastle-upon-Tyne has a huge index, arranged by places, persons and topics, and Keighley is in the process of compiling an alphabetical index on cards to its local history collection, which now contains 6,500 cards and which it is said is not a catalogue but an index to local history.

The number and complexity of supplementary indexes will often only be limited by the staff-time available for their compilation, for the possibilities are virtually endless. Many individual volumes lack indexes, especially the miscellaneous volumes compiled by nineteenth-century antiquaries and scrapbooks of newspaper cuttings assembled by local collectors. At Croydon the staff has compiled indexes to several of the older published histories, while Liverpool has indexed its early poll-books. Transcripts of parish registers are rendered much more useful by carefully compiled indexes, and collaboration with the Society of Genealogists may provide indexes to these, since the society has a band of volunteer transcribers and in return for the temporary loan of a register transcript to enable a copy to be made for the society's library, will often present a typed copy of the index to the library. In several libraries, including Derby and Shrewsbury the staff has indexed the local registers.

The files of local newspapers contain much valuable information hidden away in a more or less inaccessible form, and a comprehensive index to the significant items in these not only unlocks the door to a veritable storehouse of local knowledge, but incidentally contributes to their preservation by diminishing unnecessary handling of the files. Many queries involve the staff in slow and tedious researches in the absence of efficient indexes to this kind of material. Sometimes an index to the files of the local newspaper is compiled by the library staff as at Chester, where a selective index to three Chester newspapers for the years 1955–59 was published in 1964, and a further index for the period 1960–64 appeared in 1970.

An increasing number of libraries are finding that it is possible to enlist the services of volunteers who derive considerable enjoyment and satisfaction from visiting the library each week to compile such an index. Volunteers have been working at Nottingham since 1963 on a card index to the *Nottingham Journal* and have so far completed an index of persons, places and subjects for the years 1801–20. At Warrington an invitation published in the local newspaper in November 1970 resulted in twenty-six volunteers offering their services to compile a similar index to the files of the *Warrington Guardian*. An instruction sheet was prepared to assist these volunteers and as only items of local interest are to be included in the index (names of persons, places and subjects) a map was also duplicated showing the area covered by the local collection. Volunteers produce about eight hundred cards every week and these are edited daily by a member of the library staff. Each worker indexes one month's issues at a time and as the file of the newspaper had been previously cut for microfilming, the pages of the early files have been separated into months in manila folders so that each volunteer has no difficulty in working on the part allocated whenever a visit is made to the library for this purpose.

Manchester has compiled special handlists and indexes in the library for various special purposes including (*a*) an index to Manchester maps; (*b*) a biographical index; (*c*) a subject and place index; (*d*) a subject index to prints and cuttings and (*e*) handlists to various deed collections. Other libraries have found a general biographical index or 'Who's Who' of local

9

personalities, giving brief references to sources of information in newspapers, periodicals and books, of great and permanent value. A separate index to photographs and portraits of such people can be kept or even incorporated into the above. It can also be kept up-to-date by adding the biographical clippings and obituaries as they are culled from local papers weekly, or by sending printed forms to local notabilities for completion and inclusion in the index, and forming an up-to-date local 'Who's Who'. A similar index to family history and pedigree has proved its worth at Shrewsbury and a pedigree index has been printed by Newcastle, whilst indexes to the wills in the Commissary Court of London in the custody of the Guildhall Library are being compiled and the first of these has recently been published by the British Record Society.

A gazetteer or index of all place-names and minor names, buildings and other features on the 6 in. ordnance survey maps of the locality is another indispensable key which has answered many hundreds of questions. In Derbyshire this was compiled by the staff of the Derby Public Library; in Shropshire it was undertaken by a clerk in the county council offices, Mr H. G. D. Foxall. Birmingham has found an index to the streets of the city, giving references to and from former names and the approximate date when these changed to be of value. A detailed index to the smaller local plans is another desideratum. Many of these are included in books, sale catalogues, conveyances of property, etc. and if the index can be extended to include plans in the offices of the planning authority, the borough engineer or surveyor and other places, so much the better.

These examples, a few of many which could be cited, indicate the value of special indexes in the local collection. Local conditions may point to the desirability of others and it can be said that any index which enhances the value of the collection and makes its contents more readily available amply justifies the labour and cost of its compilation.

The permanent nature of the local history collection and its interest to people in many parts who cannot visit the library regularly has induced many librarians to consider publishing the catalogue, and certain problems arise in this connection. The principal one is the cost of printing which has deterred all but a small number of enthusiasts from emulating the numerous catalogues which appeared in the first half of the century when nearly every reputable local collection had its printed catalogue. They are nearly all out-of-print today.

Apart from the printed catalogues of county collections mentioned in Chapter 10 of this book, printed catalogues of collections in public libraries have been published since the war by Belfast (2 vols., 1965); Eastbourne (1956); Gillingham (1951); Guildford (1957); and Reading (1959). Supplements to some of these catalogues have also been produced and a printed catalogue is projected at Liverpool where in 1955 Liverpool City Libraries decided to allocate its small re-cataloguing staff to the preparation of a local history catalogue. Because of pressure of other work the project is not yet complete but so far 100,000 entries are prepared.

Local bibliography, as opposed to the cataloguing of a specific collection, has been receiving critical attention in the last few years, following the revival of interest in local history and the need for the wide dissemination of bibliographical information on its sources. In many areas libraries have entered into co-operative schemes for the production of county or area bibliographies.

A North Midland Bibliography, edited by R. A. H. O'Neal and published by the North Midland Branch of the Library Association commenced quarterly publication in 1963 on the basis of material submitted by co-operating libraries in the counties of Derby, Nottingham, Lincoln, Leicester, Rutland, Northampton and the Soke of Peterborough. The Hertford-shire Local History Council issued two parts of a county bibliography covering newspapers and periodicals in 1956 and 1959, both of which were compiled by the former County Librarian, Mrs M. F. Thwaite; and in Surrey, the Surrey Librarians Group have been concerned with a union list of directories published by the Surrey County Library in 1965 as well as with the publication of a handlist of Surrey newspapers in 1961. The Bedfordshire Historical Record Society published *A Bedfordshire Bibliography* by L. R. Conisbee in 1962 and issued a Supplement in 1967 which gives locations in seventeen libraries. In Oxfordshire, *A Bibliography of Printed Works relating to Oxfordshire, excluding the University and City of Oxford*, by E. H. Cordeaux and D. H. Merry was published by the

Oxford University Press in 1955 and was also issued by the Oxford Historical Society. Addenda and Corrigenda have subsequently appeared in the *Bodleian Library Record*, whilst *A Bibliography of Printed Works relating to the University of Oxford* by the same authors was published by the Clarendon Press in 1968.

A Current Bibliography of Published Material relating to North Staffordshire and South Cheshire, edited at the time of writing by N. Emery and D. R. Beard, and published by the Stoke-on-Trent Public Libraries commenced quarterly publication in 1954. The *East Anglian Bibliography*, which commenced quarterly publication in 1960, is organised and published by the Eastern Branch of the Library Association. This bibliography covers the counties of Cambridge, Isle of Ely, Huntingdon, Norfolk and Suffolk and now includes items listed in the *British National Bibliography* although this material was originally excluded. An East Anglian library survey of historical material has also been prepared at the University of East Anglia and a contribution towards the salary of a bibliographer engaged upon this project was made by the Norwich Libraries Committee. This survey, published in 1971 under the title *History Collections in Norfolk and Suffolk Libraries*, consists of three parts, of which the first part is a guide-book to relevant collections in the region, and parts 2 and 3 are respectively a union list of serials and a list of pre-1700 books.

In Essex the bibliography has been published as a volume of the Victoria County History and it acknowledges a great debt to the librarians in the county and concludes with an historical account of the public library movement in Essex. In particular the lists of books and pamphlets prepared by the various libraries and the county record office were collated by Miss I. E. M. Kennedy, then of the Ilford Public Libraries, and the chairman of the informal committee which planned the work was Mr E. R. Gamester, former Borough Librarian of West Ham. It covers all printed matter and local transactions and periodical literature have been dissected, including parliamentary papers and blue books. The headings of the general county section will provide valuable hints and assistance to anyone faced with the preparation of a similar bibliography, and are therefore given here.

General Works (divided by period)
 Includes also Sources (Essex Record Office, Bibliography, Historians)
Agrarian History (Agricultural Societies and Shows: Estates, Tenures and Landowners: Farmers and Labourers: Smallholdings and Gardens)
American Connexions
Architecture and Art
Charities
Church (Archdeaconries and Deaneries: Art, Music and Drama: Bells, Chests and Plate: Briefs: Churches and Chapels: Civil War and Interregnum: Clergy: The Diocese: Diocesan Records: Glass, Goods and Furnishing: Parish and its records: Religious Houses and Guilds: Sepulchral Monuments: Sunday Schools)
Dialect, Folklore and Customs
Drama
Earthquake of 1884
Education
Fisheries
Food
Forests
Geography and Geology
Guides and Directories
Handwriting
Health and Public Services (General: Diseases: Electricity: Gas: Housing: Sewage: Water Supply)
Industry and Trade (General: Banking and Insurance: Coins and Trade Tokens: Cloth: Miscellaneous industries)
Jews
Local Government (General: Crime and the Law: Finance: Hundreds: Police: Poor Relief: Prisons and Punishment: Towns)
Maps
Maritime History
Military History
Music
Natural History
Newspapers and Magazines (this section is based on the British Newspaper Library at Colindale)
Non-Conformity, Protestant
Parliamentary Representation
Place-Names
Planning, Town and Country
Population
Railways (General: Railway Guides: Individual lines)

Rivers and Canals
Roads
Roman Catholicism
Royalty
Societies (General: Essex Archaeological Society: Essex Field Club: Freemasons)
Sports (subdivided by particular sport)
Topography
Transport and Travel
Weather
Witchcraft

Part 2 of the bibliography deals with biography and family history, the major part being devoted to a *Directory of Persons and Families* in alphabetical order, in which even DNB references are given. Part 3 deals with individual places and regions, also in alphabetical order of place. This first Victoria County History Bibliography to appear was edited by W. R. Powell and in 1962 a Supplement to the Essex bibliography was compiled and published by J. G. O'Leary.

Further north, the Lancashire bibliography began in 1950 as a project of the Community Council of Lancashire, the North Western Branch of the Library Association and the North Western Regional Library System. Other bodies were also represented on the Joint Committee and grants and subscriptions were received from local authorities, the universities of Liverpool and Manchester, the Community Council, industrial and commercial firms and local history societies. In 1970 the Community Council withdrew from the project and the Joint Committee was re-formed with the Manchester City Libraries taking a prominent role in the future of the bibliography which has always had its office in the Manchester Central Library. At the same time increased support for the project was given by many of the former contributing authorities and it was decided to up-date the material published in future volumes.

Material for the bibliography was submitted by contributing authorities and was edited originally by Dr G. H. Tupling, a special lecturer in local history at the University of Manchester, who did much to further local history studies in the North-West. On the death of Dr Tupling in 1962 he was succeeded as editor by Sidney Horrocks, formerly chief assistant librarian in the Manchester City Reference Library. Publication of the bibliography began with two volumes based on material printed to the end of 1957. The first part published covered *Lancashire Directories 1684–1957* and was published by the Joint Committee in 1968. The second part to appear dealt with *Lancashire Acts of Parliament 1266–1957* and was published by the committee in 1969. The third part, *Lancashire Business Histories*, includes material printed to the end of 1970 and was published in 1971.

Another co-operative scheme for the compilation of a county bibliography is now taking place in Cheshire, where the Cheshire librarians have decided to compile a bibliography of Cheshire. No details of this scheme have been published so far, and the advantages to be derived from the co-operative production of county and regional bibliographies will no doubt appeal to other counties and areas as the effects and methods of the existing schemes become more widely known.

Chapter 16

Classifying Local Material

Although the material contained in any local history library must be classified to facilitate its use, the classification scheme selected cannot be applied to the material on the shelves with the same degree of effectiveness as in a general reference or lending library, because the diversity of material in the local history library usually necessitates a much larger number of separate sequences than are found in other departments. In any well-established local history library, unbound pamphlets are likely to outnumber bound books and the sizes of both books and pamphlets will vary considerably. All size sequences, therefore, are likely to be duplicated if it has been found more convenient to separate books and pamphlets and to arrange the pamphlets in boxes. Press-cuttings, photographs, broadsides, microfilms, and other material will also be shelved or stored in their own appropriate fittings and sequences. The effect of applying any classification scheme to the material on the shelves of a local history library, therefore, is not going to result in the single location of all the material on any given topic, and since in many local history libraries the material is either shelved in bookcases with locked doors, or is otherwise not openly accessible to users, the consideration of the most effective classification scheme for local history material should be influenced more by the suitability of the scheme for the construction of a classified catalogue, than as a scheme to be used primarily for application to the arrangement of the material on the shelves.

Many of the arguments used in favour of dictionary and classified catalogues become superfluous when it is considered that the benefits of having three arrangements of material in a local history library can be obtained by classifying the entries in the catalogue; supplying the classified catalogue with an alphabetical subject index; and arranging the material on the shelves in a chronological or other useful order. Such a scheme has proved effective at Warrington for nearly forty years. In 1932 a local classification scheme was devised in order to produce a classified catalogue of the local history collection. This catalogue was equipped with appropriate alphabetical author and subject indexes as well as an index of books printed locally to the year 1800. The books and pamphlets so catalogued were placed on the shelves in size sequences, and the material in each sequence was arranged chronologically. Call marks of the items in the catalogue are numbers that are treated decimally so that any item may be inserted at the appropriate place in any size and chronological sequence. One of the advantages found from this arrangement has been that whilst subject and author enquiries can be answered without difficulty it is also possible to indicate readily the literature relating to any period. This ability is proving to be of increasing value as students present research assignments confined to watertight periods, but the chronological arrangement on the shelves only applies to the printed books and pamphlets in the collection as the classification scheme is used for the arrangement of press-cuttings, photographs, broadsides and other material.

One of the reasons often given for the use of a classification scheme especially formulated for a local history library instead of using an adaptation of some established scheme such as Dewey, is that any adaptation results in a long or complicated class number. W. C. Berwick Sayers has stated 'that the adoption for a special library of any general scheme is notationally undesirable'.[1] The validity of this reason diminishes if the classification scheme is not applied to the material on the shelves. It is also apparent that the principal need for a classification scheme that is most suitable for shelf arrangement arises from the use of a dictionary catalogue. In any dictionary catalogue, groupings of related material can only be achieved by some abandonment of true dictionary principles and even such groupings cannot achieve the effect of a good classification

1. W. C. Berwick Sayers. 'Thoughts on Library Classification in Retrospect and Prospect'. *Library World*, vol. 60, April 1959. pp. 206–12.

scheme. If a dictionary catalogue is used, therefore, it is much more essential to apply the most effective scheme of classification to the order of the material on the shelves.

It is perhaps significant that the largest collection of local literature in a British public library – at Birmingham – is now classified in accordance with a local scheme based on the *Classification for London Literature* devised and used in the Guildhall Library and that at Birmingham a dictionary catalogue is used.

On the other hand, it is necessary to observe at once that in the local history libraries of 14 principal British cities, 13 use adaptations of Dewey and 1 uses an adaptation of the Library of Congress scheme. If all these libraries also used classified catalogues the reasoning of the first paragraphs of this chapter would be largely vindicated, but only 8 of the 14 use classified catalogues, 5 use dictionary catalogues and 1 uses an author catalogue. It would appear, therefore, that the choice of an adaptation of an established scheme in so many principal collections, and indeed, in a substantial majority (70 per cent) of all local history libraries (in which libraries only 58 per cent use classified catalogues), depends to a greater extent on the desirability of having the same scheme of classification in all departments of the library than on the suitability of such adaptations to the material of the local history library.

Of 246 British libraries using classification schemes for local history material in 1970 163 use Dewey; 60 use locally devised schemes; 8 use Brown; 5 use Hobbs; 4 use Ormerod's Derby scheme; 2 use the Library of Congress; 1 uses the Guildhall scheme and 1 an alphabetico classification.

When the Dewey decimal classification is adapted for use in a local history library it is first necessary to ensure that all aspects of certain topics should be brought together at one location. If such decisions are not made, 'roads' could be classed at three places and the economic aspects of transport separated from the mechanical. Hospitals could be placed under medicine or sociology and radio under engineering, communications or amusements. In local work all aspects and phases of a subject should be kept together. Where Dewey has been adapted the tables are used for subject division and they are often preceded by a simple notational topographical arrangement where this is felt to be necessary. The Dewey adaption used at Plymouth may be cited as typical. Subjects which are specially applicable to Plymouth use 'P' as a distinguishing letter before the subject number. Thus 385 = Railways of Devon and Cornwall and P385 = Railways in Plymouth. The Dewey history numbers 940-999 are dispensed with as being unnecessary and in their place a topographical sequence based on the administrative map of Devon and Cornwall is provided, with an alphabetical sequence for individual places. Thus:

950	West Country in general
960	Devon
960.1	Gazetteers
960.2	Directories
966	Dartmoor
966 WM	Widecombe-in-the-Moor

Classes P940-999 are used for Plymouth's connections with other parts of the world, e.g.

P973.22	Pilgrim Fathers
P974.48	Plymouth, Massachusetts

Leeds uses Dewey numbers, preceded by 'Y' for Yorkshire and 'L' for Leeds, but has devised a special scheme, evolved from the existing collections, for its photographs and prints. Sheffield uses Dewey subject numbers followed by the topographical number for Sheffield, omitting the initial 9. Some libraries prefer to use the Cutter-Sanborn author tables to provide a means of alphabetical notation by place for the small towns and villages.

In addition to several universities, two public libraries, Edinburgh and Wigan, use the Library of Congress scheme,[2] which is in use in the rest of the library. At Edinburgh, Dr Savage adapted the Library of Congress schedules, using the vacant Class Y for the purpose, and he found it well suited to the needs of a homogeneous city collection. It was necessary, however, to extend the topographical schedule to provide a

2. The Surrey Archaeological Society's library at Guildford is classified by a modified version of the Library of Congress scheme, and a classified catalogue is being compiled by members.

distinct number for each district, street, river or other feature. This was done by dividing the directory map of the city into squares, working in an anti-clockwise direction from a central point, and the arrangement of topographical material is primarily geographical. A similar system could be adapted to any collection for a single city.

A diminishing number of libraries use Brown's subject scheme for local purposes and yet of all the major classifications, the subject scheme is perhaps the most readily adaptable for the purpose of arranging local material, having some highly commendable features from this point of view. James Duff Brown explained how this could be done in the original introduction to his scheme, recommending the use of the vacant Class Y for the purpose, and dividing the county into parishes or other suitable administrative units, represented by the numbers Y000-Y999. Subject division within these topographical classes is effected by means of the categorical tables, in which many of the topics are of local significance.

The classification used for the Kent Collection in the Margate Public Library, compiled by a former librarian, Mr A. J. Gritten, is based on the subject scheme. A summary of the tables will be found in the printed catalogue of the collection, published in 1934.

Dr Bliss's system of bibliographical classification includes an 'anterior numeral' Class 8 – Collections of historical, local and institutional interest, but there is no provision for subdivision, other than the implied method of dividing by the main classification. Although Dr Bliss's schedules are better co-ordinated than any other scheme, they are no more apposite, as they stand, to the restricted purview of the local collection.

Dr Ranganathan's colon classification, based fundamentally upon an extension of the principles of Brown's categorical tables, has attracted much attention from classifiers in recent years. Even more important than the scheme itself has been the development since the war of his technique of indicating phases and facets of a subject to meet the problems of close classification and synthesis made necessary by modern documentation. Brian C. Vickery has shown in his *Classification and Indexing in Science* (Butterworth, London, 1958) how classification schedules for a special subject may be compiled by using Ranganathan's principles of facet analysis.[3] Although the technique is perhaps less easily adaptable to historical collections there is little doubt that it *could* be successfully used for a local history collection, and a wide field of experimentation awaits the librarian willing to study Ranganathan's ideas and to develop his methods.

The only serious work in the classification field today is being carried on at the documentation level, and mainly by special librarians, especially in the scientific field. Reclassification is not a matter to be embarked on lightly in any sizeable library and it is only in its special collections that the librarian can afford to experiment. And of these it is the local collection which offers the greatest scope, particularly at the documentation level, for it is specially fitted for the adoption of certain of the more obvious aspects of Dr Ranganathan's 'faceting' technique, in view of the opposing factors of subject and place which have to be considered. Few of the enquiries received in the local history room are for histories of the town or county as a whole. The enquiry is often much more elusive – the date and history of a particular building, details of an event or occurrence, or an account of a local society. Only by detailed indexing, allied to close synthetical classification, therefore, can we easily find the answer to these and many other questions asked of us.

Many librarians, debarred from exercising their logical and critical faculties in classification by the standardisation 'according to Dewey' which has been imposed upon them in their general collections, have turned their minds and abilities to local classification as a means of putting their theoretical knowledge to practical test by devising a scheme for their own local history collections.

Very few of these local classification schemes have been published or printed in library journals although some of them have been adapted for use in other libraries. As so many of the problems to be encountered in the construction of a local scheme are inherent in the nature of local classification and have been solved, in different ways, by schemes that have been published, it would be wiser for the local classifier to study these schemes in detail and model his own arrangement upon

3. See also J. A. Mills. *A Modern Outline of Library Classification*. Chapman and Hall, London, 1960.

them rather than to formulate an entirely new scheme for local use.[4]

Whilst it is true that a few of the unpublished local schemes have been adapted for use in one or two other libraries, such as the Eccles local classification which was applied at the neighbouring library of Swinton and Pendlebury, most of the unpublished and published local schemes have found little acceptance outside the libraries for which they were primarily devised. But any librarian contemplating the adoption of a local scheme may be interested in looking at those of Ormerod of Derby, the Guildhall scheme, and the local classification scheme which appears as Chapter 17 of this book and which is based on Ormerod's scheme. It is not proposed to comment on local schemes other than these three, therefore, and those who wish to study other schemes are referred to the comments about them in chapter 17 of the 1962 edition of this book and *Libraries and the Materials of Local History* (already cited, chapter 12).

In view of the decision taken at Birmingham to classify the large collection of local literature in the Birmingham local history library on a scheme based upon the Guildhall scheme, it would appear that this scheme has especial merit, and is clearly capable of adaptation for use in large cities. The scheme is published and currently appears as a third edition: *Classification for London Literature Based upon the Collection in the Guildhall Library* (Library Committee Corporation of London, London, 1966). This expansive and well-proportioned scheme was originally prepared by Mr Raymond Smith and first published in 1926, and evolved from a close study of the existing literature. It is a decimal scheme, the main classes having two figures with subdivisions extending generally to a further two, and occasionally to three, places of decimals. The summary of the main classes is:

Preliminary and General Class		00–09
Ecclesiastical History		10–19
Social Life		20–59
Social Life	20–29	
Administration-Public Bodies	30–39	
Administration-Special Subjects	40–49	
Arts and Learning	50–59	

4. See John L. Hobbs. *Libraries and the Materials of Local History.* pp. 161–2.

Economic History	60–69
History	70–79
Topography	80–89
Local Divisions	90–99

The sections of Administration – Special Subjects 40–49 are:

40	Statistics, Yearbooks etc.	45	Markets
41	Social Welfare	46	Public Health and lighting
42	Crimes. Police	47	Medicine. Hospitals
43	Prisons	48	Transport. Traffic
44	Laws. Courts	49	Education

Examples of decimal subdivision extending to two and three places in section 46 Public Health and lighting are:

46.1	Air Pollution. Smoke
.2	Water Supply
.201	Early methods of supply; details. Conduits. Pipes
.21	Individual companies, arranged A–Z
.24	Drinking fountains
.3	Sewers, sewage and municipal refuse
.9	Lighting
.91	Oil
.92	Gas
.93	Electricity

In order that no possible confusion should exist with Dewey numbers in the Birmingham Reference Library in the Birmingham adaptation of the Guildhall scheme, the letter 'L' for 'Local' has been placed before the figures in the notation.

The Derby scheme which was formulated by James Ormerod, former Librarian of Derby, was originally used at Derby and was described in 'The Classification and Cataloguing of Local Literature and Antiquities', in the *Library World* (vol. 29, 1926–27, pp. 168–74; and vol. 30, 1927–28, pp. 14–22 and pp. 119–23. The revised schedules appear in vol. 30 pp. 119–23).[5] One librarian who currently uses Ormerod's original scheme described it, with perhaps more truth than he realised, as 'a two figure adaptation of Dewey'. The scheme is distantly derived from Dewey and its schedules are much better balanced

5. This scheme was also used at Shrewsbury where it was extended by John L. Hobbs for application to the Shropshire Collection and thus was the basis of the Hobbs' scheme [George A. Carter].

for local purposes since they concentrate upon subjects strongly represented in local collections.

The third scheme, as stated above, is that outlined in the following chapter.[6]

In all general schemes of classification and in all other departments of the library the *subject* of the book is the paramount factor in deciding its appropriate place in the classification scheme, but a book is usually assigned to the local collection because of its connection with the locality. The topographical factor must therefore be made the primary basis of division in a local classification, and the golden rule is 'Classify first by locality, as precisely as possible, and then by topic'.

A pamphlet dealing with the architecture of a parish church *may* interest the student of architecture; it will certainly interest the prospective historian of the village. In material on churches and other ecclesiastical buildings, castles, historic houses, archaeological sites, local industries, and many others, the local interest is paramount. There may be subjects, such as the physical sciences, where the subject matter might seem to transcend the topographic interest and where all material might conveniently be brought together at the county or general number. The flora or geology of a particular area are examples of this. In such cases James Duff Brown's criterion – 'where will it be most constantly useful?' – should be followed, but generally the primary division will be topographical.

In a small, compact town topographical considerations may be less important and may be ignored, but in a large town or city collection topography can and should take priority where necessary, in spite of the fact that much of the material will be general in character. The minuteness of topographic expansion and the intensity of subject coverage can radiate outwards from the centre according to the law of inverse squares. Near to

6. This scheme formulated by John L. Hobbs, the original author of this book is now used by a number of libraries and has been selected by some librarians to replace older schemes and adaptations. Since it has become apparent to me that John Hobbs felt very deeply about classification for local history purposes I have allowed his own words to stand exactly as they appeared in the original edition from the next paragraph onwards in order that his own scheme may continue to enjoy the most appropriate preamble and introduction from the man responsible for its construction [George A. Carter].

the centre of the city every street, perhaps most of the buildings, will receive separate numbers; farther out it will be sufficient to denote each major thoroughfare. This is necessary not so much for the book literature, but to deal adequately with pamphlets, news-clippings, photographs and similar material.

Assuming, however, that the collection covers a wider area, perhaps a whole county, we must next decide what shall be the unit on which this topographical division is to be based. Berwick Sayers proposed that counties should be divided into their hundreds or wapentakes, in order to bring contiguous places together to some extent, while to attain the same object Jast proposed division according to the 6 in. ordnance survey map sheets. Unfortunately the attempt to group places into adjacent areas can succeed only at the expense of a longer notation, and there are many advantages in using the local government administrative areas (municipal boroughs, urban and rural districts and civil parishes) as the basis of division. Indeed the only disadvantages are the often considerable differences in area and population, and the uncertainty concerning their future.

The area covered by the collection will be divided into county and non-county boroughs, followed by county districts, the latter being further subdivided, where necessary, according to the civil parish, these being arranged alphabetically or grouped topographically. The writer's preference for the civil parish as the basic unit rests on the facts that they are small enough to include most of the chief villages, especially in the south of England; they have great historical significance and often coincide with the ecclesiastical parish, and they are still in use for modern administrative purposes. They are not, of course, so apposite to parochial records or archives but, as we have previously stated, the classification is not intended for such records.

The librarian who is faced with the task of arranging a collection of local literature will therefore be well advised to consider his collection as an entity and, bearing in mind the area it covers, to devise a simple topographical arrangement based on the latter. To this should be applied a simple literal notation consisting of one, or at most, two symbols. Since many collections take the administrative county as their area, it will be convenient to illustrate how this is done by using the county as a basis.

SHROPSHIRE

A Authors, Local, arranged A–Z
B Biography, Local, arranged A–Z
C County of Salop (works dealing entirely or mainly with the county)
D Shrewsbury Borough
E Atcham Rural District
F Oswestry Borough and Rural District
G Ellesmere U.D. and R.D.
H Whitchurch Urban District
I Wem U.D. and R.D.
J Market Drayton U.D. and R.D.
K Newport U.D.
L Wellington U.D. and R.D.
M Wenlock Borough
N Dawley and Oakengates Urban Districts
O Shifnal R.D.
P Bridgnorth Borough and R.D.
Q Ludlow Borough and R.D.
R Church Stretton U.D.
S Bishop's Castle Borough
T Clun R.D.
U Other districts of county which cannot be included in the above, e.g. UO=Offa's Dyke, US=Severn River, UT=Teme River, UW=Wye Valley, etc.
V Other English counties, VC=Cheshire, VS=Staffordshire, etc.
W Wales and Welsh Collection, subdivided by counties, A–Z
X, Y Special Collections
Z Special Bindings, Rare Books, Curiosa

The general literature of the county, and that of cities, borough and urban districts will need further subdivision by subject, a matter which we shall discuss shortly. For rural districts, whose literature will not normally be sufficient to warrant subdivision, it may be necessary only to provide a distinctive number for the civil parish, and the following examples show how this can be done. Thus, in most counties, a two-figure notation will provide a symbol for the smallest unit, the civil parish.

WELLINGTON URBAN AND
RURAL DISTRICTS

L   Wellington Urban District
LA Wellington Rural District
LB Bolas Magna
LC Cherrington
LD Chetwynd
LE Chetwynd Aston
LF Church Aston
LG Edgmond
LH Ercall Magna
LI Eyton-on-the-Weald-Moors
LJ Hadley
LK Kinnersley
LL Lilleshall
LM Longdon
LN Longford
LP Preston-on-the-Weald-Moors
LR Rodington
LT Tibberton
LU Waters Upton
LW Woodcote
LX Wrockwardine

MARKET DRAYTON URBAN
AND RURAL DISTRICTS

J   Market Drayton
JA Adderley
JC Cheswardine
JE Childs Ercall
JG Hinstock
JH Hodnet
JI Ightfield
JM Moreton Say
JN Norton-in-Hales
JS Stoke-upon-Tern
JT Sutton-upon-Tern
JW Woore

The alphabetical arrangement shown here is not really logical and some libraries may prefer a sequence designed to integrate the parishes into contiguous areas. This could be based on a series of concentric circles radiating from the central place (e.g. Wellington, Market Drayton). A systematic arrangement of this kind is perhaps preferable to alphabetical order, except in small sections where the simplicity of the A–Z order probably outweighs the advantages.

Class A of the main classification is designed to accommodate those books by local authors which do not otherwise relate to the area covered by the collection. Only works whose sole interest lies in the fact of their local authorship are placed here. The need to collect such material has been explained in Chapter 3, and it is more convenient to bring it together at one place rather than to distribute it throughout the classification according to the author's place of residence. In a small collection the latter might be preferred and a place is provided in the subject tables for this purpose, but it is generally more convenient to arrange such books in one alphabetical sequence by using the Cutter-Sanborn author tables (two-figures only). Thus Charles Darwin's books are classed at AD22 and Samuel Butler's at AB98. Different titles by the same author could be distinguished by arranging them alphabetically by title, but a further letter or number could be added to the class mark if necessary. Voluminous collections relating to local authors will be treated as special collections and classed at x or y, with a special classification.

Biographies of local people can similarly be dealt with in two ways, as in the lending library. They may be distributed throughout the classification according to the place where they lived (*not* by subject) or they may be kept in one sequence. For those preferring the latter method, Class B is provided, a simple alphabetical sequence again being all that is required. A life of Darwin would be classed at BD22 and of Sir Philip Sidney at BS56. It may also be convenient to include family histories and genealogy in this biographical sequence, where they fall into place alongside the lives of individual members of the family. On the other hand, family histories often shed a great deal of light on the past of the locality with which they were connected, and there is a strong justification for classing them at the place number, especially where the family has a long and intimate association with that place. The final decision may well rest on the nature of the book.

Classes x, y and z are reserved for special collections which it may be desirable, for some reason, to keep in a separate sequence. This may be a collection of general works bequeathed by a local personage, an assembly of material relating to a local industry, or one about a famous individual connected with the district. They are often large enough to require a classification scheme to themselves, but even where they are treated as part of the local collection special schedules need to be provided. Such special collections relating to individuals range from the magnificent Shakespeare Collection at the Birmingham City Library, probably the finest collection of Shakespeariana in the world and a veritable library in its own right, down to quite small collections of local worthies.

Printed catalogues are available for some of these special collections, such as the *Bibliography of Edward Carpenter: A*

Catalogue of Books, Manuscripts, Letters, etc. By and About Edward Carpenter in the Department of Local History of the Central Library, Sheffield (Sheffield City Libraries, 1949) and the *Catalogue of Robert Burns Collection in the Mitchell Library, Glasgow* (Glasgow Public Libraries, 1959). The arrangement of the latter should be studied by anyone compiling a bibliography or classification of an author's work.

Schedules for a specific author must be based upon the existing literature, and the librarian must compile a schedule fitted to his own needs. The material generally falls into four main groups:

1. The man's own writings, including translations, selections and quotations.
2. Biographical and autobiographical material.
3. Critical material, including reviews, essays and lectures.
4. Miscellanea, concerning the man and his family, with pictorial material, news-cuttings, autographs, portraits, sale catalogues and everything not readily accommodated in the other groups.

Bibliographies of other authors will give the librarian a basis on which to found his own table, and those attached to some of the general bibliographic schemes will also be helpful, though not universally applicable. Quite the best of these is Bliss's schedule 6, for subdivision under an author, and a study of this will furnish excellent hints for the appropriate headings to apply to a local author. Dewey, too, has a special author table, while one of the appendices to the subject scheme is a *Table for Arranging an Author's Works*, but these merely provide the superstructure or framework on which the schedules for a voluminous local writer must be constructed. The Library of Congress classification treats English Literature in great detail: well-known writers are allocated a block of numbers, varying according to their importance, and several tables are provided for the subdivision of an author, but modern writers are excluded.

Sometimes the subject of a special collection is not an author, but has achieved fame in another walk of life, in which case the scheme of arrangement is conditioned to a large extent by the circumstances and events of the person's life and the basic order is usually chronological. The classification applied to the small, but remarkably complete, collection relating to James Nasmyth, the engineer, at Eccles, is a good example of a special table for a non-literary personage. Its main classes are as follows:

SN00	Biography
10	Life in Eccles
20	Industry
30	Business organisation
40	Nasmyth, Wilson and Company
50	Inventions, Patent Specifications
60	Steam Hammer
70	Drawings and Paintings
80	Technical publications
90	Astronomy

The catalogue of the collection on William Wilberforce and Slavery in the Kingston-upon-Hull Public Libraries also illustrates the principles of arrangement for a non-literary personage. Its main headings are:

1 The Historical background, 1750–1850
2 Kingston-upon-Hull, 1750–1850
3 William Wilberforce – Biography
  Wilberforce and his circle
  Election to Parliament
  Religious activities
4a The Anti-Slavery campaign, as represented in contemporary pamphlets
  i   Up to the time of Abolition in 1807
  ii From abolition to emancipation in 1833
  iii After emancipation
4b As represented in Parliamentary Debates and Official Reports
4c Modern histories of Slavery and its abolition

Returning to the question of subject subdivision. The main topographical classes of the scheme will, as we have said, need further division by subject and to avoid confusion it is desirable that a numerical notation should be applied to the subject tables. This results in a 'mixed' notation, but it seems impossible to avoid this in a local classification where the dual bases of place and subject have to be provided for. The following subject table is based broadly on the Dewey decimal classification, using a two-figure decimal notation, but it could easily be expanded on a three-figured basis if this were considered necessary. It seeks to give greater prominence to those subjects which assume an added importance in local work, such as Local Government, Heraldry and Genealogy, Military History, etc. Other topics, such as Foreign Languages and Literature have no place in a local scheme, while others such as the Physical sciences, Philosophy and Doctrinal Theology need far less emphasis than in a general scheme.

OUTLINE OF CLASSIFICATION
(The full tables are printed in Chapter 17)

00	GENERAL WORKS, SCIENTIFIC AND BACKGROUND STUDIES
10	GEOGRAPHY AND DESCRIPTION: TOPOGRAPHY
20	SOCIOLOGY: ECONOMICS
30	TECHNOLOGY: INDUSTRY: COMMUNICATIONS
40	ADMINISTRATION: LOCAL AND NATIONAL
50	BIOGRAPHY, GENEALOGY AND HERALDRY
60	ARCHAEOLOGY: RECORDS: HISTORY
70	ARTS AND CRAFTS: CUSTOMS
80	LANGUAGE AND LITERATURE
90	PHILOSOPHY AND RELIGION

There is undoubtedly a logical and orderly progression to be observed in the development of any human community and the local literature tends to conform loosely to this, and upon it the local classification should be based. This order has been perceived, in its essentials, by several local classifiers, notably by L. A. Burgess in his Southampton scheme and the compiler of the Eccles scheme, and by local historians such as Dudley Stamp and Professor Hoskins. Geology constitutes the basic factor and is the governing force behind the local topography. Physical features, geography, the flora and fauna, settlement patterns and land utilisation, and man's use and adaptation of his environment all follow and are conditioned by the basic structure of the land. From these stem the industrial and economic development of the area, its social structure and political organisation, history, the arts, literature and spiritual life.

One of the basic problems in local classification is whether to bring the relative aspects of a subject together or not. Many subjects can be treated from the general or administrative standpoint, e.g. Education, Medicine and Public Health, Law,

Public Works and others, and in local work the administrative aspect is frequently the more important. We can bring these together under the local or national administration, or provide a subject number for them, or do both and follow Dewey in trying to separate the two aspects. Historically they were often unconnected or had only loose affiliations with local government, but today they are intrinsically tied up with the system of modern administration. Many local schemes subordinate them to Central or Local Government, but the writer has preferred to make Medicine, Law and Legislation, etc. separate classes, considering that the specific subject is all-important in the local collection and that relative phases should be left for the catalogue. Societies should similarly be classed under the subject represented by the organisation, not kept together in a special class. Turnpike roads will be classed with their successors, the county roads, and the administrative aspects of hospitals and asylums will not be separated from the professional and social aspects. It may not seem strictly logical to place the annual reports of the medical officer of health with the general works on medicine, rather than under the appropriate local government department, but it must be remembered that the latter are subject to changes which may increase in the future. Similarly the technical and the economic aspects of transport and industries should be grouped together. This is one reason why the extremely 'relative' nature of the decimal classification tables with its extensive division of specific topics according to 'aspect' makes the scheme unsuitable for local work.

Allied to the above is the difficulty met in local classification of catering adequately for both the historical and current literature of a subject. In many cases the literature of the medieval or Tudor periods differs so materially from that of the modern period that each really requires its own schedule and there may be little common ground between them. A medieval trade as organised through the craft guild, for instance, has little in common with the modern industrial combine, or the manorial system of land tenure with modern agricultural organisation. Even the Industrial Revolution entirely reorganised the basis of many aspects of local history. Although in the scheme outlined here the history numbers can, as in

Dewey, be used like common form subdivisions (.01–.09) at many points of the scheme, the historical aspects of a subject may in some instances need detailed treatment far beyond the capacity of these. The arrangement in many local history classes needs to be based upon historical rather than functional subdivisions, and this is another aspect in which Ranganathan's synthetic approach could be applied successfully.

The general rules for classifying local material can be summarised briefly. Unless the collection is limited to a small area, classify first by place, then by subject, then by form. It may occasionally be convenient to class primarily by subject certain topics which are usually studied in relation to the district as a whole, and where the student may reasonably expect to find *all* relevant material brought together at the general or county number. Examples of this are specific historical events, such as the Civil War or the Jacobite Rebellion; certain trades such as Coalmining (for coalfields pay no attention to administrative boundaries); means of transport, such as Railways, Canals; and subjects like Local Dialect. In such cases any specific local significance in the material should be brought out in the catalogue.

In all special collections the old, but well-established primary rule of practical classification, that of placing the book where it will be most permanently useful, should be followed. In the local collection some special, and even incidental, feature of the book may be the primary factor which has decided its inclusion in the collection, and other aspects or facets, even the subject of the book, are secondary and unimportant, so far as classification is concerned. The basic rule is that it should be classed according to its connection with the locality. The subject matter of such works, although ignored in the classification process, will be brought out in the catalogue. The local connection may be because of its subject, its authorship, or because it was printed or published within the area. A few books and pamphlets may be included for even less apparent reasons – because they belonged to some prominent local celebrity; or were written during a stay in the locality; it may contain local autographs or bookplates; it may be a sermon preached in a local church, or may be about some local emigrant who achieved prominence.

No special merits are claimed for the classification scheme outlined in this chapter and the writer is conscious that whatever merits it may have are due almost entirely to the many librarians who have devised such schemes before him and to whose labours he owes much, and especially to its originator, the late Mr James Ormerod. Nevertheless he believes it to be a simple, workable scheme which could be applied, without radical alteration, to any other area and to most library local collections of average size. It is based upon practical experience, over thirty years, of two large and varied local history collections at Derby and Shrewsbury, and has been found to work well in practice. Most books can be defined, by subject in relation to a place, with a notation of from three to five symbols, as the following examples will show.

Griffith, E. C. *The Bishop's Castle Railway, 1865–1935.*   S35.7

Great Britain. Historical Manuscripts Commission. *Report on the Records of the Corporation of Bridgnorth.*   P45

Shropshire Parish Register Society. *The Register of Wrockwardine, 1591–1812.* 1907.   LX55.1

Mendenhall, T. C. *Shrewsbury Drapers and the Welsh Wool Trade.* 1953.   D37.12

With little variation, too, it can be applied to most of the miscellaneous material which comprises an integral part of any reputable local collection. Archives, naturally, are expressly excluded, since any attempt to force these into a rigid bibliographical scheme is foredoomed to failure. More has been said of this subject elsewhere. Pamphlets, newspaper cuttings, broadsides and visual material such as prints and drawings, illustrations, photographs and lantern slides could, however, be classified without much difficulty, although photographs and slides may need a more detailed topographical basis.

In the local collection pamphlets are classified and treated exactly like books. Indeed, since many are equally as important as the books published in stiff covers, we endeavour to bind as many as possible and to place them alongside books on the shelves. Some of those which are not bulky enough to take spine lettering can be made so by interleaving or by binding two or more pamphlets on the same subject together. The practice of binding them in miscellaneous volumes should be avoided, but many libraries have several such legacies from private libraries which defy close classification. Other pamphlets are similarly classified and stored in vertical files or pamphlet boxes.

Newspaper clippings can also be classified with the number at the right-hand corner of the mount, and filed like pamphlets. When there are sufficient on any particular subject they may be bound into volumes for permanency. Some librarians do not classify fugitive material of this nature but file the mounted sheets in a self-indexing alphabetical sequence. Much of the material is biographical, personal accounts, literary criticism, obituary notices, etc. which can be arranged by name. Substantial articles in periodicals should be treated as pamphlets and classed and catalogued as books.

Chapter 17

A Local Classification Scheme

oo General Works and Background Studies

01 GENERAL WORKS
- .1 Collections
- .2 Dictionaries
- .3 Cyclopedias
- .4 Miscellaneous pamphlets
- .5 Essays
- .6 Scrapbooks
- .7 Miscellanea
- .8 Notes and queries
- .9

02 NEWSPAPERS AND PERIODICALS
- .1 Newspapers
- .2 Newscuttings and clippings
- .3 Magazines (general)
- .4 Journalism
- .5 Sale catalogues
- .6 Congresses
- .7 Festivals
- .8 Almanacs
- .9 Yearbooks

03 SCIENTIFIC INSTITUTIONS. Museums, Field Clubs

04 GEOLOGY AND PALAEONTOLOGY
- .1 Petrology, Rocks

.2 Ores and Stones
.3 Gems, Ornamental stones
.4 Mineralogy
.5 Seismology, Earthquakes
.6 Erosion and Deposition, Glaciation
.7 Palaeontology, Stratigraphy
.8 Palaeobotany, Fossil plants
.9 Palaeozoology, Fossil animals

05 PHYSICAL GEOGRAPHY. DESCRIPTION OF AREA
.1 Physical description and surface features
.2 Mountains, Hills
.3 Caves, Speleology
.4 Forests and Woods
.5 Moors, Heath
.6 Plains, Mosses and Low country
.7 Lakes and Meres
.8 Rivers and Streams
.9 Springs and wells

06 GENERAL SCIENCE
.1 Mathematics
.2 Astronomy, comets, meteorites
.3 Surveying
.4 Physics
.5 Physical chemistry
.6 Chemistry
.7 Crystallography
.8 Meteorology
.9 Climate, floods

07 BOTANY. FLORA
.1 Structural botany
.2 Trees
.3 Wild flowers
.4 Cultivated flowers
.5 Ferns
.6 Mosses
.7 Lichens
.8 Fungi and moulds, Mushrooms
.9 Ecology, distribution

08   ZOOLOGY FAUNA
- .1   Insects, Entomology
- .2   Butterflies and Moths
- .3   Bees, Apiculture
- .4   Fishes and Amphibia
- .5
- .6   Reptiles
- .7   Birds
- .8   Mammals
- .9   Biochemistry

09   NATURAL HISTORY
- .1   Physical anthropology, Ethnology (original inhabitants of area)
- .2   Migrations of races
- .3   Natural History of Men
- .4   Influence of climate and surroundings
- .5   Pathology (deformities, dwarfs, giants)
- .6   Evolution and Environment
- .7
- .8   Psychology
- .9   Social Psychology

10   Geography and Description. Topography

11   GEOGRAPHY AND TRAVEL
- .1   Early guide books (topographical)
- .2   Road Books
- .3   Railway guides and handbooks
- .4   Modern road travel
- .5   Hiking, Rambler's guides
- .6   Tourist guides
- .7   Travel, Exploration
- .8
- .9   Books of views

12   DIRECTORIES
- .1   General directories
- .2   Street guides
- .3   Commercial directories

.4 Telephone directories
.5 Gazetteers
.6
.7
.8 Itineraries
.9

13 PLACE-NAMES
.1 Etymology, derivation
.2 Village names
.3 Field names
.4 River and stream names
.5 Hill and minor names
.6 Street-names
.7
.8 Personal element in place-names
.9 Study of place-names, elements

14 MAPS AND PLANS. CARTOGRAPHY

15 REGIONAL AND SOCIAL SURVEYS. TOWN AND COUNTRY
PLANNING (general). Rural settlement

16 LAND UTILISATION
Soil surveys

17 AGRICULTURE: HISTORY (divided by period)

18 AGRICULTURAL SYSTEMS
.1 Farming: agricultural methods
.2 Dairying and Dairy products
.3 Animaliculture, Flocks, Veterinary practice
.4 Agricultural machinery and technology
.5 Vegetable and field crops
.6 Gardening and allotments, Horticulture
.7 Fisheries
.8 Forestry and Forests
.9 Preservation of game

.8 Liquor traffic

.9 Licensing system

24 LAW AND LEGISLATION

  .1 Medieval law (ancient jurisdictions, assize of Bread and Ale)

  .2 Borough Courts

  .3 County Court and Quarter Sessions

  .4 Modern magistracy and Justices of the Peace

  .5 Court officials: Clerk, Coroner, etc.

  .6 Criminal trials: hangings

  .7 Penology. Prisons and reformatories, byegone punishments

  .8 Police system

  .9 Probation service, juvenile delinquency

25 EDUCATION. SCHOOLS

  .1 Elementary education

  .2 Secondary education

  .3 Grammar schools

  .4 Technical and vocational training

  .5 Endowed schools, church and board schools

  .6 Other schools, private, Bell, Lancastrian

  .7 Public schools, training colleges

  .8 Adult education, extension training, W.E.A.

  .9 Teaching profession and teaching systems

26 SOCIAL GROUPS AND COMMUNITIES

  .1 Gilds and Livery companies

  .2 Societies, Clubs and Associations (general), Social clubs

  .3 Youth groups: Scouts, Guides, Y.H.A., etc.

  .4 Community centres

  .5 Benevolent and Friendly Societies (e.g. Oddfellows, Druids)

  .6 Secret Societies. Freemasonry

  .7 Foreign communities. Race problems

  .8 Inns, taverns, etc.

  .9 Family life and marriage

10

27 SOCIAL PATHOLOGY
  .1 Philanthropy (Red Cross, Order of St John)
  .2 Charities, Almshouses
  .3 Care of the old and infirm
  .4 Care of the blind
  .5 Care of the deaf and dumb
  .6 Mental defectives
  .7 Orphanages, Foundling Hospitals
  .8 Workhouses, Poor Law Institutions, House of Industry
  .9 Social Ethics (e.g. Betting and gambling. Alcoholism)

28 AMUSEMENTS AND SPORTS. Public entertainments
  .1 Theatre
  .2 Music Halls
  .3 Cinemas
  .4 Assemblies and concerts
  .5 Dancing and balls
  .6 Shows, Fetes, and Carnivals
  .7 Fairs, circuses, menageries
  .8 Animals and pets (local shows)
  .9 Community Recreation Centres

29 SPORTS AND GAMES
  .1 Athletics
  .2 Cricket
  .3 Football
  .4 Other ball games (Tennis, golf, bowls, etc.)
  .5 Aquatic sports (Swimming, boating, rowing)
  .6 Other outdoor sports (Angling, riding, motoring, archery, climbing, hiking, etc.)
  .7 Other sports, A–Z (Boxing, wrestling, fencing, judo)
  .8 Animal sports (Cock and bull-fighting, coursing, horse and dog racing)
  .9 Indoor sports and games. Hobbies

30 Technology. Industry. Communications
  .1–.9 Industrial history and archaeology (divided by period)

31 MEDICINE AND PUBLIC HEALTH
   .1 Epidemics: Plagues
   .2 Diseases and remedies
   .3 Medical profession. G.P.'s
   .4 Hospital services
   .5 Nursing and nursing services. Convalescent homes
   .6 Clinics and special services
   .7 Asylums and mental hospitals
   .8 Public health
   .9 Disposal of the dead. Cemeteries and crematoria

32 DOMESTIC ECONOMY AND SANITATION
   .1 Domestic science
   .2 Food: Cookery
   .3 Clothing and toilet
   .4 Laundry facilities
   .5 Home pests and home sanitation. Slum clearance
   .6 Atmospheric pollution, smoke and fumes
   .7 Drainage and sewerage. Water pollution
   .8 Sewage disposal
   .9 Refuse disposal

33 BUILDING AND BUILDING TRADES
   .1 Housing, municipal and private
   .2 Materials, local stone, etc.
   .3 Carpentry and joinery. Roofing
   .4 Plumbing
   .5 Heating
   .6 Ventilation
   .7 Finishing: Painting
   .8 Lighting
   .9

34 ENGINEERING INDUSTRIES
   .1 Automobile engineering
   .2 Aeronautical engineering
   .3 Electrical engineering
   .4 Hydraulic engineering
   .5–.9 Local Industries

35 COMMUNICATIONS
  .1 Roads. Turnpike trusts and highway overseers
  .2 Modern road systems
  .3 Early road transport. Coaches and coaching
  .4 Passenger transport services, municipal or other
  .5 Goods transport. British Road Services
  .6 Canals and Canal transport (Divided A–Z by name of canal)
  .7 Railways
  .8 Bridges and bridge construction. Tunnels
  .9 Air transport

36 MINING AND MINERAL INDUSTRIES
  .1 Metallurgy. Ironworks. Ironfounding
  .2 Coal and coal mining
  .3 Lead, Copper and Tin mining etc.
  .4 Prospecting and exploration. Plant equipment
  .5 Practical mining and boring
  .6 Quarrying and Quarries
  .7 Gravel, sand, lime, etc.
  .8 Special stones, e.g. Alabaster
  .9 Mine hazards and accidents

37 TRADES AND HANDICRAFTS
  .1 Textile trades
       .11 Cotton; .12 Wool; .13 Linen Flax; .14 Silk; .15 Rayon, Artificial silk, etc.; .16 other fabrics; .17 Ropes; .18 Paper-making; .19 Rubber
  .2 Leather industries, Tanning, Boots and shoes, Saddlery
  .3 Clocks and Watches
  .4 Metal manufactures. Cables
  .5 Other manufactures, tobacco pipes, etc., local industries
  .6 Blacksmithing, farriery
  .7 Milling, Wind and water mills
  .8 Glass-making, pottery and tiles
  .9 Woodwork, Toymaking

38   CHEMICAL TECHNOLOGY
- .1   Chemicals, Industrial
- .2   Explosives, Fuels
- .3   Beverages
- .4   Food Production
- .5   Gas
- .6   Petroleum
- .7   Dyes and dyeing
- .8   Plastics and other organic products
- .9   Other industries

39   MILITARY AND NAVAL SCIENCE
- .1   Marine engineering
- .2   Shipbuilding
- .3   Barges, coracles and other river craft
- .4   Harbours, Navigation
- .5   Military science
- .6   Castles and fortifications
- .7   Barracks and regimental depots, Drill Hall, etc.
- .8   Ordnance. Arsenals
- .9   Military Transportation

40   Administration: Local and National

- .1   History, general
- .2   Manorial administration. Court rolls
- .3   Early borough administration, bailiffs and six-men
- .4   Medieval court of Assembly
- .5   Shrievalty
- .6   Custos Rotulorum
- .7   Mayors and Corporation
- .8
- .9   Forms of regional government (i.e. Council of the Marches, Duchy of Lancaster)

41   CENTRAL GOVERNMENT
- .1   Relations with local government
- .2   Local Acts of Parliament
- .3   Ministries

.4   Crown Officials (Sheriff, Lord Lieutenant)
.5   Judicature
.6   Government departments and inspectors
.7   Local Government Board auditors
.8   Fire Protection
.9   Civil Defence

42   LOCAL GOVERNMENT (Borough Corporation or County Council)
Subdivision will vary according to the type of authority
.1   Council or Corporation (Borough, County or Parish)
.2   Officials: Mayor, Alderman and Councillors
.3   Committees, standing and statutory
.4   Special committees
.5   Byelaws, rules and standing orders
.6   Minutes and Proceedings
.7   Meetings, Council and Vestry
.8   Overseers, parish constables, etc.
.9

43   MUNICIPAL FINANCE
.1   Valuation. Rateable Value
.2   Sinking Fund, Balances
.3   Loans, securities
.4   Rates and local taxes
.5   Assessments and collection of Rates
.6   Audits and Accounts
.7   Annual estimates and Abstracts of Accounts
.8   Tenders
.9   Municipal trading. Central purchasing

44   AREAS AND BOUNDARIES. Ancient liberties, wards, etc.
Regalia, Seals, Insignia and Plate

45   CHARTERS AND RECORDS (for *official* records only)
(subdivided by type of record, e.g. for Borough)
.1   Charters and Letters Patent
.2   Gild merchant rolls

.3 Assembly books and Minutes of House meetings
.4 Admissions of burgesses
.5 Subsidy rolls, house, land and window tax assessments
.6 Bailiffs' Accounts
.7 Records of Borough Courts
.8 Petitions to Mayors
.9 Quarter sessions records

46 FRANCHISE: SUFFRAGE: ELECTIONS
.1 Parliamentary representation
.2 Election of Burgesses and M.P.'s
.3 Election squibs and cartoons
.4 Election addresses
.5 Poll-books, Voting procedure
.6 Local Government elections
.7 Electoral Registration
.8 Ward associations
.9 Freedom of the Borough

47 MUNICIPAL SERVICE
.1 Officials. Heads of departments
.2 Staffs, Clerical and technical. N.A.L.G.O.
.3 Town Clerk's department
.4 Treasurer's and Finance department
.5 Surveyor and Engineer
.6 Public Health and Sanitation
.7 Estates and Housing
.8 Watch Committee. Weights and Measures
.9 Other departments

48 OFFICES AND BUILDINGS
.1 Town Hall or Guildhall
.2 Council chamber or Assembly Hall
.3 Other civic buildings
.4–.9 Housing estates

49 PUBLIC WORKS AND PUBLIC UTILITIES
Electricity, Gas and Water

50   **Biography, Genealogy and Heraldry**

51   BIOGRAPHY, COLLECTIVE. Obituaries (divide like classification)

52   BIOGRAPHY, INDIVIDUAL (divide A–Z) (include Letters, Diaries, Journals and Funeral sermons, etc.)

53   PORTRAITS, PERSONALIA. Caricatures, Silhouettes, busts, death-masks, etc.

54   AUTOGRAPHS (single letters and signatures)

55   PERSONAL NAMES
   .1   Registers of Births, Marriages and Deaths
   .2   Bishop's transcripts
   .3   Burgess rolls and lists
   .4   Episcopal registers
   .5   Wills and Administrations
   .6   School Registers
   .7   Poll-books and Electoral Registers
   .8   Epitaphs and Monumental Inscriptions
   .9   Monumental Brasses

56   ANECDOTES. Personal and miscellaneous material

57   GENEALOGY
   .1   Genealogies, Pedigrees and sources
   .2   Family history
   .3   Epitaphs and Inscriptions
   .4   Inquisitions post mortem
   .5   Heraldic Visitations
   .6   Other visitations
   .7   Sequestrian records
   .8   Census returns

58   COUNTY AND ROYAL FAMILIES. Peerage, Landed Gentry, etc.

59 HERALDRY
   .1 Armorial bearings, Coats of Arms
   .2 Authorisation from the College of Arms
   .3 Crests
   .4 Mottos
   .5 Flags
   .6 Heraldic book-plates
   .7
   .8 Orders of Knighthood
   .9 Civic Heraldry

60 History

61 ARCHAEOLOGY AND ANTIQUITIES (divided by period)
   .1 Old Stone Age and Middle Stone Age
   .2 New Stone Age or Neolithic (*c.* 2500–1900 BC)
   .3 Early Bronze Age (*c.* 1900–1500 B.C.)
   .4 Middle Bronze Age (*c.* 1500–1000 B.C.)
   .5 Late Bronze Age (*c.* 1000–450 B.C.)
   .6 Iron Age (*c.* 450 B.C. to A.D. 43)
   .7 Roman period
   .8 Saxon period
   .9 Medieval and later

62 ANTIQUITIES AND MONUMENTS
   .1 Cave dwellings
   .2 Barrows and Burial mounds
   .3 Cromlechs and Stone circles
   .4 Late Bronze enclosures and pounds
   .5 Hill-forts
   .6 Stone implements
   .7 Flint implements
   .8 Bronze implements

63 INSCRIPTIONS NUMISMATICS. Miscellaneous antiquities
   .1 Coins
   .2 Tokens
   .3 Medals and medallions
   .4 Local Mints
   .5 Seals

.6　Carving, Wood
.7　Stone carving
.8　Arms and Armour

64　SOURCES. ARCHIVES AND RECORDS. National and Private
　　Records (for Official Records, see 45)

65　HISTORY, GENERAL
.1　Prehistory
.2　Roman period
.3　Saxon and Danish, pre-Conquest
.4　Norman, 1066–1399
.5　Tudor, 1399–1603
.6　Stuart, 1603–1714
.7　Hanoverian, 1714–1837
.8　Victorian, 1837–1900
.9　20th century

66　HISTORY, SOCIAL AND ECONOMIC (divide by period, as
　　65)

67　MILITARY AND NAVAL HISTORY. REGIMENTAL HISTORIES
.1　Pre-Conquest, Saxon battlefields
.2　Pre-Reformation, Medieval battlefields
.3　Wars of the Roses
.4　Civil War
.5　Jacobite Rebellion
.6　Napoleonic Wars
.7　Victorian campaigns
.8　The First Great War, 1914–18
.9　The Second Great War, 1939–45 and after

68　HISTORICAL, ARCHAEOLOGICAL AND RECORD SOCIETIES
　　(divide A–Z, by name of Society)
69　FOREIGN CONNECTIONS

70　Arts and Crafts, Customs

71　CUSTOMS, PRIVATE AND PUBLIC
.1　Customs of birth and baptism
.2　Marriage customs

.3 Burial customs
.4 Calendar customs: Christmas and New Year
.5 Other Calendar customs
.6 Mumming plays
.7 Farming and country customs, corn-dollies, rush-bearing, harvest lore, etc.
.8 Country dancing
.9 Well dressing and similar customs

72 FOLKLORE, PROVERBS, LEGENDS
.1 Folklore, traditional beliefs
.2 Children's rhymes and games
.3 Proverbs and sayings
.4 Chap-books
.5 Haunted houses and places
.6 Supernatural occurrences
.7 Witchcraft
.8 Legends
.9 Gypsies and Nomads

73 CELEBRATIONS AND SPECIAL OCCASIONS
.1 Royal Visits
.2 Coronation celebrations
.3 Victory celebrations
.4 Pageants
.5 Official pageantry
.6 Civic functions
.7 Banquets, feasting
.8 Conferences

74 COSTUME AND DRESS
.1 Men's dress
.2 Ladies' dress
.3 Children's costume
.4 Hats and head-gear
.5 Shoes and footwear
.6 Gloves, fans and accessories
.7
.8 Care of the person
.9 Hairdressing, wigs, beards

75   TRADITIONAL ARTS AND CRAFTS
     Byegones, Country crafts, Antiques

76   FINE ARTS
     .1   Sculpture
     .2   Monumental masonry
     .3   Carving and woodwork
     .4   Graphic arts, drawing and design
     .5   Painting
     .6   Engraving
     .7   Pottery and Porcelain
     .8   Decoration and Ornament
     .9   Stained Glass

77   PHOTOGRAPHY, FILMS, PHOTOGRAPHIC AND PRINT
     COLLECTIONS

78   ARCHITECTURE
     .1   Town Planning, Regional Planning
     .2   Gardens and Open spaces. Public Parks
     .3   Housing schemes. Planning
     .4   Domestic architecture. Historic houses
     .5   Public buildings. Civic architecture
     .6   Commercial buildings (Shops, Cinemas, Hotels)
     .7   Educational and Scientific Institutions
     .8   Ecclesiastical architecture. Churches
     .9   Church Furniture and Ornament

79   MUSIC (including local music societies)
     .1   Sacred music, Oratorios, Cantatas
     .2   Choral music
     .3   Orchestral music
     .4   Pianoforte music
     .5   Vocal music. Songs, folk-songs, ballads
     .6   Campanology. Church bells, change ringing
     .7   Operatic and Theatre music
     .8   Concert programmes
     .9   Musical Festivals, Eisteddfods, etc.

80 Language and Literature

.1 Philosophy and theory
.2 Handbooks
.3 Dictionaries and Encyclopedias
.4 Essays
.5 Periodicals
.6 Literary Societies
.7 Study and Teaching
.8 Literary associations of area
.9 History

81 LANGUAGE PHILOLOGY

.1 Etymology
.2 Grammars
.3 Early Text-books, spellers
.4 Phonology
.5 Glossaries and Word-books
.6 Dialect
.7 Slang
.8 Debating

82 LITERATURE: POETRY (with a local setting)

83 DRAMA (with a local setting)

84 FICTION AND ROMANCE (with a local setting)

85 SATIRE AND HUMOUR (also miscellanies)

divide by period, if necessary

86 BIBLIOGRAPHY AND BOOK ARTS

.1 Bibliography. Book Production
.2 History and description
.3 Book printing
.4 Publishing
.5 Bookbinding
.6 Book Clubs, etc.
.7 Bookplates, Local
.8 Rare books
.9 Special presses

87 LIBRARIES, LOCAL (including Catalogues)
  .1 Early libraries
  .2 Church libraries: chained libraries
  .3 Parish libraries
  .4 Other early libraries (e.g. Philosophical Society library)
  .5 Mechanics' Institute libraries
  .6 Private subscription libraries
  .7 Private libraries
  .8 Rate-supported public libraries
  .9 National and special libraries

88 BOOKS BY LOCAL AUTHORS, EDITORS, TRANSLATORS, ETC., A–Z

89 BOOKS PRINTED OR PUBLISHED LOCALLY (A–Z by publisher)

90 Philosophy and Religion

91 PHILOSOPHY AND ETHICS
  .1 Local Philosophic systems
  .2 Ethics
  .3 Logic
  .4 Occult sciences, local ghosts
  .5 Witchcraft, local witches
  .6 Magic
  .7 Temperance
  .8 Vivisection
  .9 Gambling

92 RELIGIOUS HISTORY (divided by period)

93 DEVOTIONAL AND PASTORAL RELIGION
  .1 Evangelistic writings
  .2 Hymnology
  .3 Family worship
  .4 Preaching
  .5 Sermons
  .6 Church and parish administration

.7 Welfare work
.8 Other parish activities

94 CHURCH ORGANISATIONS
  .1 Church organisation
  .2 Sacraments
  .3 Missions, Home and Foreign (local branches)
  .4 Societies within the Church
  .5 Y.M.C.A. and Y.W.C.A.
  .6 Religious education
  .7 Sunday schools
  .8 Evangelistic work, Revivals

95 ROMAN CATHOLIC CHURCH (including Pre-Reformation church, Monastic history, Abbeys)

96 ANGLICAN CHURCH (divided by churches in towns, A–Z)

97 NONCONFORMITY
  .1 Early Protestant sects, Dissenters and early history of Nonconformity
  .2 Presbyterian churches
  .3 Quakers. Society of Friends
  .4 Congregational churches
  .5 Puritanism
  .6 Baptist. Seventh Day Adventist
  .7 Methodist church
  .8 Unitarian church
  .9 Other Christian sects (Salvation Army, Christian Science, Jehovah's Witnesses, etc., A–Z)

98 NON-CHRISTIAN RELIGIONS, A–Z

99 AGNOSTICISM. ATHEISM

Appendix 1

The Place of Archives and Manuscripts in the Field of Librarianship¹

A statement of policy approved by the LA Council, November 1968

I GENERAL POLICY

a. The acquisition of archives and manuscripts is a legitimate purpose of libraries serving the interests of scholarship and research. Such materials may be appropriately consulted alongside collections of printed books, which are often needed to supplement or elucidate the manuscript material.

b. Archives and manuscripts differ from printed books in being unique and incapable of wide distribution or standard treatment. Archives should be gathered in as few large repositories as is compatible with ease of access and storage.

c. A good repository for archives and manuscripts should
i have permanence and a secure income;
ii have adequate strongroom accommodation, fire and water proof, with temperature and humidity control;
iii have a staff trained to deal with documents and, where appropriate, qualified archivists;
iv be open during all reasonable hours, including evenings and lunch hours;
v be readily accessible from all parts of the area served;
vi provide proper working space for staff and students;
vii provide finding lists, catalogues, indexes and other aids to searches;
viii provide reference books needed by research workers;
ix provide for repair of documents and seals and fumigation of documents;

1. Reprinted from the *Library Association Record*, vol. 71, January 1969. p. 15.

x provide adequate facilities for documentary reproduction;

xi provide for the examination of documents by ultra-violet and infra-red lamps.

d. The creation of new repositories in areas already covered should not be undertaken without due regard to established facilities. Where existing repositories are adequate they should be utilised as centres for an agreed area. All those institutions which substantially fulfil the conditions listed in *c.* should be included in any national scheme which may be formulated.

2 QUALIFICATIONS

A distinction in staffing qualifications must be made between those responsible for handling non-archival and archival materials.

a. Non-archival materials. Qualified archivists or qualified librarians may take charge of non-archival materials, according to circumstances.

b. Archival materials. The Associateship of the Library Association with, in the case of the Library Association's professional examinations, passes in papers B.91 (Archive administration and records management) and B.92 (Palaeography and diplomatic) in the case of non-graduates, or papers G.13 (Archive administration) and G.14 (Palaeography) in the case of graduates, or other qualifications regarded by the Library Association as equivalent, may be accepted as a suitable qualification for:

i A librarian in charge of archives and directing the work of archivists.

ii A librarian working in a special department or on a special branch of work alongside archivists.

c. Such librarians should keep abreast of professional developments in the field of archives, and acquaint themselves with the professional publications and activities of archivists.

d. A qualified archivist may be defined as a person who has

i successfully completed a recognised course of training in archive administration, and has practical experience in this field.

ii has been accepted for membership by the Society of Archivists.

3 SMALL REPOSITORIES

No existing repository for archives can be considered satisfactory unless the quantity of material is sufficient to justify the employment of a qualified archivist.

Long-established small repositories unable to conform to the majority of the conditions in 1*c.* above should consider either handing over their archival deposits to a nearby large repository, or employing suitably qualified persons to calendar and list all documents and employing a neighbouring record office or suitable commercial firm to carry out repairs with adequate safeguards to preserve the continuous custody of the records.

4 ARCHIVISTS IN LIBRARIES

Archivists employed in libraries should not be expected to undertake routine library duties not connected with the departments in which they work. Where special departments may appropriately be staffed either by archivists or by librarians, their chances of advancement within the department should be equal.

Archivists should have full facilities for attending professional meetings. Production of MSS without consultation with an archivist should only be undertaken by librarians when no investigations of a complex character are involved, and all documents should be replaced by the archives' staff.

Just as library authorities should not be in charge of archives without employing qualified archivists, so records committees or similar employing bodies should not be in charge of considerable libraries without engaging qualified librarians.

There should be complete mobility of archivists between libraries and other employing bodies.

Appendix 2

Ministry of Housing and Local Government Circular No. 44/62[1]

Ministry of Housing and Local Government
Whitehall, London, S.W.1
3rd September, 1962

LOCAL GOVERNMENT (RECORDS) ACT, 1962

1. I am directed by the Minister of Housing and Local Government to draw attention to this Act which comes into force on 1st October, 1962.

2. Broadly the effect of the Act is to give all local authorities in England and Wales additional powers:—

(a) to make records in their possession available for study (section 1);

(b) to contribute towards the expenses of persons looking after local records (section 4); and

(c) in the case of councils of counties and county boroughs to buy local records, accept them by way of gift, or accept deposit of them by their owners (section 2).

Notes on the provisions of the Act are annexed.

3. The Minister hopes that authorities will make full use of these new powers, and will also take the opportunity to review their existing arrangements for the care and storage of records under the powers contained in section 279 of the Local Government Act, 1933 (in London, section 169 of the London Government Act, 1939). In particular they should ensure that they have made adequate provision, according to the scale of their individual requirements, for

1. Reprinted by permission of the Controller of HMSO.

the storage of their permanent records under conditions which will afford sufficient protection, especially from fire and damp, and will provide space for future accruals. For this purpose it is suggested that authorities who do not have sufficient records to justify the employment of an archivist might seek the advice of an archivist employed by another authority.

4. The problem of securing that the right records are kept for future study is particularly difficult under modern conditions, as the volume of material is so great that it would be quite impossible to keep it all for an indefinite period. It is therefore important that an adequate system be established to ensure that records are reviewed after a suitable period, and a selection made for retention. Broadly, this selection should include all the key documents, and a sample of case histories and other documents of the council's detailed work. Before establishing a method of selection authorities without an archivist of their own may again find it helpful to seek the advice of an archivist employed by another authority.

5. Selection involves disposal of documents not selected for retention, and the Minister is advised that the power of local authorities (under section 279 of the Act of 1933 or the London provision) to issue directions with regard to any records under their control are sufficient to permit the destruction or disposal of unwanted records. This power extends to records given to the local authority or deposited with them, but the Act specifically provides in section 1(2) that the council may not act in contravention of the terms of any agreement under which documents are held. It is suggested that local authorities accepting the gift or deposit of records should take great care to ensure that the terms on which the records are given or deposited are clearly set out and fully understood by both parties.

6. Similar care is needed where one local authority deposits its records with another. The Act ensures (through section 2(5) and section 8(2)) that in such a case all the powers relating to records are available to both authorities and it is for them to decide, preferably when the records are first deposited, how the different functions are to be exercised and by whom.

7. The selection and preservation of records are clearly the first essential. But to be of real value records need to be adequately catalogued and accommodated in a well-staffed and well-equipped records department where they are readily accessible to students. A

service of this character can only be provided by records departments with substantial resources, and their number must necessarily be limited. The Act therefore provides that the additional powers for local authorities to take in records other than their own should be available only to the councils of counties and county boroughs and such county districts and metropolitan boroughs as the Minister may specially authorise.

8. Although the Act is designed to make local records more accessible it makes no change in the law on rights of access: existing statutory rights of the public to inspect registers or other documents and secure copies are untouched, as is the law relating to subpoenas and orders for discovery. Similarly where an existing provision requires documents to be treated as confidential that status is preserved, and any conditions under which records are held (for instance conditions made by a donor or depositor) are also protected. The local authority's discretion in cases not covered by these specific considerations remains, and the Minister trusts that authorities will make records available for study (subject if necessary to conditions on publication) unless real considerations of confidentiality forbid.

9. Parish councils already have power under section 281 of the Local Government Act, 1933, to deposit their records for safe keeping with the county council and many have already done so. Parish councils will not often have suitable premises for the safe keeping of their records, and even where they have, the records may well be more readily available for study if they are deposited with other parish records in the archives department of the county council. The Minister recommends therefore that parish councils which have not already deposited their records should now consider whether it would not be best for them to do so.

10. Other authorities may also wish to deposit records where they can be more readily made available for study, or several authorities may find it convenient to establish a joint committee to look after their records. Similarly a county council and a county borough council with offices in the same town may find it convenient to work together, each specialising in different classes of records.

I am, Sir,
Your obedient Servant,
W. M. FOX,
Assistant Secretary.

The Clerk of the Authority.
   County Councils
   County Borough Councils
   Metropolitan Borough Councils
   County District Councils
   Parish Councils
      England and Wales
   (96208/1/16)

Notes on the Provisions of the Act

   1. *Section 1* provides a broad general power for local authorities to do anything necessary to enable adequate use (i.e., use for study as well as for purposes of administration) to be made of records under the authority's control. This broad power is conferred in the opening words of the section, and includes the specific powers listed but is not limited to them.

   2. The power in section 1(1)(d) enables an authority to make charges for admission to exhibitions or lectures, but this does not override the prohibitions on charging for admission to certain buildings contained in section 5 of the Museums and Gymnasiums Act, 1891, and section 11(3) of the Public Libraries Act, 1892.

   3. The power in section 1(1)(e) to entrust records to other persons for exhibition or study enables authorities to send records to another local authority's record office for the use of a student visiting the search room there. It is not intended to provide a general lending service for students to take away records for study.

   4. Subsection (2) provides a protection for copyright, and debars authorities from acting under subsection (1) in contravention of conditions under which they hold records. This bar applies both to statutory conditions such as those relating to certain youth employment service records, and contractual conditions such as those made by a donor or depositor of records that the records be treated as confidential for a certain period.

   5. *Section 2* empowers the councils of counties and county boroughs to acquire records or receive them by way of gift, and to accept the deposit of records belonging to other persons or bodies.

The Minister can by order extend these powers to a county district or metropolitan borough.

6. The power in subsection (1)(a) for the purchase of records from rate moneys is limited to records which, in the council's view, are of local interest. The power in subsection (1)(b) however, enabling these authorities to accept the gift of records, extends also to records of general interest.

7. *Section 2* also provides power (in subsections (2) and (3)) for counties and county boroughs to accept the deposit of records which belong to other persons or bodies and will remain in the ownership of those other persons or bodies. This includes acceptance of deposit of the records of another local authority and also (under subsection (3)) public records such as local court records deposited under arrangements made by the Lord Chancellor with the agreement of the receiving authority.

8. Subsection (4) provides the complementary power for a local authority to deposit any of its records with an authority to whom the receiving powers of subsection (2) apply, or (with the Minister's consent) with any other person. This last provision would enable a local authority to deposit records with such bodies as the great national libraries in the way some Welsh authorities have already deposited records with the National Library of Wales. The section does not deal with the deposit of records by a parish council or parish meeting, as this is already covered by section 281(2) of the Local Government Act, 1933.

9. *Section 3* deals with committees. For the appointment of committees the general powers of section 85 and 91 of the Local Government Act, 1933 apply (in London, section 59 of the London Government Act, 1939). The section does, however, give an additional power for a committee or joint committee to delegate powers to subcommittees. Where executive powers are so delegated, the section requires at least a two-thirds majority to be members of the appointing council (or appointing councils in the case of a joint committee), but this requirement does not apply to a subcommittee which is purely advisory.

10. *Section 4* deals with finance. It enables local authorities to pay other people for doing, in respect of records under the control of the council, anything the council could themselves do. This provision

would for instance enable a local authority to make payments to another authority with whom they have deposited records.

11. The section also enables local authorities to meet all or part of the expenses of persons making other local records available to the public, and to contribute similarly to the expenses of persons in looking after local records in any case where the council are satisfied that there will be adequate provision for access.

12. *Section 5* deals with local Acts. It empowers the Minister to amend or repeal local Act powers in this field, but only on the application of the authority concerned.

13. *Section 7* enables local authorities to accept the deposit of manorial or tithe records if the Master of the Rolls wishes to direct the persons responsible for those records to deposit them with the local authority for safe keeping.

14. The section also amends the basic power of section 279 of the Local Government Act, 1933 (on which the new powers in this Act are built) so as to put on a common basis the powers of local authorities to issue directions with regard to their records.

15. *Section 8* gives the term 'records' a wide definition. This includes not only documents but materials *recording* information in any way. Thus it would not extend to cover for instance the manuscript of a novel, but would cover a wide range of records, including not only documents, plans or maps, but sound recordings, photographs, film, and microfilm copies of other records.

16. *Section 9* provides a saving for existing provisions with regard to records, both provisions made in statutes themselves and the Rules of the Supreme Court and other subordinate legislation.

Bibliography

The bibliography presented here does not attempt or claim to be a complete conspectus of the material available on local history, a subject now so vast and with so many aspects that it would need a volume to itself. It is, in general, limited to those items which are considered to be of greatest value to the librarian in charge of a local history collection and to the student librarian.

A general list of sources for the study of the subject is provided by the *English Local History Handlist* published for the Historical Association (London, 4th ed. 1969), and in books of the calibre of Professor W. G. Hoskins' *Local History in England* (cited below). Reference should also be made to the appropriate sections of *Guide to Reference Material* (3 vols., Library Association, London, 2nd ed. 1966–67), edited by A. J. Walford. In the field of archives and record preservation excellent bibliographies will be found in Redstone and Steer's *Local Records* and Sir Hilary Jenkinson's *A Manual of Archive Administration* (both cited below). Each volume of the *Bibliography of British History*, which covers the period 1485–1789 in three volumes (Oxford, 1933–51) has sections dealing with local history, social history and economic history. Current literature is listed in *Writings on British History*, published by the Royal Historical Society (see pp. 49–50) and in the Library Association's *British Humanities Index* (annual) as well as in the *British National Bibliography*.

There are also several series of booklets or articles which are important for the study of local history. The Historical Association pamphlets and the S.P.C.K. series, 'Helps for Students of History', though in many instances dated and out-of-print today, are still useful and they have not been entirely superseded by the post-war 'Local History Series' issued by the Standing Conference for Local History in association with the National Council of Social Service. Local history sources are dealt with in both a general and specific manner in the pages of the *Amateur Historian* (now the *Local Historian*) (1952 to date) and also, to a lesser extent but with greater authority, in the *Bulletin of the Institute of Historical Research*, especially in the series devoted to Bibliographical Aids to Research.

For archive matters, the publications of the British Records Association and of its Records Preservation Section, are invaluable. A list of the former appears in the Association's annual report, while its magazine, *Archives,* contains a useful series of contributions detailing the contents and sources of many local record offices and libraries. The *Journal of Documentation* and the *Journal of the Society of Archivists* both contain much useful data on the problems of record preservation and use.

Finally, many societies, national and local, are concerned in one way or another with the preservation of local records and their publications often reflect this interest. Although local sources in the national repositories and university libraries have been dealt with in periodical articles, recourse should still be had to their handlists, annual reports and journals for more detailed accounts of particular records or archive groups.

LOCAL HISTORY – GENERAL

CELORIA, FRANCIS. *Teach Yourself Local History.* English University Press, London, 1959.

EMMISON, F. G. *Archives and Local History.* Methuen, London, 1966.

GALBRAITH, V. H. *An Introduction to the Study of History.* C. A. Watts, London, 1964.

HOSKINS, W. G. *English Local History: the Past and the Future.* University Press, Leicester, 1967.

HOSKINS, W. G. *Fieldwork in Local History.* Faber, London, 1967.

HOSKINS, W. G. *Local History in England.* Longmans, London, 1959.

KUHLICKE, F. W. and EMMISON, F. G. (eds.). *English Local History Handlist, A Select Bibliography and List of Sources for the Study of Local History and Antiquities.* Helps for Students of History, no. 69. Historical Association, London, 4th ed. 1969.

PERRY, G. A., JONES, E. and HAMMERSLEY, A. *Handbook for Environmental Studies.* Blandford, London, rev. ed. 1971.

STOCKHAM, P. *et al. British Local History: A Select Bibliography.* Dillons University Bookshop, London, 1964.

SOURCES – GENERAL

BAILLIE, H. M. G. 'The Use of the Resources of the Historical Manuscripts Commission'. *Journal of the Society of Archivists,* vol. 3, no. 9, April 1969. pp. 462–6.

BAIRD, KENNETH D. 'Use of Scottish Registers at H. M. Register House in Edinburgh'. *Amateur Historian*, vol. 3, no. 3, Spring 1957. pp. 112–14.

BOND, M. F. *Guide to the Records of Parliament*. HMSO, London, 1971.

CLARK, G. KITSON and ELTON, G. R. *Guide to the Research Facilities in History in the Universities of Great Britain and Ireland*. University Press, Cambridge, 2nd ed. 1965.

COUNCIL FOR BRITISH ARCHAEOLOGY. *Archaeological Bibliography for Great Britain and Ireland*. Council for British Archaeology, London, 1949– . Published annually. Also published by the C.B.A. is *Current and Forthcoming Off-prints on Archaeology in Great Britain and Ireland*. Council for British Archaeology, bi-annually, 1950– .

CRUMP, C. G. *History and Historical Research*. Routledge, London, 1928.

GALBRAITH, V. H. *Introduction to the Use of Public Records*. Oxford University Press, London, 2nd ed. 1952.

GILSON, J. P. *A Guide to the Manuscripts of the British Museum*. Helps for Students of History, no. 31. S.P.C.K., London, 1920.

HEPWORTH, PHILIP. *How to Find Out in History*. Pergamon, Oxford, 1967.

HISTORICAL MANUSCRIPTS COMMISSION. *List of Record Repositories in Great Britain*. HMSO, London, 4th ed. 1971.

HISTORICAL MANUSCRIPTS COMMISSION. *Manuscripts and Men*. HMSO, London, 1969.

HISTORICAL MANUSCRIPTS COMMISSION. *Report of the Secretary to the Commissioners:* 1968–1969, HMSO, London, 1969; 1969–1970, HMSO, London, 1970.

JONES, P. E. and SMITH, RAYMOND. *A Guide to the Records in the Corporation of London Records Office and the Guildhall Library Muniment Room*. English Universities Press, London, 1951.

MULLINS, E. L. C. *A Guide to the Historical and Archaeological Publications of Societies in England and Wales, 1901–1933*. Compiled for the Institute of Historical Research. University of London, The Athlone Press, London, 1968.

MULLINS, E. L. C. (comp.). *Text and Calendars: An Analytical Guide to Serial Publications*. Royal Historical Society, London, 1958.

NORTON, JANE E. *Guide to the National and Provincial Directories of England and Wales, Excluding London, Published before 1856*. Royal Historical Society, London, 1950.

PARKER, DONALD D. *Local History: How To Gather It, Write It, and Publish It*. Rev. ed. by Bertha E. Josephson. Social Science Research Council, New York, 1944.

POWELL, W. R. *Local History from Blue Books: A Select List of the Sessional Papers of the House of Commons*. Helps for Students of History, no. 64. Historical Association, London, 1962.

PUBLIC RECORD OFFICE. *Guide to the Contents of the Public Record Office.* 2 vols. HMSO, London, 1963.

PUGH, R. B. *How to Write a Parish History.* Allen and Unwin, London, 1954.

SKEAT, T. C. *British Museum. The Catalogue of the Manuscript Collections.* British Museum, London, 1951.

TATE, W. E. *The Parish Chest.* Cambridge University Press, London, 3rd ed. 1969.

SOURCES – SPECIAL

CHALONER, W. H. 'Business Records as a Source of Economic History with Special Reference to their Selective Preservation in Libraries'. *Journal of Documentation*, vol. 4, June 1948. pp. 5–13.

DAVIS, G. R. C. *Medieval Cartularies of Great Britain: A Short Catalogue.* Longmans Green, London, 1958.

EMMISON, F. G. and GRAY, I. *County Records.* Historical Association, London, rev. ed. 1967.

FOWLER, G. HERBERT. *The Care of County Muniments.* County Councils Association, London, 2nd ed. 1928.

GARRETT, R. E. F. *Chancery and Other Legal Proceedings.* Pinhorns, Shalfleet Manor, Isle of Wight, 1968.

GROSS, CHARLES. *A Bibliography of British Municipal History.* Leicester University Press, Leicester, 2nd ed. 1966.

HEPWORTH, PHILIP (ed.). *Select Biographical Sources: the Library Association Manuscripts Survey.* Library Association, London, 1971.

HOBSBAWM, E. J. 'Records of the Trade Union Movement'. *Archives*, vol. 4, no. 23, 1960. pp. 129–37.

JAMES, R. L. M. 'Brewing Records: An Inquiry and its Lessons'. *Archives*, vol. 7, no. 36, 1966. pp. 215–20.

JAMES, R. L. M. 'Friendly Society Records'. *Archives*, vol. 6, no. 32, 1964. pp. 223–4.

JOHNSON, L. C. 'British Transport Historical Records Department: the First Decade'. *Archives*, vol. 6, no. 31, 1964. pp. 163–71.

KELLAWAY, WILLIAM. 'Record Publications of Societies'. *Archives*, vol. 7, no. 20, 1965. pp. 46–9.

KER, NEIL R. (ed.). *The Parochial Libraries of the Church of England.* The Faith Press, London, 1959.

LE HARDY, WILLIAM. 'Records of Clubs and Societies'. *Archives*, vol. 1, no. 3, 1950. pp. 29–39.

MACLURE, J. STEWART. *Educational Documents England and Wales, 1816–1968.* London, Chapman and Hall, 2nd ed. 1968.

MATHIAS, PETER. 'Historical Records of the Brewing Industry'. *Archives*, vol. 7, no. 33, 1965, pp. 2–10.

OTTLEY, G. *et al*. *Bibliography of British Railway History*. Allen and Unwin, London, 1965.

OWEN, DOROTHY M. *The Records of the Established Church in England. Excluding Parochial Records*. British Records Association, London, 1970.

POWELL, W. R. 'The Sources for the History of Protestant Nonconformist Churches in England'. *Bulletin of the Institute of Historical Research*, vol. 25, no. 72, 1952. pp. 213–27.

PURVIS, CANON J. S. *An Introduction to Ecclesiastical Records*. St Anthony's Press, London, 1953.

PURVIS, CANON J. S. *Educational Records*. Borthwick Institute of Historical Research, York, 1959.

TWINN, KENNETH. 'Sources for Church History. 2. Dr Williams's Library'. *Local Historian*, vol. 9, no. 3, August 1970. pp. 115–20.

GENEALOGY AND PARISH REGISTERS

CAMP, ANTHONY J. *Wills and their Whereabouts*. Phillimore for the Society of Genealogists, Canterbury, 1963.

FERGUSON, JOAN P. S. *Scottish Family Histories Held in Scottish Libraries*. Scottish Central Library, Edinburgh, 1960.

GARDNER, DAVID E. and SMITH, FRANK. *Genealogical Research in England and Wales*. 3 vols. Bookcraft Inc., Salt Lake City, Utah, 1956–65.

HARLAND, DEREK. *A Basic Course in Genealogy*. 2 vols. Bookcraft Inc., Salt Lake City, Utah, 1958.

KAMINKOW, MARION J. *Genealogical Manuscripts in British Libraries*. Magna Charta Book Co., Baltimore, Maryland, 1967.

KAMINKOW, MARION J. *A New Bibliography of British Genealogy with Notes*. Magna Charta Book Co., Baltimore, Maryland, 1965.

MARSHALL, G. W. *The Genealogist's Guide*, 1903. Reprinted by Genealogical Publishing Co., New York, 1967.

MATTHEWS, W. *British Autobiographies*. California University Press, 1955.

MATTHEWS, W. *British Diaries*. Cambridge University Press, London, 1950.

SMITH, FRANK (comp.). *A Genealogical Gazetteer of England*. Genealogical Publishing Co., New York, 1968.

SOCIETY OF GENEALOGISTS. *Catalogue of the Parish Registers in the Possession of the Society of Genealogists*. Society of Genealogists, London, rev. ed. 1963.

THOMSON, T. R. *A Catalogue of British Family Histories.* Oxford University Press, London, 2nd ed. 1935.
WAGNER, SIR ANTHONY R. *English Genealogy.* Oxford University Press, London, 1960.
WHITMORE, J. B. *A Genealogical Guide.* Walford, London, 1953.

THE CARE AND ADMINISTRATION OF ARCHIVES

JENKINSON, SIR HILARY. *A Manual of Archive Administration.* Lund, Humphries, London, 1965.
REDSTONE, LILIAN J. and STEER, FRANCIS W. (eds.). *Local Records: their Nature and Care.* Society of Local Archivists, London, 1953.
SCHELLENBERG, T. R. *Modern Archives: Principles and Techniques.* F. W. Cheshire, Melbourne, Australia, 1956.

ARCHIVES AND LIBRARIES

ELLIS, ROGER H. 'Local History, Archives and Libraries.' *Proceedings of the Annual Conference of the Library Association, Scarborough, 1960.* Library Association, London, 1960. pp. 9–16.
HEPWORTH, PHILIP. *Archives and Manuscripts in Libraries.* Library Association Pamphlet, no. 18. 2nd ed. 1964.
HOBBS, JOHN L. 'Local Records and the Library'. *Library Association Record*, vol. 51, no. 6, June 1949. pp. 177–9.
RENSHAW, MARY. 'A University Archive Repository'. *Library Association Record*, vol. 56, March 1954. pp. 75–80.
RIDLEY, NICHOLAS. 'The Local Government (Records) Act, 1962: its Passage to the Statute Book'. *Journal of the Society of Archivists*, vol. 2, no. 7, 1963. pp. 288–92.
SOCIETY OF ARCHIVISTS. *Recommendations for Local Government Archive Services.* Society of Archivists, London, 1971.
STEPHENS, GEOFFREY B. 'Archives and Libraries'. *Proceedings of the Annual Conference of the Library Association, Llandudno, 1953*, Library Association, London, 1953. pp. 50–4.
WALTON, MARY. 'Local Records and the Public Library'. 1938. An unpublished thesis accepted for the honours diploma of the Library Association. Copy in the Library Association Library.

LOCAL COLLECTIONS IN LIBRARIES

CARTER, G. A. 'Libraries and Local History'. *The Librarian and Book World*, vol. 45, nos. 7–8, August and September 1956.

HOBBS, JOHN L. *Libraries and the Materials of Local History*. Grafton, London, 1948.

HOBBS, JOHN L. (ed.). *The Librarian and Book World*. Double Number: Local Collections, vol. 44, no. 8, September–October, 1955. Contains articles by J. L. Hobbs, P. Hepworth, A. Shaw Wright, Miss D. M. Norris and Raymond Smith.

OVERINGTON, MICHAEL A. *The Subject Departmentalized Public Library*. Library Association, London, 1969.

SAVAGE, E. A. 'A Library of Local History and Affairs'. *Special Librarianship in General Libraries and Other Papers*. Grafton, London, 1939. pp. 119–39.

SAYERS, W. C. BERWICK. *Library Local Collections*. Allen and Unwin, London, 1939.

LOCAL HISTORY AND EDUCATION

DEPARTMENT OF EDUCATION AND SCIENCE. *Archives and Education*. Education Pamphlet, no. 54. HMSO, London, 1968.

DOUCH, ROBERT. *Local History and the Teacher*. Routledge and Kegan Paul, London, 1967.

FRANCE, R. SHARPE. 'Archives for Education: History Brought to Life through County Records'. *County Councils Gazette*, December 1958. pp. 363–5.

HUMPHREYS, D. W. *Local History in School: A Guide for Teachers and Students*. Standing Conference for Local History, National Council of Social Service, London, 1953.

SHERCLIFF, W. H. 'The School and the Local History Library'. *Manchester Review*, vol. 9, summer 1960. pp. 33–8.

AIDS TO INTERPRETATION OF RECORDS

CAPPELLI, ADRIANO. *Lexicon abbreviaturarum. Dizionario di abbreviature latine ed italiane*. Hoepli, Milan, 6th ed. 1961.

GRIEVE, HILDA. *Examples of English Handwriting, 1150–1750, with Transcripts and Translations*. Essex Record Office, Chelmsford, 2nd ed. 1959.

HECTOR, L. C. *The Handwriting of English Documents*. E. Arnold, London, 1958.

JENKINSON, SIR HILARY. *The Later Court Hands in England from the Fifteenth to the Seventeenth Century*. 2 vols. Cambridge University Press, Cambridge, 1927.

JOHNSON, CHARLES and JENKINSON, SIR HILARY. *English Court Hand,*

A.D. 1066–1500 Illustrated from the Public Records. 2 vols. Clarendon Press, Oxford, 1915.

LATHAM, R. E. *Revised Medieval Latin Word-list from British and Irish Sources*. Oxford University Press for the British Academy, London, 1965.

MARTIN, CHARLES T. *The Record Interpreter*, 2nd ed. Stevens, London, 1910, reprinted 1967.

PELZER, A. *Abréviations latine médiévales*. Beatrice – Nauwelaerts, Paris, 2nd ed. 1966.

PHOTOGRAPHY AND RECORDS

CHAMBERS, HARRY T. *Copying, Duplication and Microfilm: Systems and Equipment for Use in Business and Administration*. Business Books Ltd., London, 1970.

DAVISON, GEORGE H. *1962 Review of Equipment for Microtext*. Council for Microphotography and Document Reproduction, London, 1962.

FENNELL, YVONNE. 'Chester Photographic Survey'. *Library Association Record*, vol. 72, May 1970. pp. 197–9.

GOWER, H. D., JAST, L. S. and TOPLEY, W. W. *The Camera as Historian: A Handbook to Photographic Record Work for Those Who Use a Camera and for Survey and Record Societies*. Sampson Low, London, 1916.

MASON, DONALD. *Document Reproduction in Libraries*. Association of Assistant Librarians, London, 1968.

MICROCARD EDITIONS INC. *Guide to Microforms in Print*. Microcard Editions Inc., Washington D.C., 1961–   .

N.B.S. INSTITUTE FOR BASIC STANDARDS, U.S. Dept. of Commerce. 'Cause and Prevention of Microfilm Blemishes'. *British Journal of Photography*, vol. 117, no. 5745, August 1970. p. 827.

PAGE, S. B. *Modern Office Copying*. Deutsch, London, 1966.

RADMORE, D. F. 'Suggestions for a Photographic Survey'. *Local Historian*, vol. 9, no. 5, February 1971. pp. 222–5.

RUBIN, J. (ed.). *International Directory of Micrographic Equipment*. International Micrographic Congress, Saratoga, California, 1967.

SOCIETY OF AUTHORS and THE PUBLISHERS' ASSOCIATION. 'Photocopying and the Law: A Guide for Librarians and Teachers and Other Suppliers of Photocopies of Copyright Works'. *Library Association Record*, vol. 67, no. 11, November 1965.

VERRY, H. R. *Document Copying and Reproduction Processes*. Fountain Press, London, 1958.

VERRY, H. R. *Microcopying Methods*. Rev. ed. by Gordon R. Wright. Focal Press, London, 1967.

MAPS AND THEIR CARE

CHUBB, THOMAS. *The Printed Maps in the Atlases of Great Britain and Ireland: A Bibliography, 1579–1870.* Ed. J. Barrow, London, 1927. Dawson, London, 1966.

HARLEY, J. B. and PHILLIPS, C. W. *The Historian's Guide to Ordnance Survey Maps.* National Council of Social Service, London, 1964.

HODGKISS, A. G. *Maps for Books and Theses.* David and Charles, Newton Abbot, 1970.

PUBLIC RECORD OFFICE. *Maps and Plans in the Public Record Office. 1. British Isles c. 1410–1860.* HMSO, London, 1967.

RODGER, ELIZABETH M. *The Large Scale County Maps of the British Isles, 1596–1850.* Bodleian Library, Oxford, 1960.

CONSERVATION OF MATERIAL AND EQUIPMENT

BRAWNE, MICHAEL. *Libraries: Architecture and Equipment.* Praeger, New York, 1970.

BRITISH STANDARDS INSTITUTION. Recommendations for the *Storage of Documents* are due to be issued in 1973 by the British Standards Institute.

BROMMELLE, N. S. and HARRIS, J. B. 'Museum Lighting'. *Museums Journal,* vols. 61–62, 1961–2.

COCKERELL, SYDNEY M. *The Repairing of Books.* Sheppard Press, London, 2nd ed. 1960.

COLLISON, ROBERT L. *Commercial and Industrial Records Storage.* Ernest Benn, London, 1969.

ELLIS, ROGER H. 'An Archivist's Note on the Conservation of Documents'. *Journal of the Society of Archivists,* vol. 1, 1959. pp. 252–4.

ELLIS, ROGER H. *The Principles of Archive Repair.* London School of Printing and Graphic Arts, 1951.

JENKINSON, SIR HILARY. 'Some Notes on the Preservation, Moulding and Casting of Seals'. *Antiquaries Journal,* vol. 4, 1924. pp. 388–403.

LANGWELL, W. H. *The Conservation of Books and Documents.* Pitman, London, 1957.

LANGWELL, W. H. 'The Postlip Duplex Lamination Processes'. *Journal of the Society of Archivists,* 1964, vol. 2. pp. 471–6.

PLENDERLEITH, H. J. *The Conservation of Prints, Drawings and Manuscripts.* British Museum, London, 1937.

PLENDERLEITH, H. J. *The Conservation of Antiquities and Works of Art: Treatment, Repair and Restoration.* Oxford University Press, London, 1956.

THOMSON, GARRY. *Conservation and Museum Lighting*. Museums Association Information Sheet. Museums Association, London, 1970.

WARDLE, D. B. *Document Repair*. Society of Archivists, London, 1971.

CATALOGUING AND CLASSIFICATION

AMERICAN LIBRARY ASSOCIATION. *A.L.A. List of Subject Headings for Use in Dictionary Catalogues*. American Library Association, Chicago, 3rd ed. 1911.

AMERICAN LIBRARY ASSOCIATION. *A.L.A. Rules for Filing Catalog Cards*. American Library Association, Chicago, 1942.

ANGLO-AMERICAN CATALOGUING RULES . . . British Text. Library Association, London, 1967.

COATES, E. J. *Subject Catalogues: Headings and Structure*. Library Association, London, 1960.

FOSKETT, D. J. *Classification and Indexing in the Social Sciences*. Butterworth, London, 1963.

GUILDHALL LIBRARY. *Classification for London Literature Based upon the Collection in the Guildhall Library*. Library Committee, Corporation of London, London, 1966.

MILLS, J. *A Modern Outline of Library Classification*. Chapman and Hall, London, 1960.

ORMEROD, JAMES. 'The Classification and Cataloguing of Local Literature and Antiquities'. *Library World*, vol. 29, 1926–27. pp. 168–74; vol. 30, 1927–28. pp. 14–22 and pp. 119–22.

VICKERY, B. C. *On Retrieval System Theory*. Butterworth, London, 2nd ed. 1965.

VICKERY, B. C. *Techniques of Information Retrieval*. Butterworth, London, 1970.

Index

Index

See also Index of Special Collections

Index of Special Collections

Index

of the Special Collections mentioned in the text